1001 JUMBO Brain Booster Activities

PEGASUS®
www.pegasusforkids.com

Published by Kuldeep Jain for B. Jain Publishers (P) Ltd., D-157, Sector 63, Noida - 201307, U.P.
Registered office: 1921/10, Chuna Mandi, Paharganj, New Delhi-110055

Printed in India

1 Number writing practice

2 Underline the words ending with –sh sound.

3 Colour the shapes by the code below.

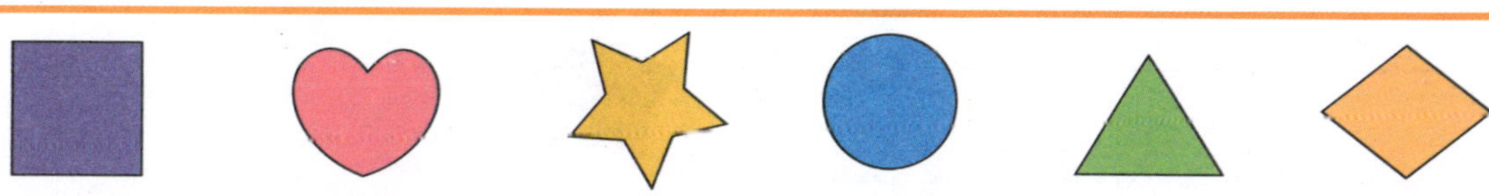

4 Colour by number.

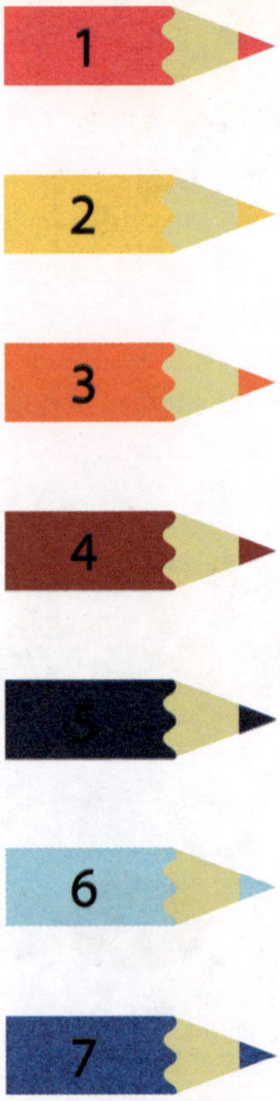

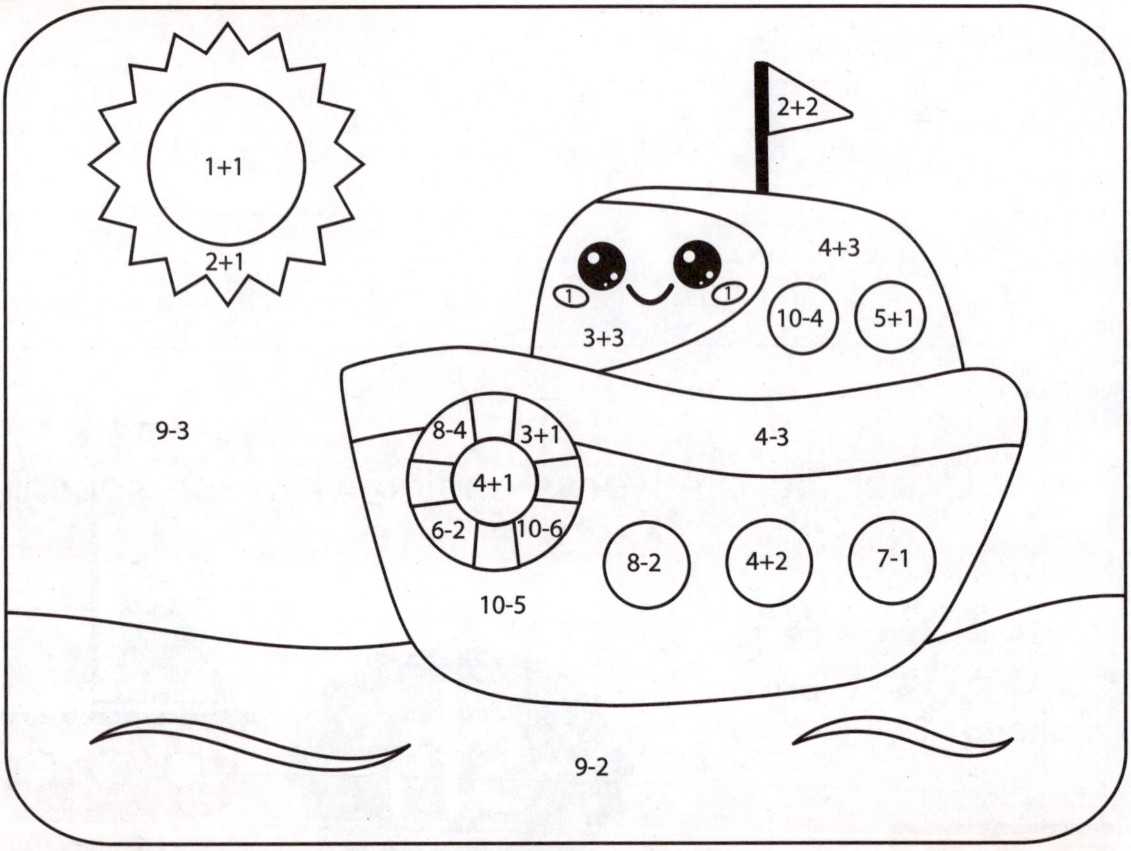

5 Number writing practice

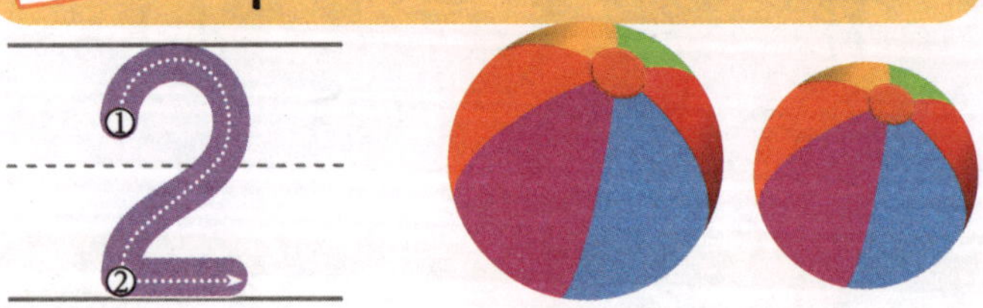

6 Count and write.

7 Fill in the missing numbers.

___ 12 ___ 14 ___ 16

___ 18 ___ 20 ___ 22

8 Underline the similar picture.

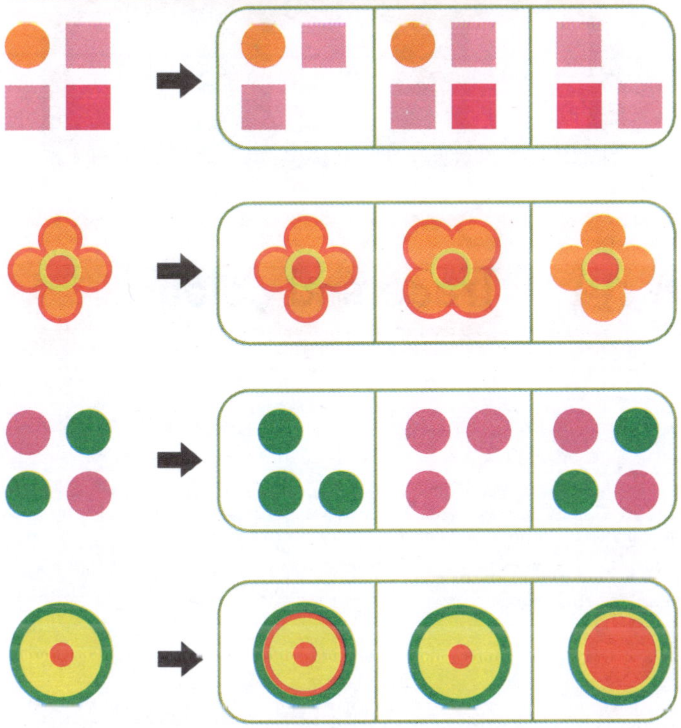

10 Add the fractions.

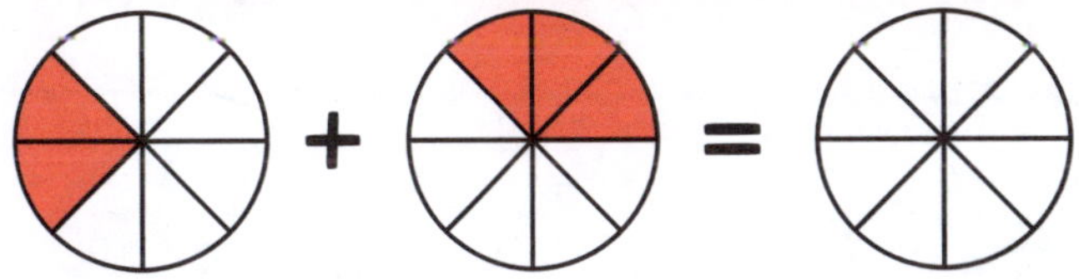

$$\frac{2}{8} + \frac{2}{8} = \frac{\square}{\square}$$

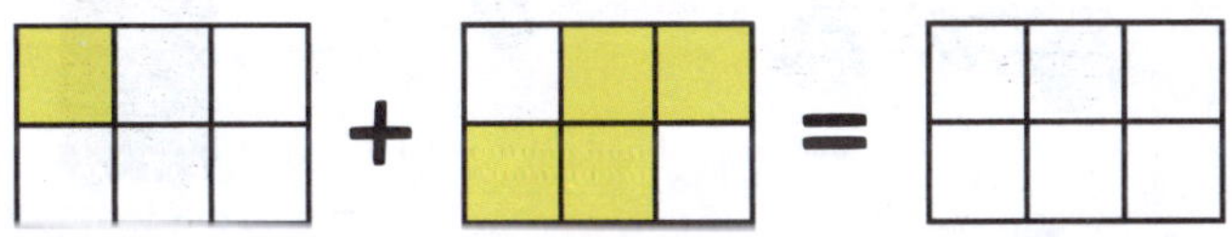

$$\frac{1}{6} + \frac{4}{8} = \frac{\square}{\square}$$

9 Help the bird find its home.

Answer: ☐

11 Match ordinal numbers with their names.

1st ✦	✦ Fifth
2nd ✦	✦ Third
3rd ✦	✦ Fourth
4th ✦	✦ Second
5th ✦	✦ First

12 How many?

13 Maths puzzle

25	-	10	=	
-		-		-
	-	5	=	
=		=		=
	-		=	9

14 Trace and colour.

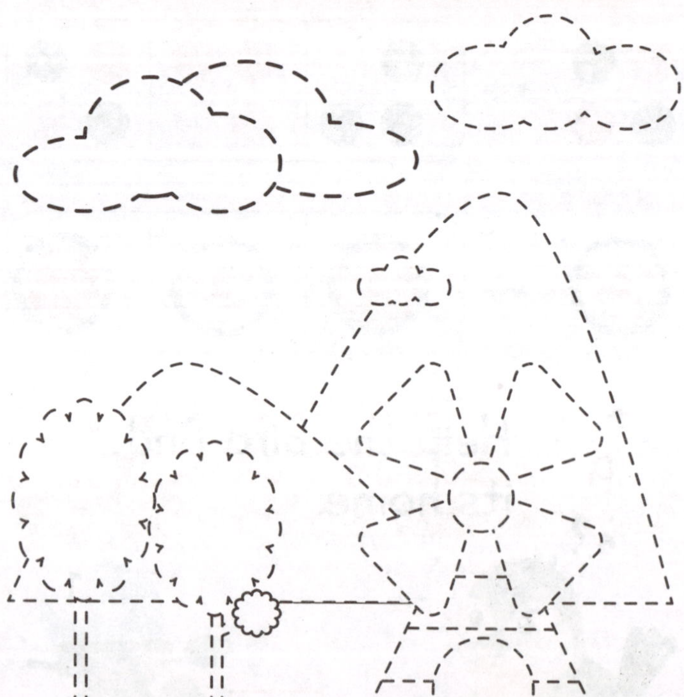

15 Dot to dot, then colour.

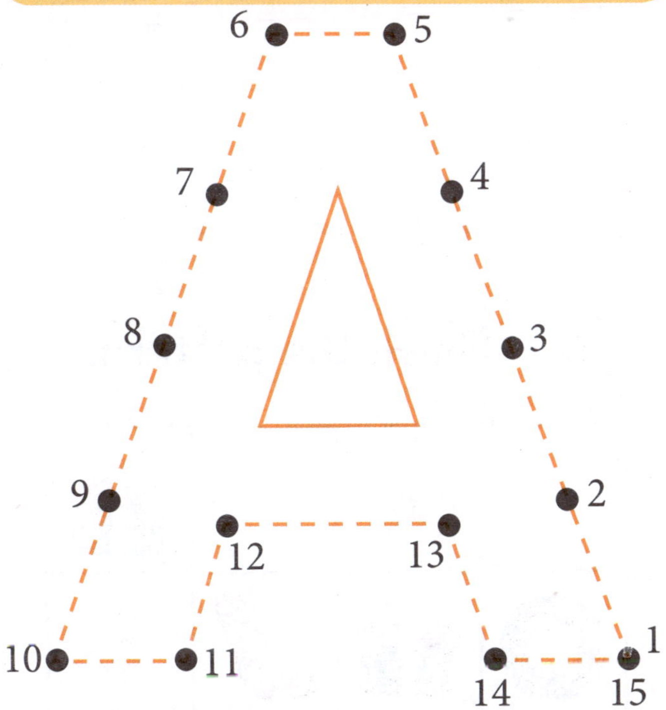

16 How much does the abacus show?

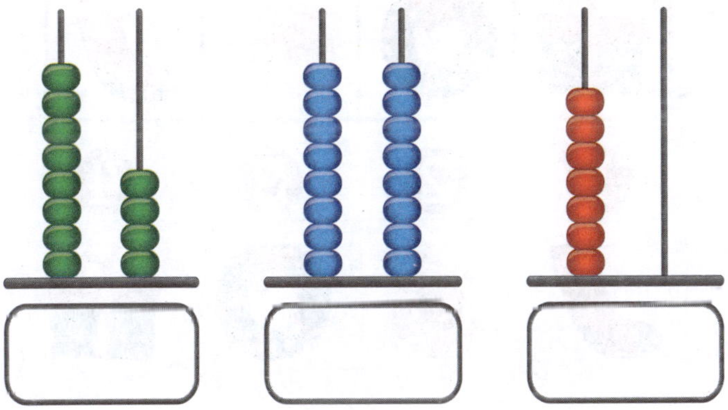

17 Trace the word and practise sound 'a'.

hat hat hat hat

hat hat hat hat

18 Which is the missing letter?

_uail

O D Q

19 What time is it?

☐ o'clock

☐ o'clock

☐ o'clock

☐ o'clock

20 Number writing practice

21 Match with their initials.

 F

 G

 H

 I

 J

23 Finish the pattern.

22 Follow directions to colour.

E	ш	Ǝ
yellow	red	blue

E	Ǝ	ш	Ǝ	Ǝ

24 Colour the fraction.

$\frac{7}{8}$

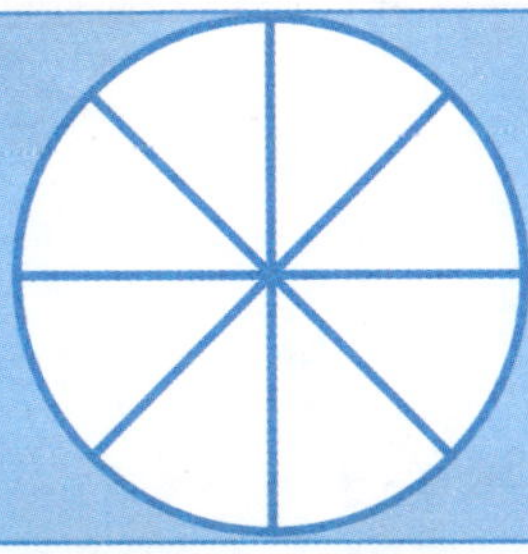

$\frac{4}{9}$

25 Mirror symmetry drawing

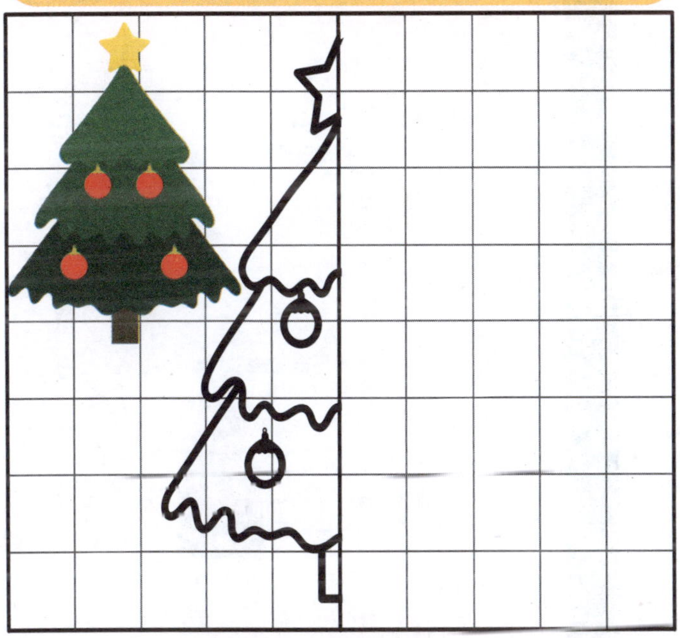

26 Letter writing practice

a a a a a

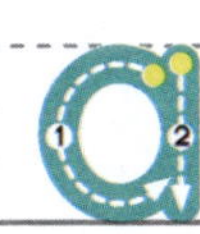

ant

a a a a a a a a a a

27 <, > or = ?

28 Add and match with the sum.

3+6 8+1 8

6

2+5 7 4+2

9 4+4 9

29 Number writing practice

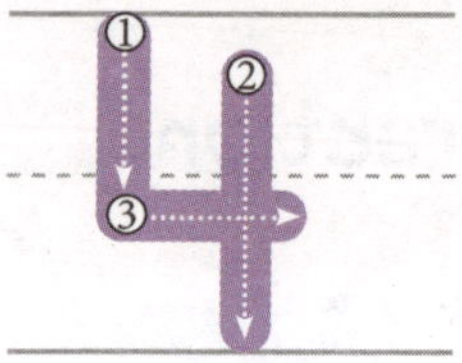

30 Tick (✓) the right number of cubes.

- 7
- 10
- 8
- 12

31 Fill numbers in sequence.

32 Find their height.

______ cm

______ cm

33 Trace the word and practise sound 'e'.

egg egg

egg egg egg

34 Follow the pattern.

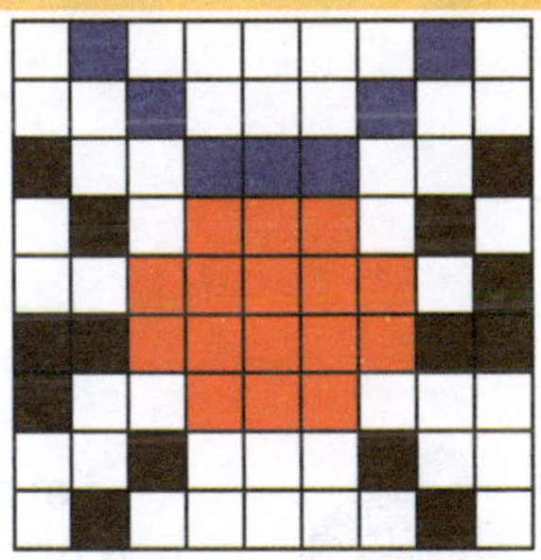

35 Trace and colour

36 Subtract and circle the correct answer.

1 2 3
4 5 6
7 8 9

1 2 3
4 5 6
7 8 9

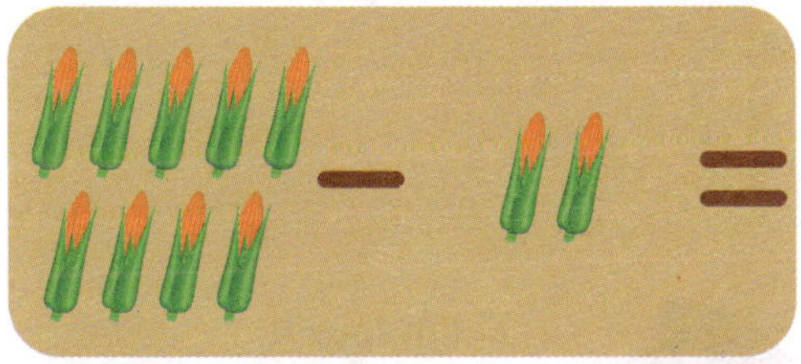

1 2 3
4 5 6
7 8 9

37 Tick (✓) the correct option.

A day has 23 / 24 / 25 hours.

There are 50 / 60 / 70 seconds in a minute.

The longest hand of a clock is the minute / second / hour hand.

38 Write the missing numbers and colour.

39 How old are they? Count the candles and match.

40 Trace the shapes.

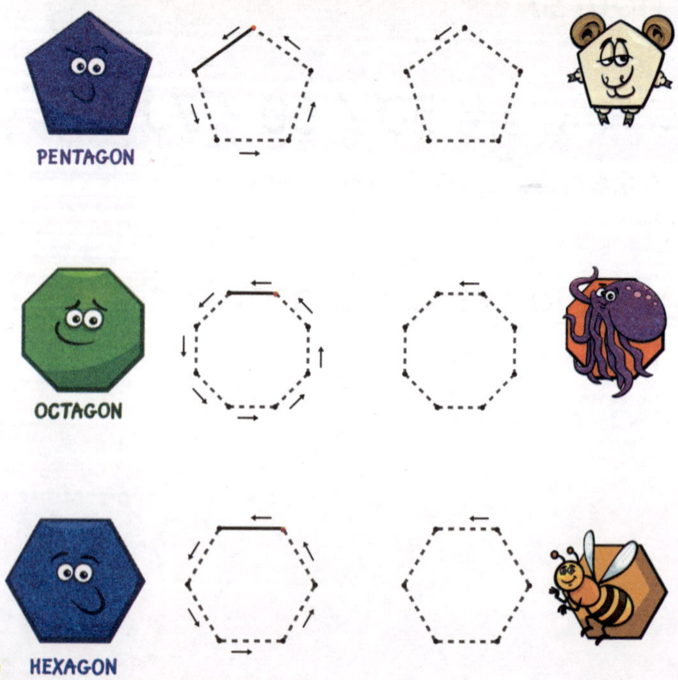

41 Multiply the following.

$8 \times 4 = \square\square$

$9 \times 5 = \square\square$

$10 \times 2 = \square\square$

$5 \times 7 = \square\square$

$6 \times 7 = \square\square$

$6 \times 6 = \square\square$

42 Dot to dot, then colour

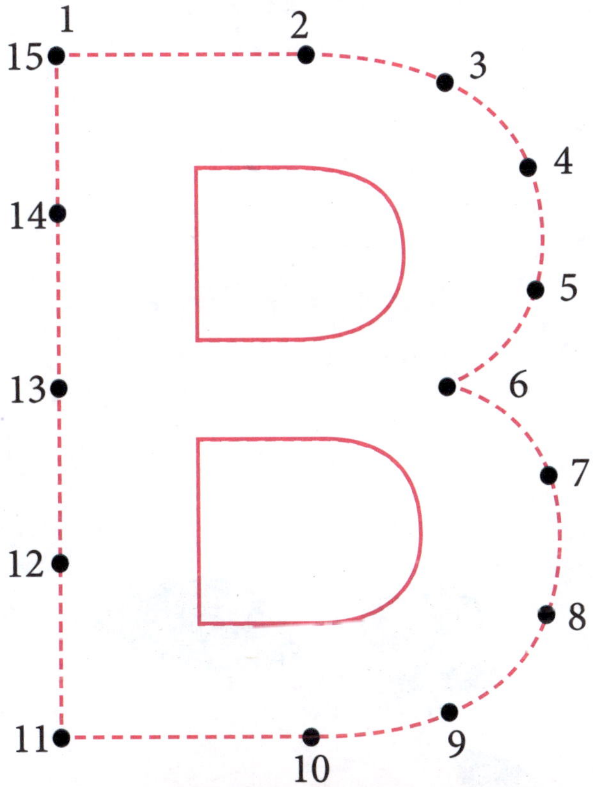

43 Which broken piece is from the mirror?

44 Solve the rebus.

45 Mirror symmetry drawing

46 Add in the candy.

47 Number writing practice

48 Match by colour.

50 Find the correct shadow.

49 Find the difference.

51 Crossword

52 Colour the blocks from the measuring line.

54 Add in the mug.

53 Eek! Who was that? Find and circle.

55 Which is next?

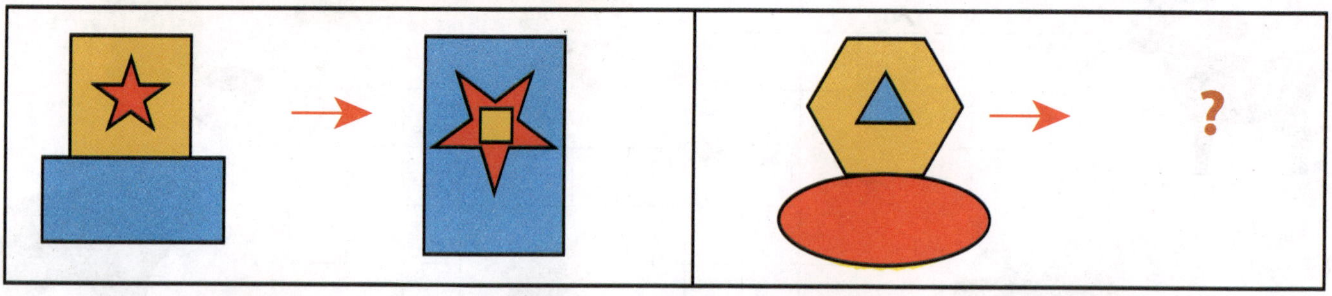

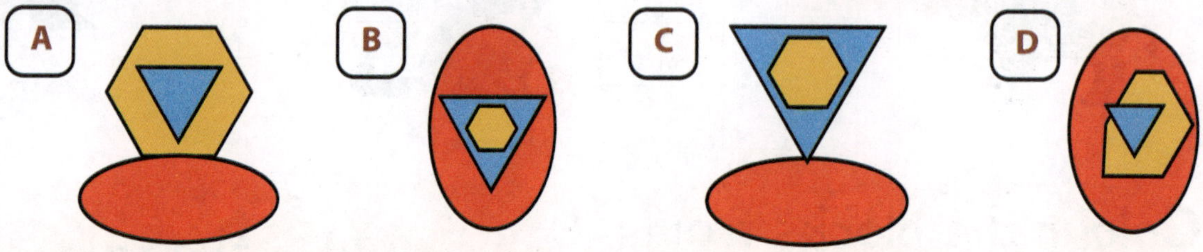

56 Count and circle.

57 Underline the words ending with –ee sound.

58 Dot to dot, then colour.

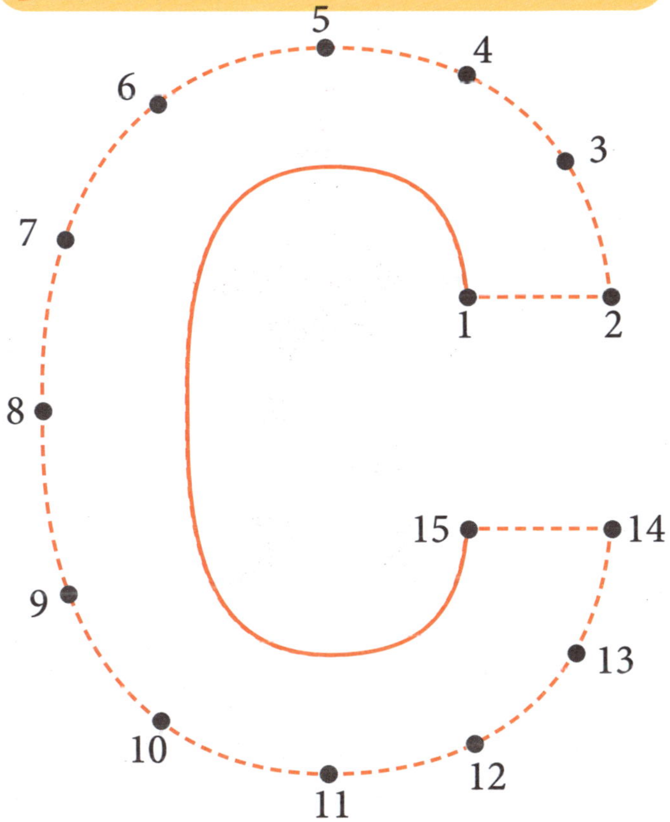

60 Sum the gifts.

59 Which can each buy?

61 Number writing practice

62 Multiply and match.

63 Collect the word.

64 Crossword

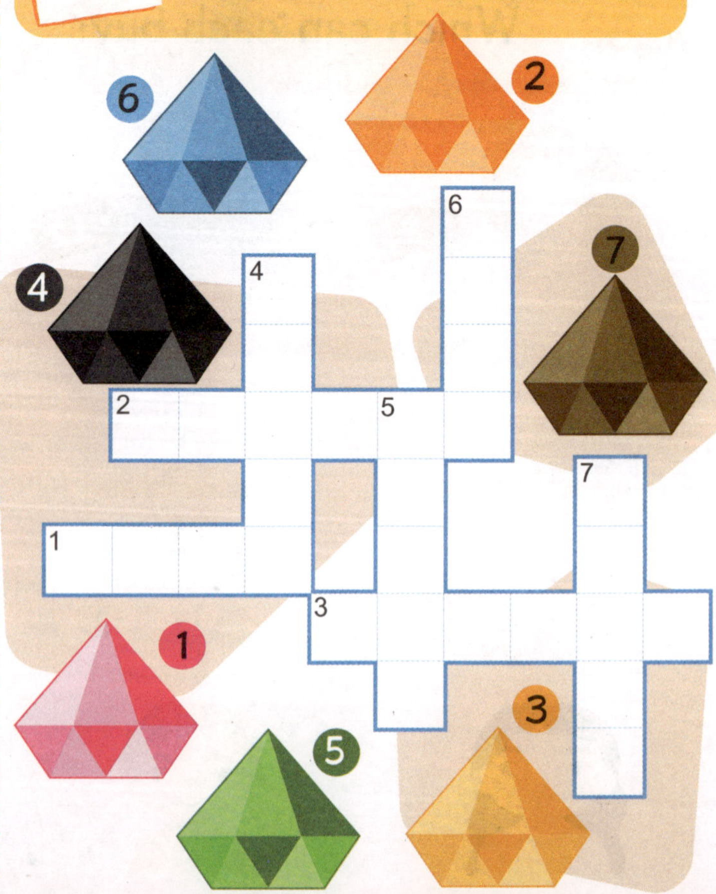

65 Circle the corresponding shape.

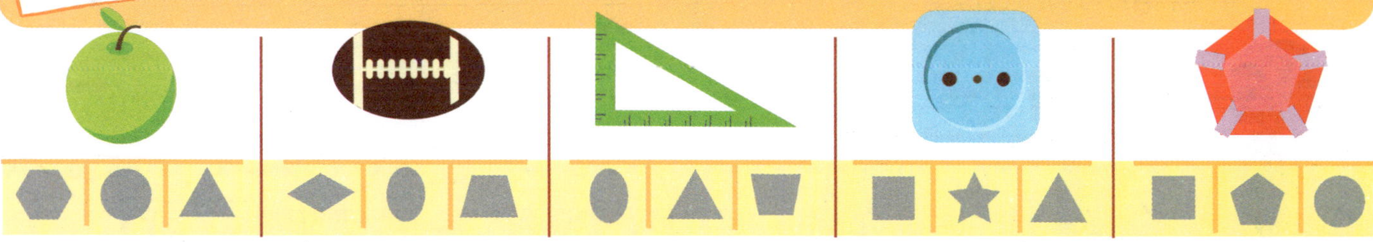

66 Find 7 differences.

68 Count and add.

69 Fill in the missing letter.

 C_R

 D_CK

 B_LL

 B_RD

67 In which vase is not three flowers, not two flowers, not five flowers, not four flowers?

70 Find the correct shadow.

72 Odd or even?

2+2 2+3 4+5 3+3

1+2 1+3 5+0 4+6

71 Join the dots and copy the shapes.

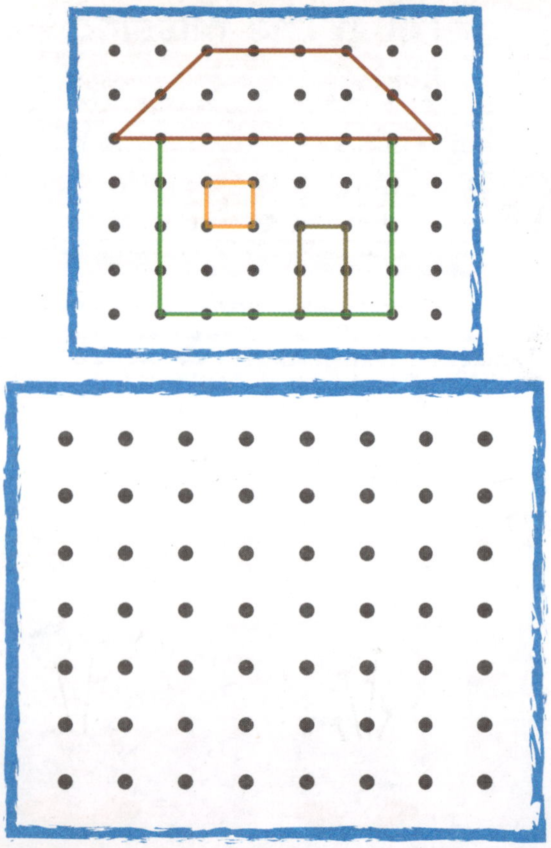

73 Decode the 3-letter words.

2 O	1 M	3 M
1	2	3

3 W	1 C	2 O
1	2	3

74 Dot to dot, then colour.

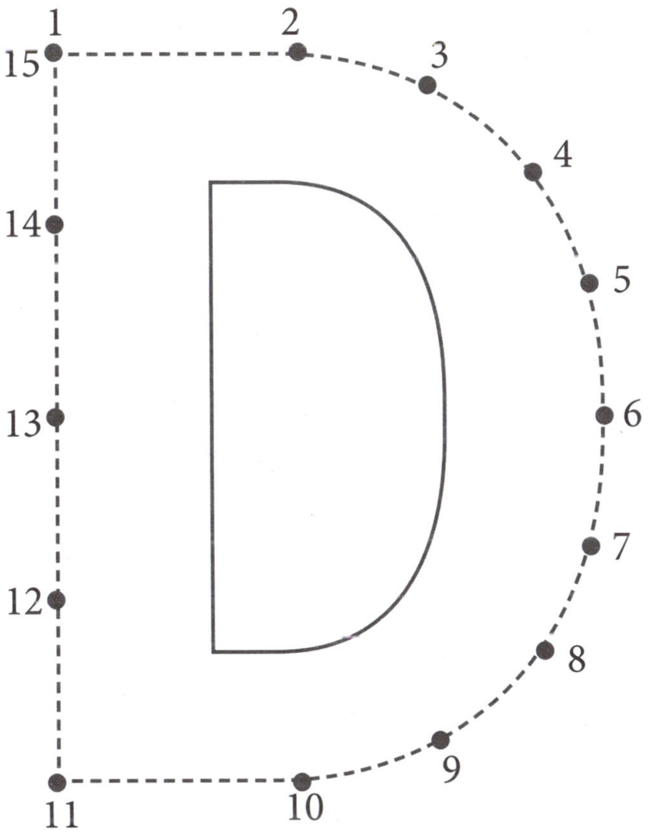

75 Subtract and circle the correct answer.

1 2 3
4 5 6
7 8 9

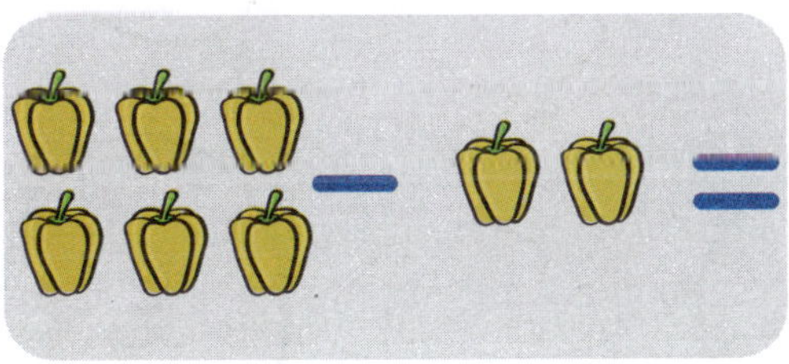

1 2 3
4 5 6
7 8 9

1 2 3
4 5 6
7 8 9

76 What should be the first letter?

_ueen Bee

D
Q
G

77 Size match

a b c d e

a b c d e

78 How many triangles?

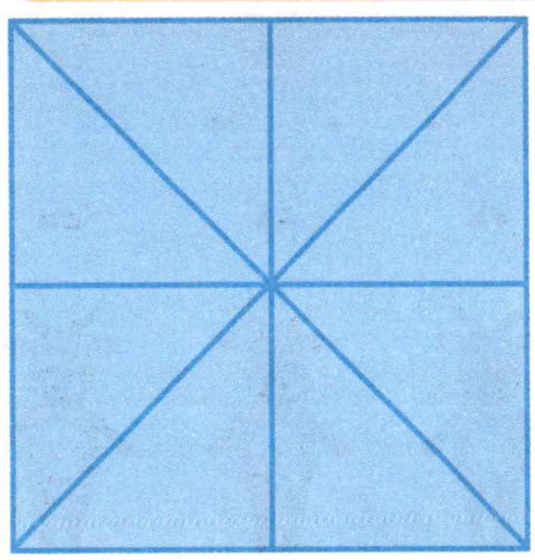

79 Colour the same number of boxes as given on the left.

5

3

7

2

80 Trace the shapes.

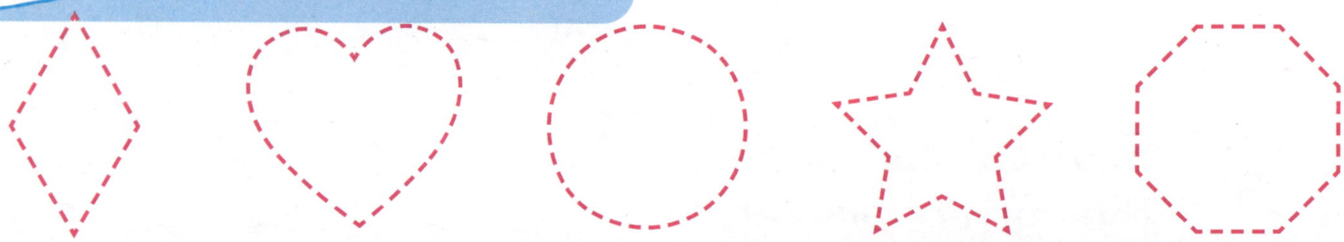

81 Odd one out.

82 Colour the odd number red.

83 Solve the rebus.

84 Across and down

85 Letter writing practice

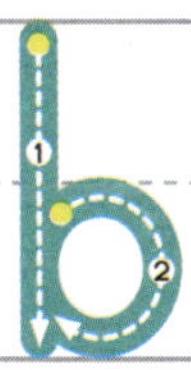

86 Maths puzzle

87 Which is different? Circle it.

88 Number writing practice

91 Colour only the triangles.

89 Fill in the missing letters.

 S__N

 FR__G

 L___N

 P__N

 W__RM

 Z__BR__

90 Colour the blocks according to the numbers written on the apples.

92 Trace small letters.

a b c d e f g h i j

k l m n o p q r s t

u v w x y z

93 Subtract the following.

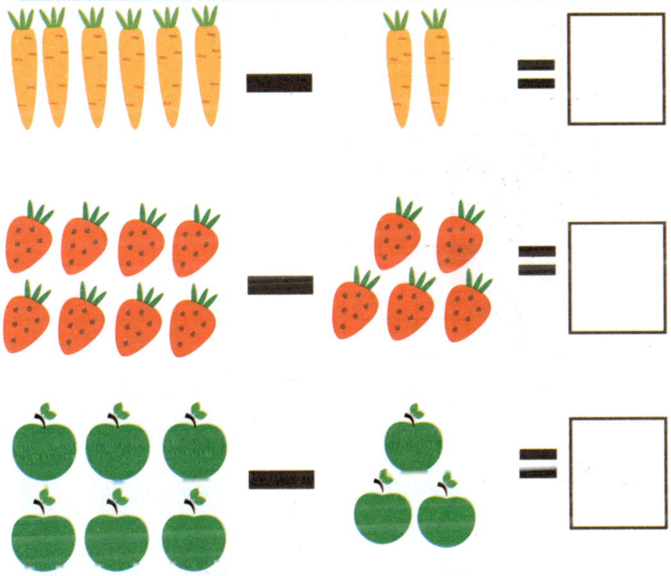

95 What is the weather like?

94 Which duck is neither small nor big?

96 Match with their initials.

T ●

B ●

F ●

C ●

P ●

97 Complete the number sentences.

☐	+	☐	+	☐	= 13
+		+		+	
☐	+	7	+	☐	= 13
+		+		+	
☐	+	☐	+	☐	= 13
=		=		=	
13		13		13	

98 Divide and match with their quotient.

8 56:7 27:9 6 36:6 3 4+2 6 8+1 9

99 Follow the pattern.

100 Find the path from 1 to 10.

3	7	6	3	4	10		
4	6	5	9	3	8		
3	2	3	4	8	8	9	10
3	1	5	5	6	7	10	7
		2	4	4	9	6	7
		1	6	3	6	5	9

101 Dot to dot, then colours

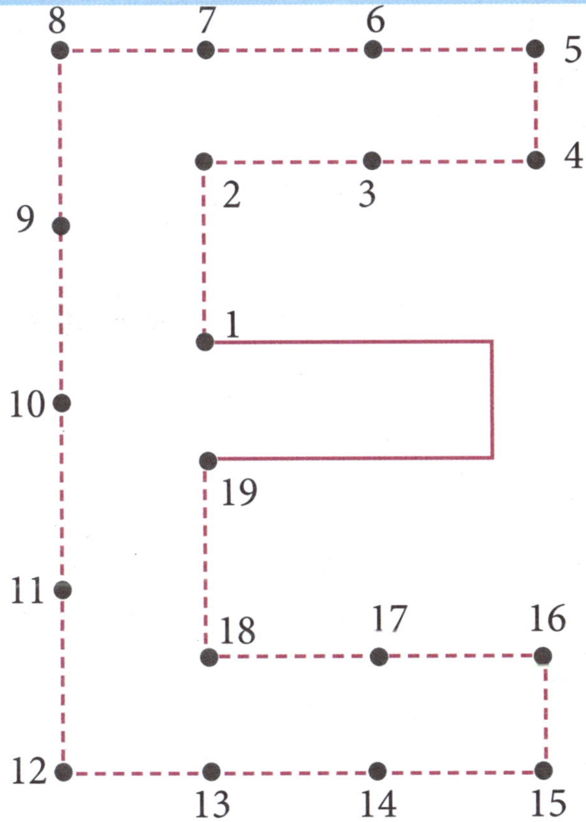

104 Find the missing numbers.

6	+		=	10
+				-
2				
=				=
	-	5	=	

9	-		=	
-				+
				4
=				=
5	+		=	11

	-	6	=	
-				+
				9
=				=
4	+		=	10

1	+	5	=	
+				+
=				=
	+	5	=	9

102 Tick (✓) the right set of shapes.

A ☐ B ☐ C ☐

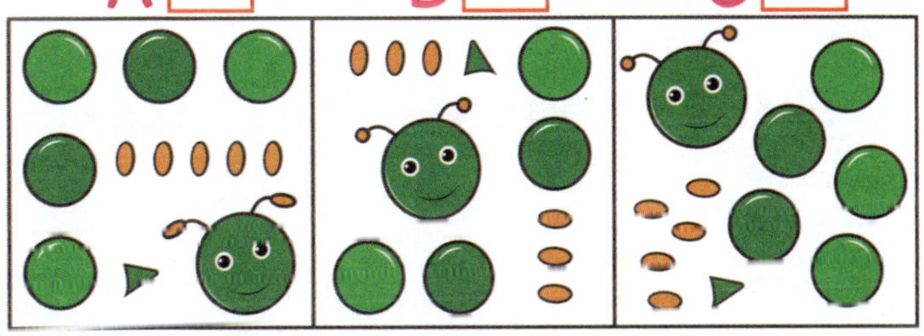

103 Addition

$73 + 25 = \_\_$

$14 + 43 = \_\_$

$28 + 61 = \_\_$

$26 + 52 = \_\_$

$25 + 53 = \_\_$

105 How many?

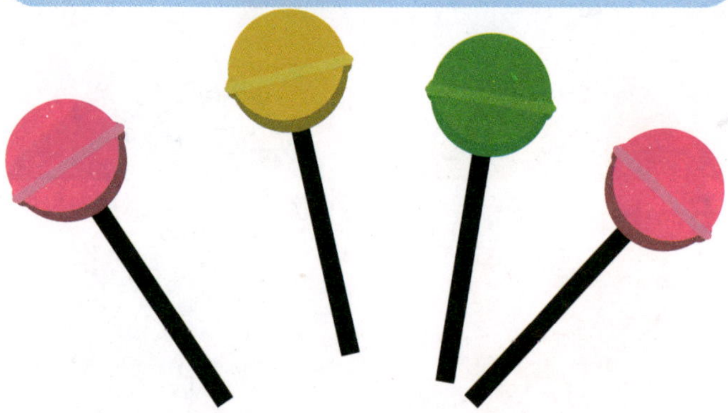

1 4 9

106 Solve and colour.

5+4 8-3 1+6

2+3 4+4 4+2

2+5 9-1 3+6

107 Handwriting practice

108 Number the body parts of the stork.

1-eye 2-head 3-beak 4-neck

5-wing 6-body 7-feather

8-leg 9-tail

109 Find the matching shadow.

110 How many cubes are in the figures?

7 6 8

6 7 5

9 10 8

9 8 10

111 Trace capital letters.

A B C D E F G H I J

K L M N O P Q R S T

U V W X Y Z

112 Trace the word and practise sound 't'.

ant ant ant

ant ant ant

ant ant ant

115 Match objects with their names.

Book

Board

Chair

Desk

Pencil

Bag

113 Add the following.

 +  = ☐

 +  = ☐

 +  = ☐

 +  = ☐

114 Number writing practice

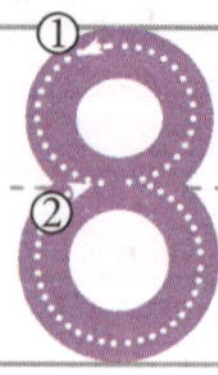

8 8 8 8 8

8 8 8 8 8 8 8

8 8 8 8 8 8 8

116 Join the dots and copy the shapes.

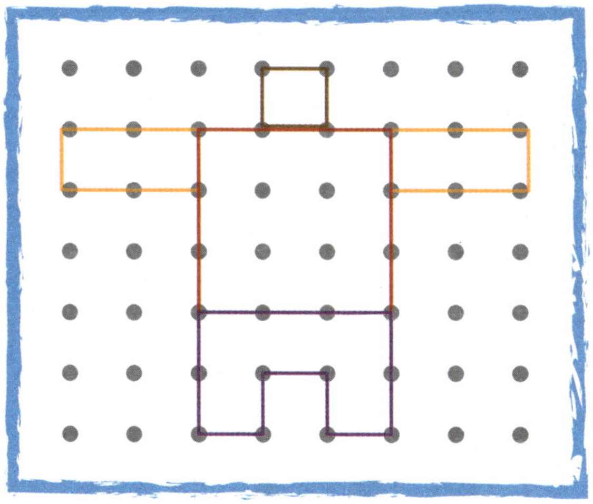

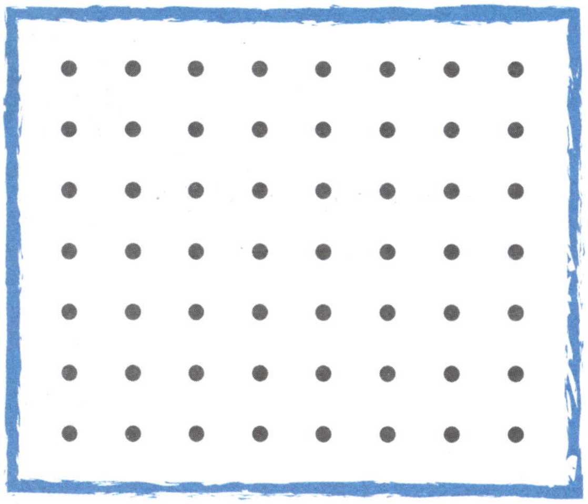

117 Riddle with numbers.

118 Solve the rebus.

119 Crack the maze.

120 What word does the picture and letters make?

HOC

121 Letter writing practice

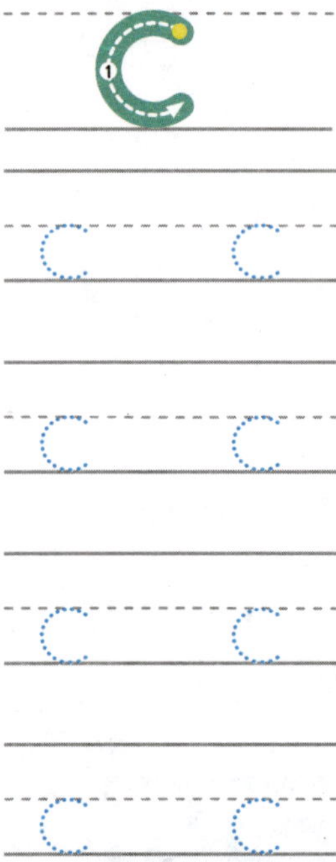

car

123 Which geometric figure is the object?

122 How many?

124 Finish the pattern.

125 Greater or smaller?

78		18	41		55	55		77
15		51	34		83	98		81
41		24	72		22	25		47

126 Match by shape.

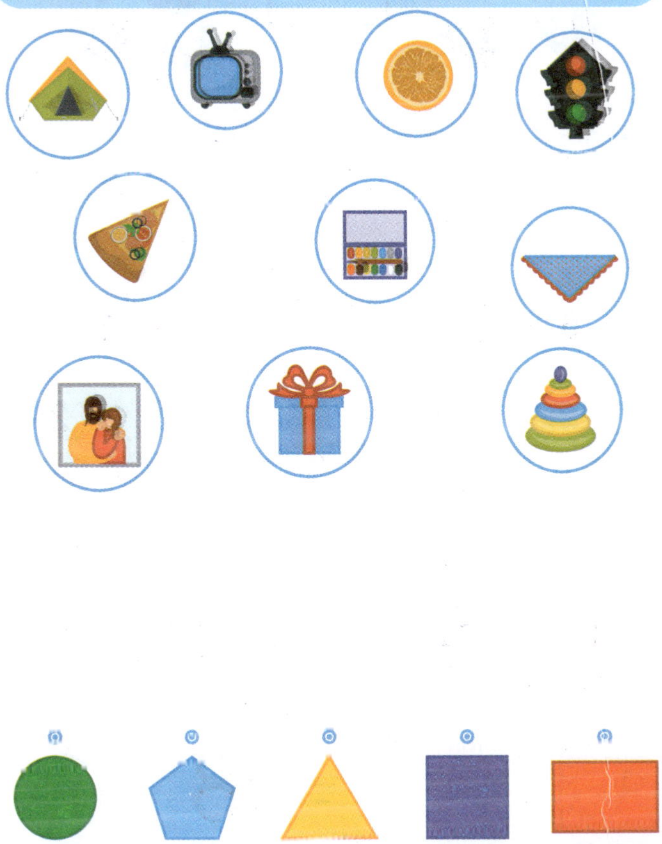

128 Draw the other half.

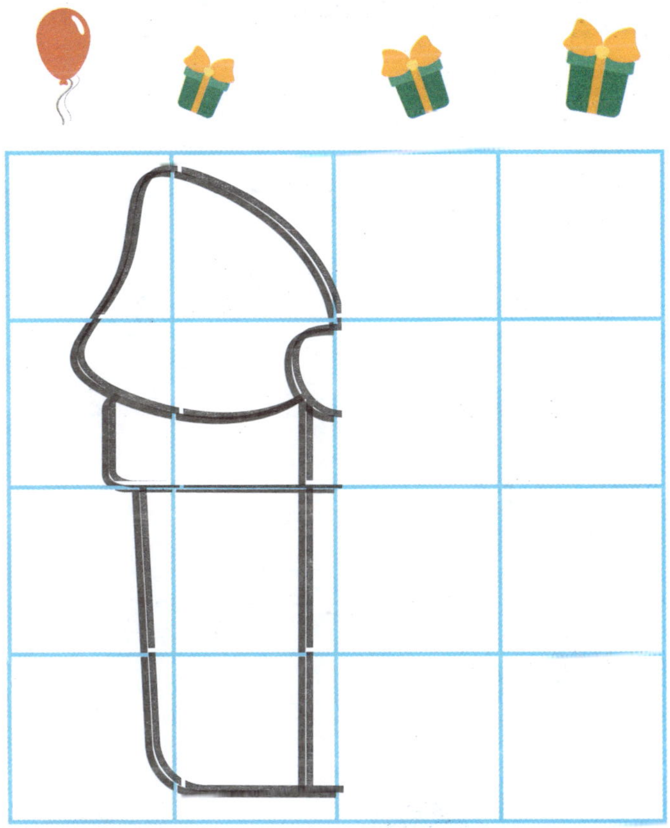

127 Circle the correct fractions.

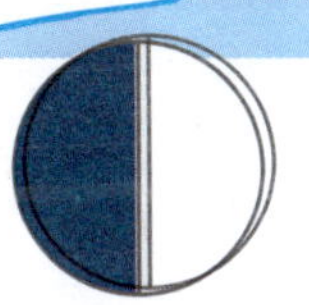 $\frac{3}{1}$ $\frac{2}{1}$ $\frac{1}{2}$ $\frac{3}{2}$

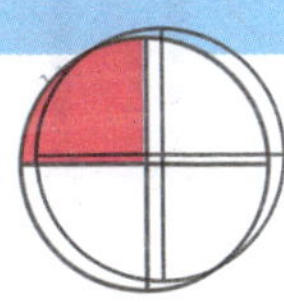 $\frac{4}{1}$ $\frac{1}{4}$ $\frac{1}{3}$ $\frac{3}{4}$

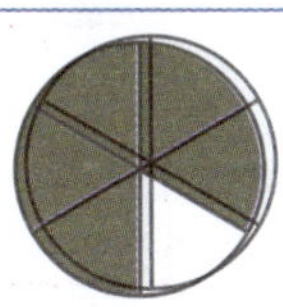 $\frac{3}{1}$ $\frac{6}{5}$ $\frac{6}{7}$ $\frac{5}{6}$

 $\frac{4}{10}$ $\frac{5}{12}$ $\frac{3}{11}$ $\frac{3}{10}$

129 <, = or >?

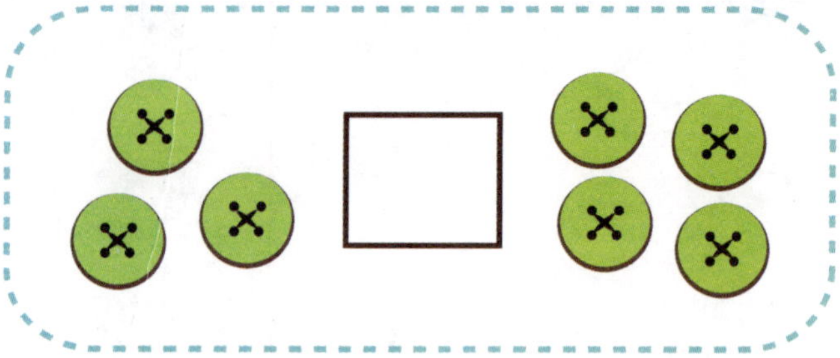

130 Subtract the following.

9 − 1 → 8 − 5 → 3	7 − 3 → ☐ − 2 → ☐	8 − 2 → ☐ − 5 → ☐	5 − 3 → ☐ − 2 → ☐

131 What is kept in a bank?

132 Guess and solve.

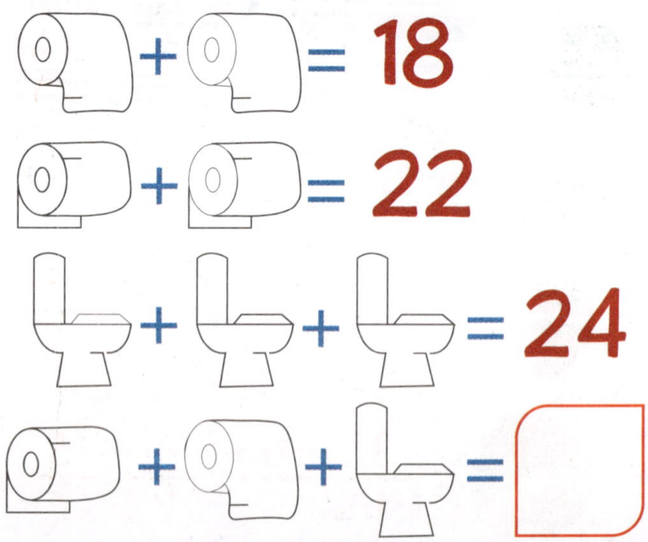

133 Drop the word and practise sound 'b'.

bed bed bed

bed bed bed

bed bed bed

134 Where do they live?

135 Drop the coin in its piggy bank.

136 Fill in the missing numbers.

137 Solve the rebus.

140 Count and add.

 + 2 = ☐

 + 2 = ☐

138 Number writing practice

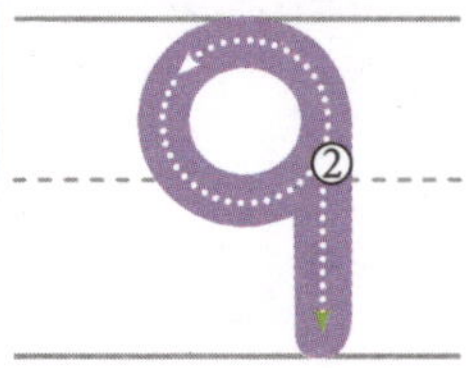

139 Pick and fill the numbers in order.

141 Decode the 5-letter words.

3 A	5 D	1 A	2 W	4 R
1	2	3	4	5

4 N	1 S	2 T	5 E	3 O
1	2	3	4	5

142 Find the difference.

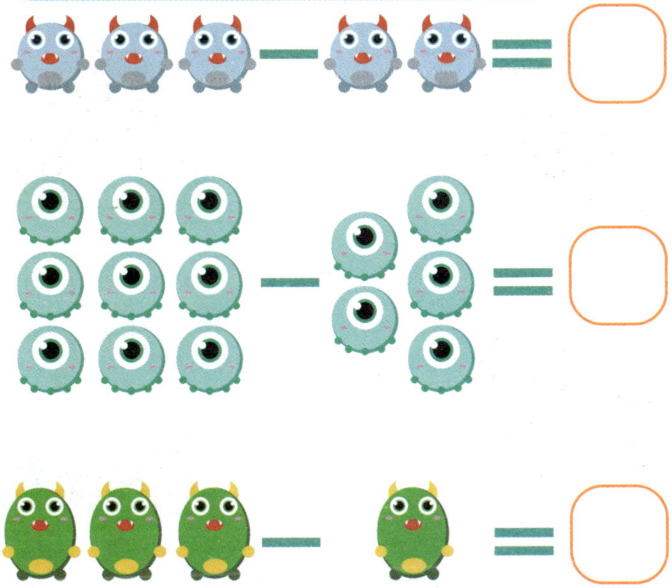

143 What word does the picture, the symbol and the letter make?

144 <, > or =?

145 Write the heavier weight.

146 Will the 3-masted ship be able to reach the island?

147 Compare the numbers <, >, =.

5	>	3	3	○	4
6	○	8	1	○	2
2	○	2	5	○	5
4	○	9	8	○	10
3	○	1	6	○	5
7	○	7	9	○	6

149 Match with their homes.

148 Help the bus reach the school.

150 Trace and colour the butterfly.

151 Dot to dot, then colour.

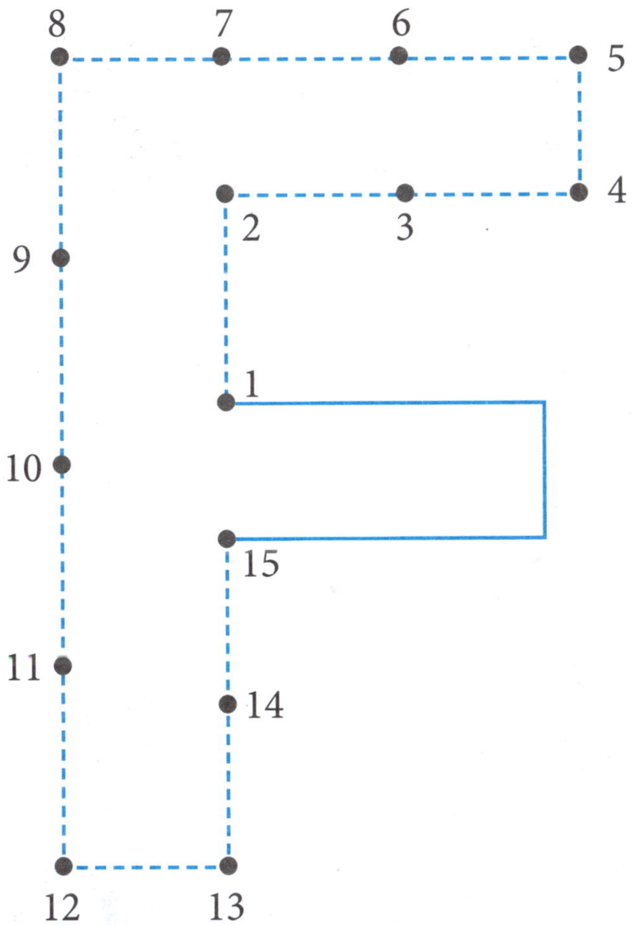

153 Fill the markers.

2	
1	1
2	

3	
1	2
2	
3	

4	
1	3
2	
3	
4	

5	
1	4
2	
3	
4	
5	

154 Find the value.

113 = 35

114 = 46

115 = 57

116 = 68

117 = 79

118 = ☐

152 Find 10 differences.

155 Make an ordered list of numbers to the exit.

		32	2	2	28	27	26	25	10
		←	31	30	29	23	9	24	29
16	18	16	10	8	17	24	6	23	10
17	21	19	14	11	19	20	21	22	11
13	14	15	16	17	18	19	7	12	10
12	9	13	12	18	10	9	8		
11	10	9	8	11	12	5	6		
16	19	15	7	9	10	7	4		
14	13	10	6	13	2	1	←		
12	11	8	5	4	3	6	10		

156 Find 7 differences.

157 Alphabet sudoku

	C		A
D			
	B		

158 Find the shapes with corners. One is done for you.

159 Match by shadow.

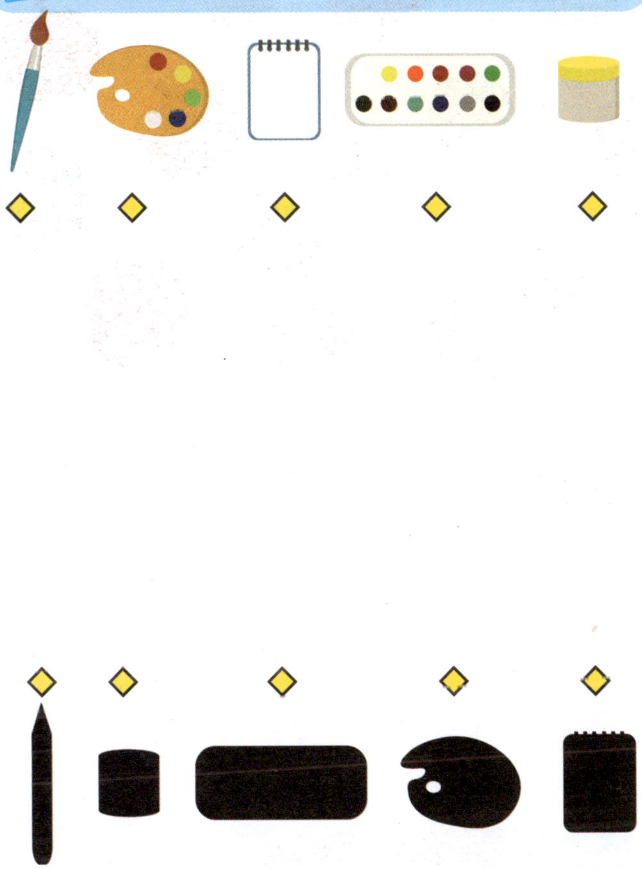

161 Draw the other half.

160 Letter writing practice

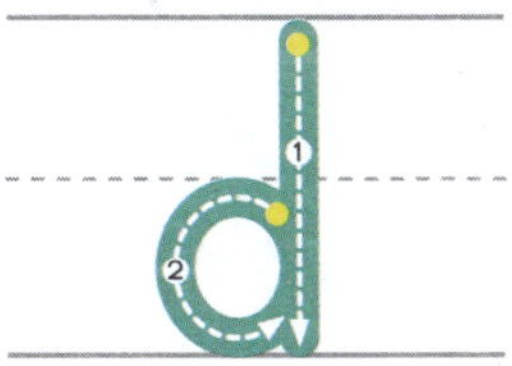

Duck

162 Trace the letters.

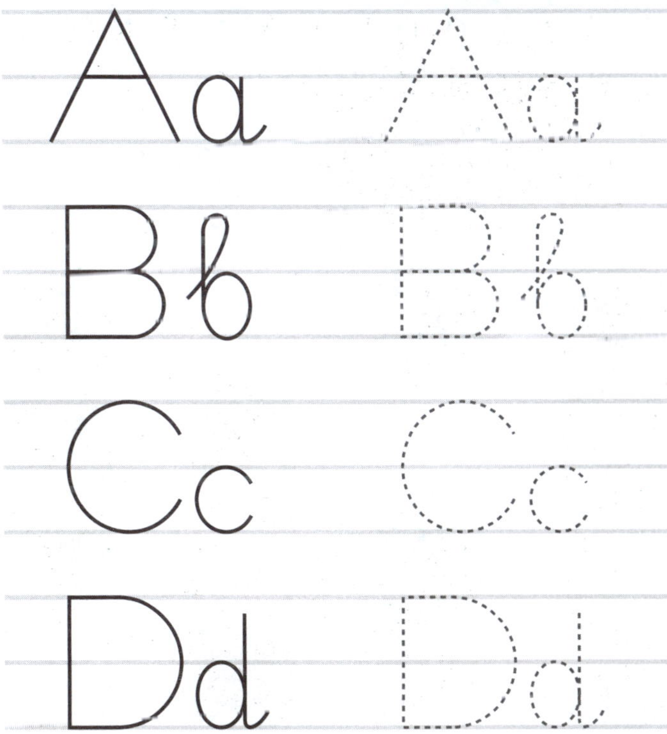

163 How many?

164 Find the number names in the grid.

Q	C	S	U	P	F	D	U	M	I	A	P	S	I
O	N	E	T	K	O	H	U	J	A	R	A	N	G
S	E	V	K	L	U	W	A	X	A	Z	Q	F	A
M	S	E	Y	M	R	C	F	E	I	G	H	T	R
A	L	N	T	P	T	Q	E	L	P	I	H	W	C
V	N	S	S	F	K	D	Z	E	A	K	X	O	H
I	I	U	Q	I	Z	V	A	V	R	Q	E	T	Y
X	T	D	Q	V	L	R	Z	E	R	O	A	M	T
D	T	H	R	E	E	H	L	N	N	N	B	M	E
E	S	Z	J	O	Q	W	S	X	C	E	N	I	N
Q	W	R	I	S	Z	X	D	J	C	I	K	L	O

165 Find what is missing in the spaces.

2	4	?	8
3	?	9	12
4	8	?	16
5	10	15	?

166 What is the weather like?

167 <, > or = ?

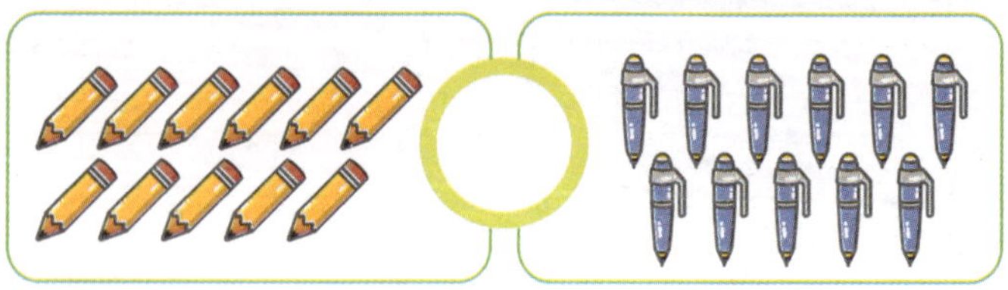

168 Trace the word and practise sound 'i'.

bib bib bib bib bib

bib bib bib bib bib

169 What are they called?

Candy

Hamburger

Bread

Ice cream

Fish

Salad

Pasta

Cheese

171 Count and write.

170 How many?

(5) (2) (9)

(7) (6) (5)

(4) (7) (1)

172 Fill in the missing numbers.

☐	–	4	=	2
–		+		+
☐		☐		6
=		=		=
3	+	☐	=	☐

9	–	☐	=	☐
–		–		+
4		☐		9
=		=		=
☐	+	5	=	☐

175 Solve the rebus.

173 Number writing practice

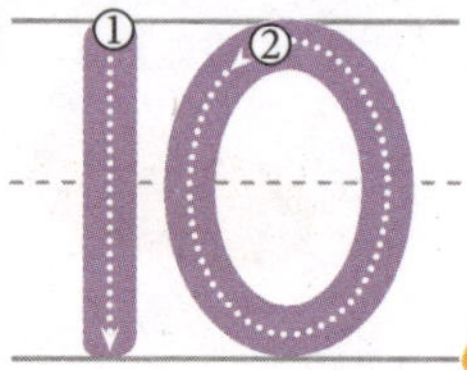

10 10 10 10 10

10 10 10 10 10 10 10

10 10 10 10 10 10 10

174 Colour using the code.

1 2 3 4 5 6

7 8 9

176 Match the money and the price.

177 Draw along the dashed lines.

178 Find 10 differences.

179 Find the right path.

180 Write the missing numbers.

181 Shadow match

183 Work out the next numbers.

	+8	+8	+8	+8
3	11	19		
1				
2				
4				

182 Take away 5 and write the new number.

184 Match the geometric figure and the object.

187 Yes or no?

Ice cream treats the throat?

yes NO

Can a rabbit fly?

yes NO

185 Count different shapes.

186 Letter writing practice

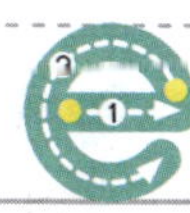

elephant

188 Compare and choose.

189 Find the numbers to make 10.

1 + 9 = 10

☐ + ☐ = 10

☐ + ☐ = 10

☐ + ☐ = 10

190 Number from smallest to biggest.

191 Match with the time.

12:45 7:15 4:00 6:40

192 Odd one out

193 Help the bear taste some honey.

194 Match by shadow.

196 Find 5 differences.

197 Greater than, less than or equal to?

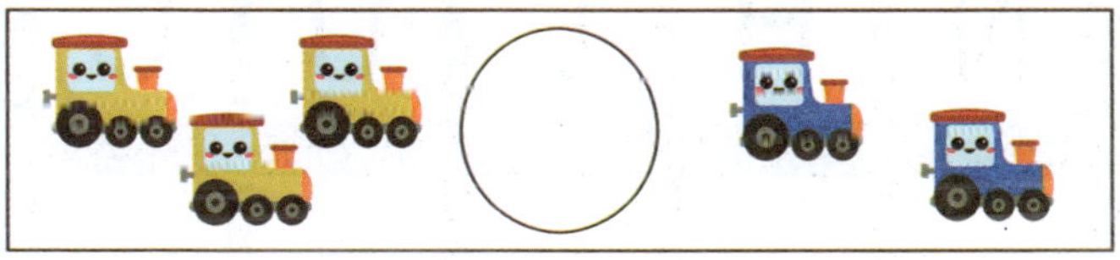

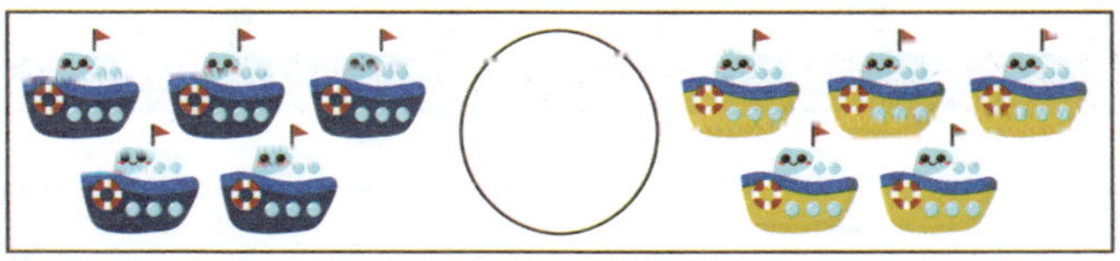

195 Write their names.

198 Write number names.

1 🍄 ______

2 🍎🍎 ______

3 🐥🐥🐥 ______

4 🦋🦋🦋🦋 ______

5 ⚽⚽⚽⚽⚽ ______

6 🧁🧁🧁🧁🧁🧁 ______

7 🐟🐟🐟🐟🐟🐟🐟 ______

8 🍓🍓🍓🍓🍓🍓🍓🍓 ______

9 🌸🌸🌸🌸🌸🌸🌸🌸🌸 ______

10 ⭐⭐⭐⭐⭐⭐⭐⭐⭐⭐ ______

199 Decode the 5-letter words.

3 N	5 H	1 L	2 U	4 C
1	2	3	4	5

2 A	4 T	5 E	1 W	3 S
1	2	3	4	5

200 Subtract in the hut.

	-	1	=	9
-		-		-
5	-		=	
=		=		=
	-		=	4

201 What is wrong in the picture?

202 Dot to dot, then colour.

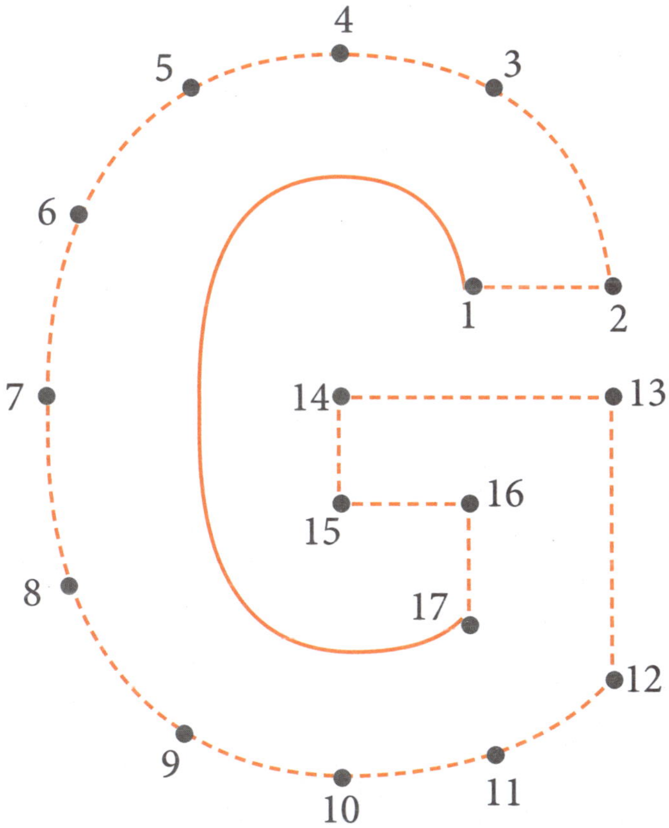

203 Match by shadow.

204 Colour the dog.

205 Find 10 differences.

206 What comes next?

+7 +7 +7 +7

1, 8, 15, ___, ___

6, ___, ___, ___, ___

4, ___, ___, ___, ___

7, ___, ___, ___, ___

207 Letter writing practice

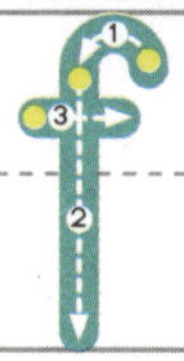

Fox

f f f f f

f f f f f

f f f f f

f f f f f

209 Help the bird find her eggs.

208 Which does not belong?

210 Let's count.

4 + 4 = ◯

5 + 3 = ◯

6 + 2 = ◯

7 + 1 = ◯

8 + 1 = ◯

211 Which should go in?

◯ 

◯ 

◯ 

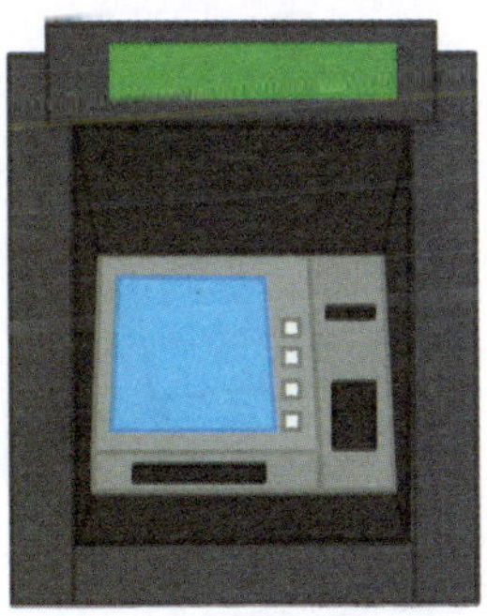

◯ 

◯ 

◯ 

212 Maths puzzle

-	7	8	9
3	4		
4			
5			
6			

213 What are they called?

 • • Urchin

 • • Umbrella

 • • Uguisu

 • • Uncle

214 Match with their sum.

216 Whose shadow is it?

215 What did the fisherman catch?

217 Fill with the corresponding letters.

218 Dot to dot, then colour.

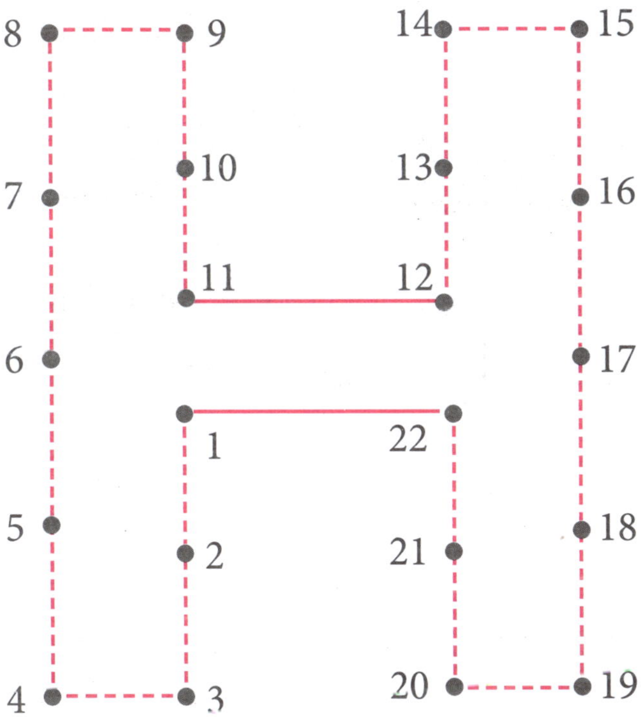

220 How much money is going into the purse?

219 Find the twin Easter bunnies.

221 Find these bird names.

B	R	Y	D	U	C	K	A
S	F	H	A	E	U	D	B
J	L	M	P	R	C	I	P
U	K	Z	A	A	K	L	I
S	P	A	R	R	O	W	W
X	Y	H	R	U	O	A	O
O	N	K	O	T	A	A	R
N	V	C	T	A	F	Y	C

CROW CUCKOO PARROT
SPARROW DUCK

222 Match the groups.

224 Match each vehicle with its shadow.

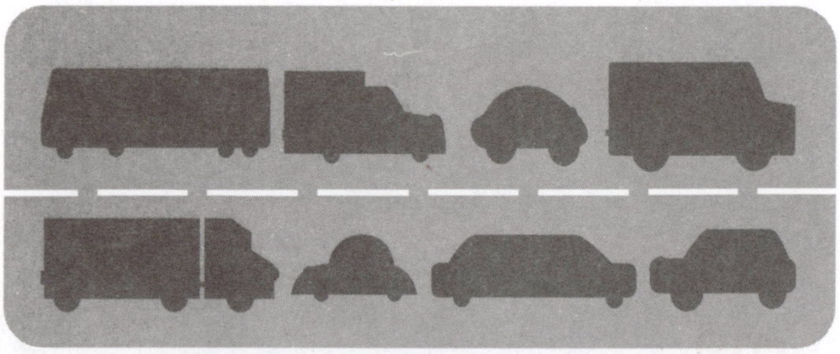

223 One shape once in each row or column.

225 Crack the maze.

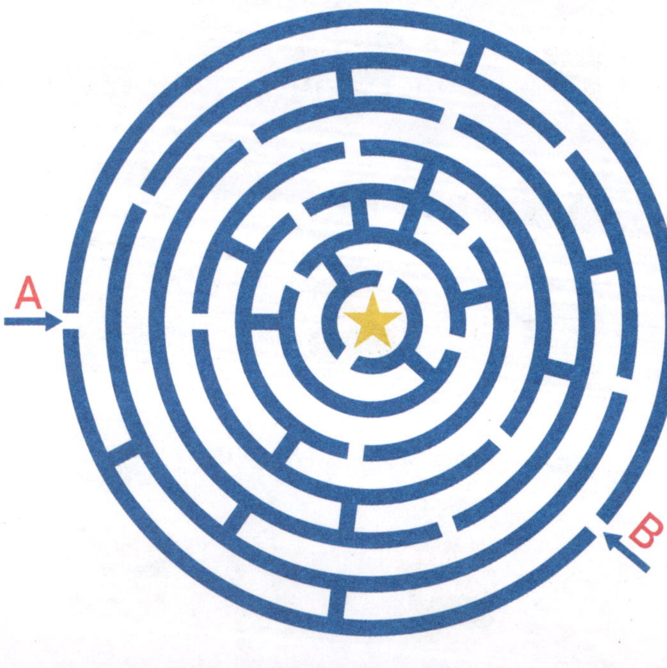

226 Find the sum.

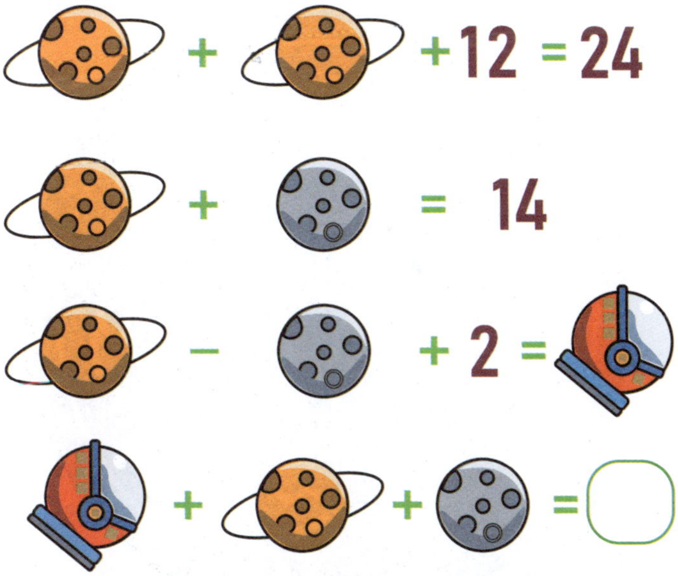

227 Which letter?

228 Write the missing numbers in sequence.

1, 2, ☐, 4, 5, ☐, 7, 8, ☐, 10

1, △, 3, △, 5, △, 7, △, 9, △

229 Letter writing practice

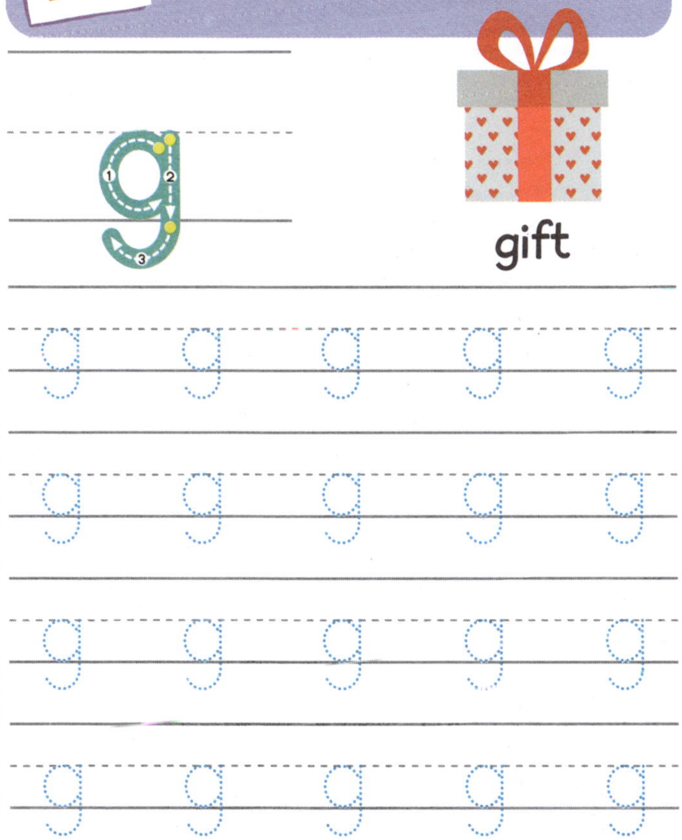

230 Trace and colour.

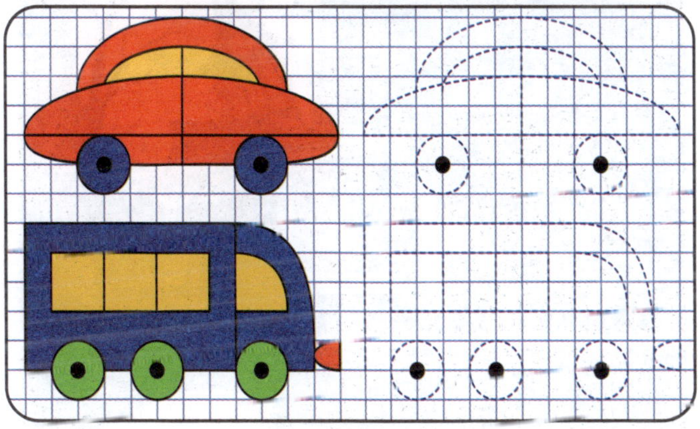

231 Which geometric figure is the object?

232 Find 14 differences.

233 Draw the cat's path to the fish.

234 Number the yellow space correctly.

235 How many?

	4 5 6 7
	1 2 3 4
	3 4 5 6
	6 7 8 9

236 Make a word with the picture and the letters.

E U

☐☐☐☐

237 <, > or = ?

☐
☐
☐

238 Number maze 1-10

		2	3	10	2	10
		1	4	6	3	4
1	3	2	3	1	2	7
7	5	4	4	7	8	9
9	1	10	5	6	5	10
7	2	7	4	6		
3	1	8	9	10		

239 Let's colour!

240 Help the crab collect some fish for its family.

242 Riddle with numbers.

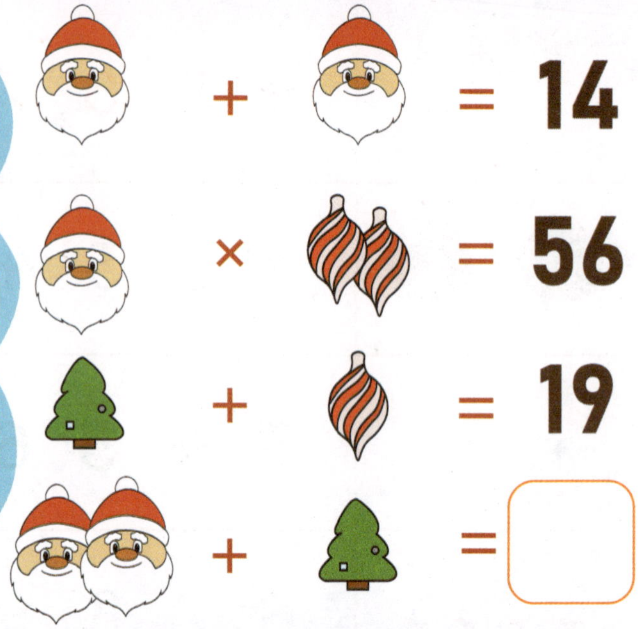

241 Count and match.

243 Cross (×) two same alarm clocks.

244 Dot to dot, then colour.

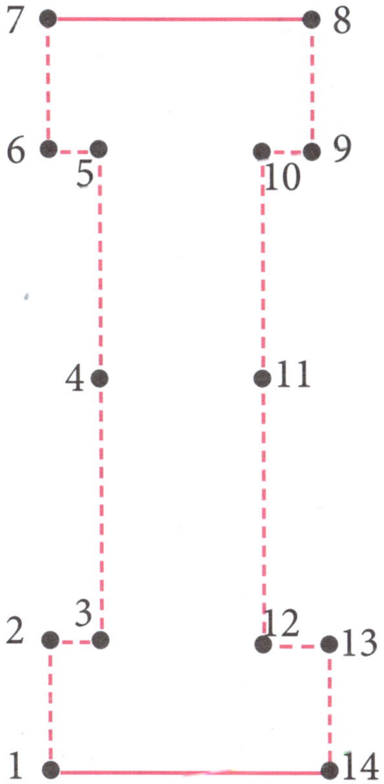

245 Colour the picture.

246 Find the correct shadow.

247 Sort by shape.

248 Choose the correct value.

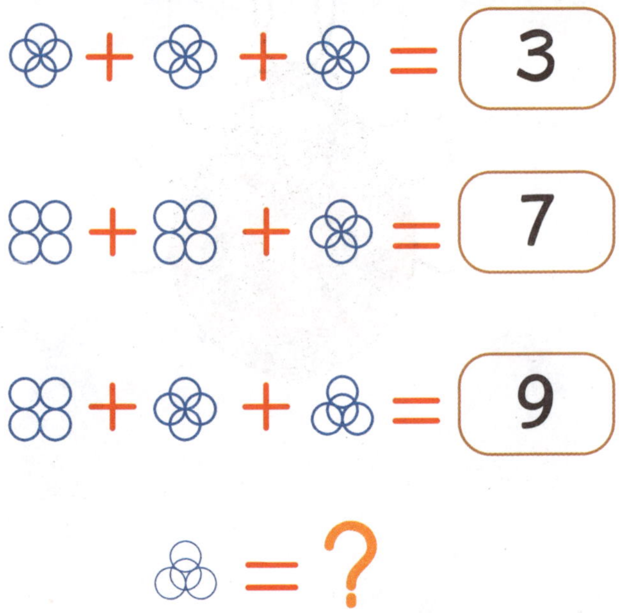

3 5 2 6

249 Find the value.

250 How many?

251 Find two same pictures.

252 Trace the word and practise sound 'u'.

bus bus bus
bus bus bus
bus bus bus

253 Shadow match

254 Use the code to colour.

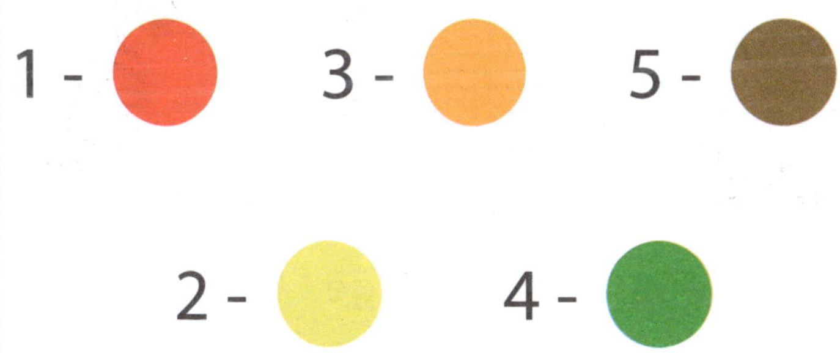

255 What comes next?

+9 +9 +9 +9

1, 10, 19, ___, ___

3, ___, ___, ___, ___

5, ___, ___, ___, ___

8, ___, ___, ___, ___

257 Match with the corresponding shape.

256 Complete the words.

t				r
h				o
s				l
s				e
z				a
l				r
m				e
s				k
e				e

emu agl ige tor

ipp ebr nak ous nai

258 Find the correct shadow.

259 Dot to dot, then colour.

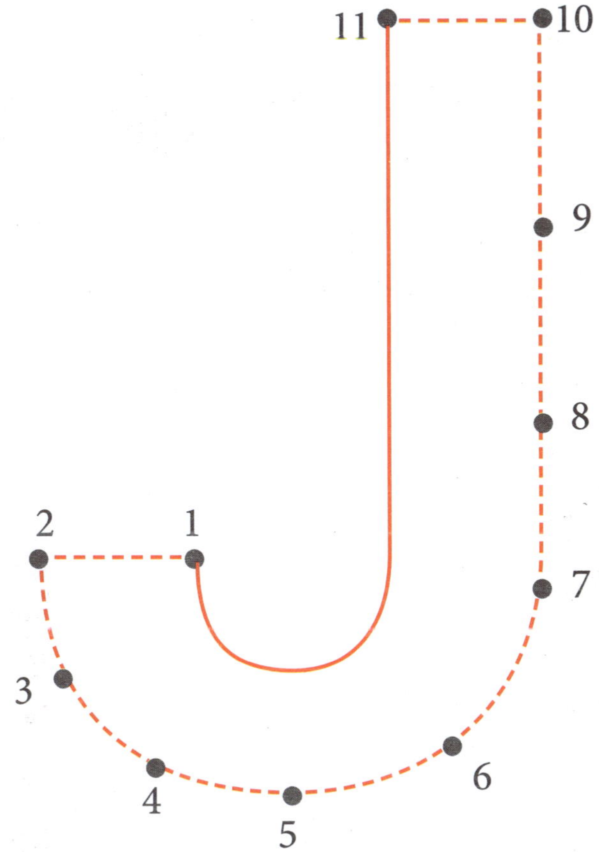

261 Find the secondary colours.

260 What time is it?

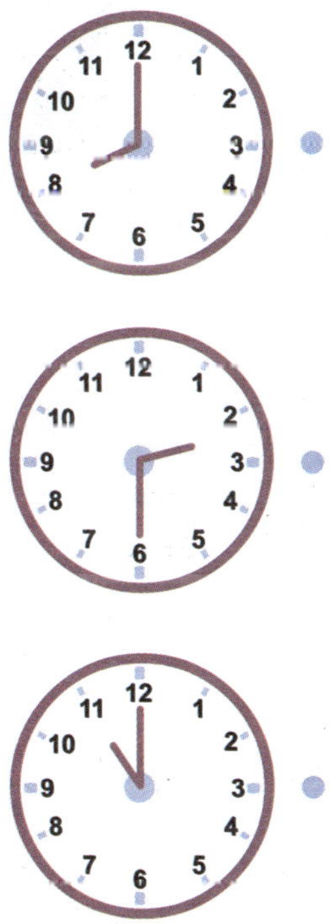

11:00

8:00

2:30

262 Add in the jam jar.

263 Letter writing practice

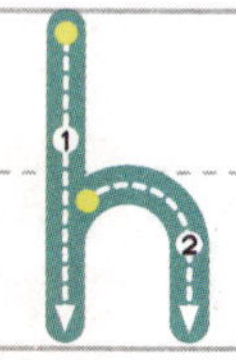

house

264 Match the image with its right spot.

265 What word do the first letters of these pictures make?

266 Match to make a whole.

267 Decode the 3-letter word.

1	3	2
N	T	E
1	2	3

268 What do the letters say?

269 <, > or = ?

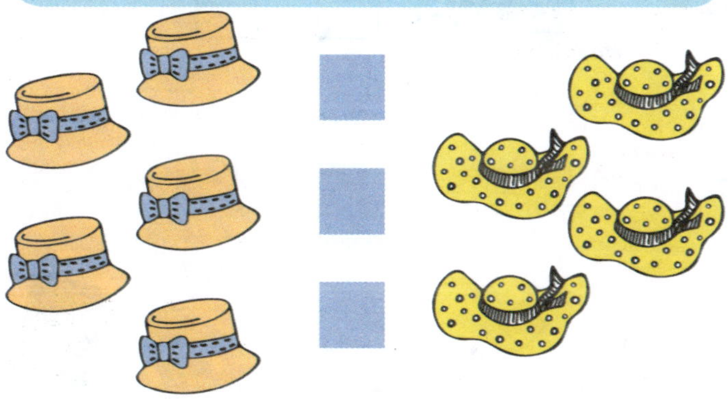

270 What is the weather like?

271 Find the value.

272 How many?

273 Write their count.

275 Write the animals names.

274 Trace the word and practise sound 'o'.

fox fox fox

fox fox fox

fox fox fox

276 Match by colour.

277 Dot to dot, then colour.

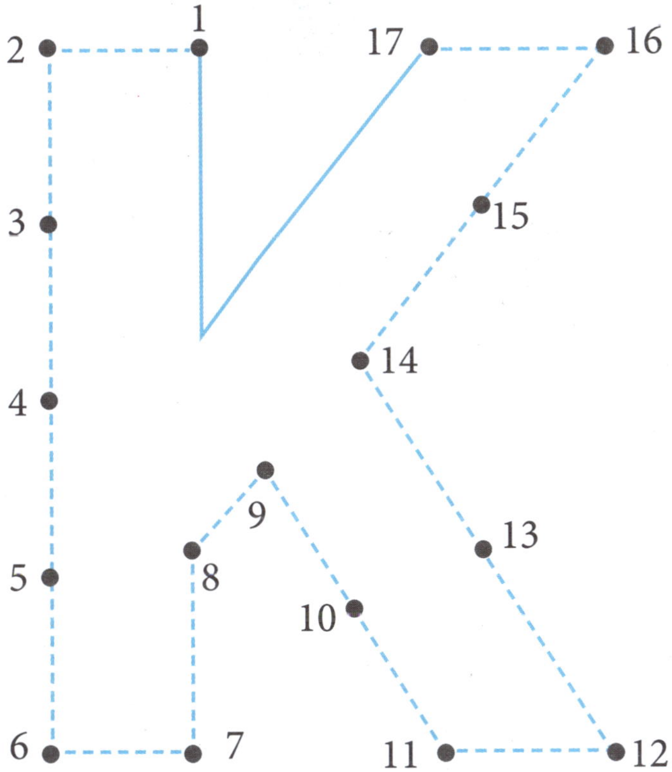

279 Find the difference.

278 Colour the bears so that they become the same.

280 Finish the pattern.

281 How many worms?

282 What is it used for?

283 What comes next?

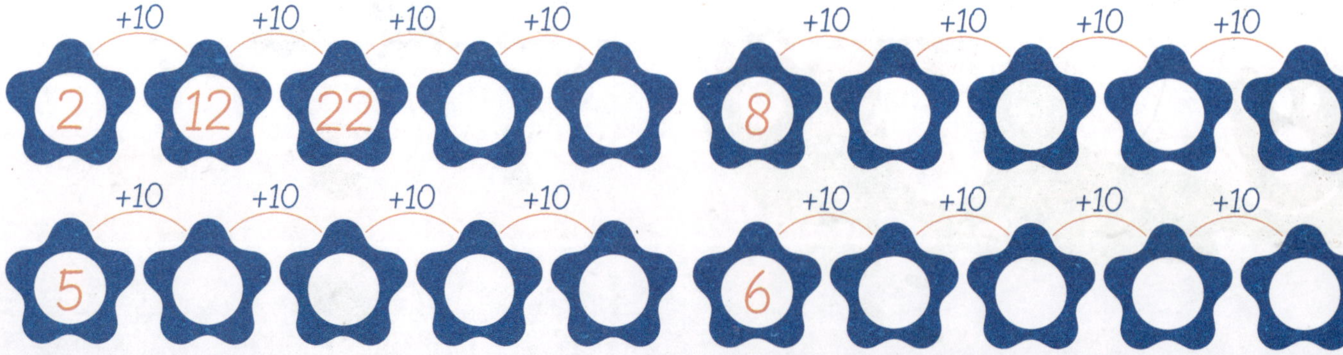

284 Trace and colour.

285 Find the value.

286 Match by shape.

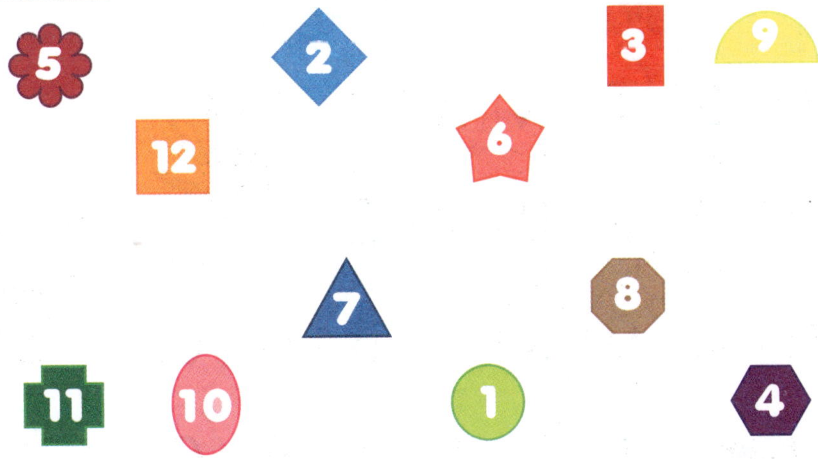

287 Circle the pictures with the same beginning sounds.

I...

J...

K...

L...

289 Riddle with numbers.

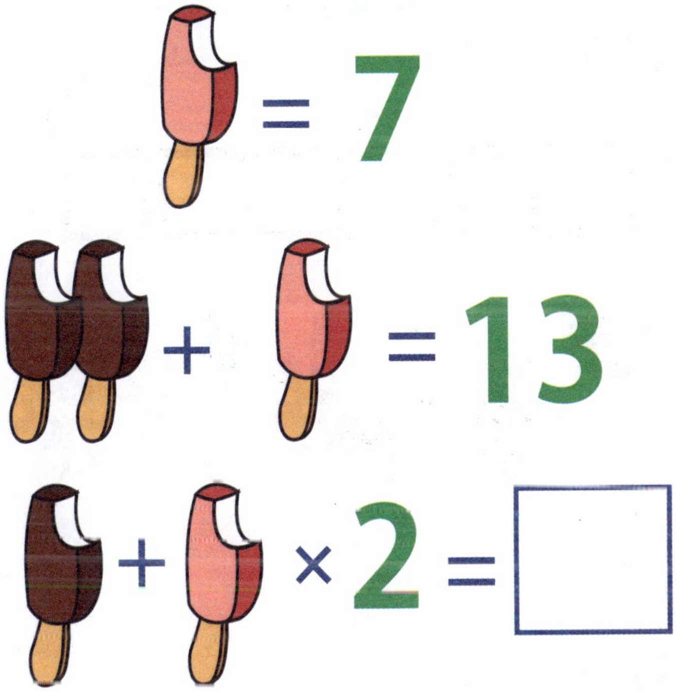

288 Count by 2s.

290 Connect letters from A to Z to help the girl get the flowers.

291 Solve the rebus.

292 <, > or = ?

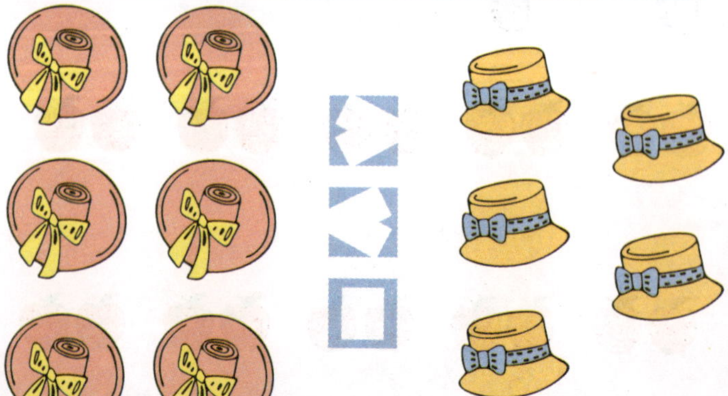

293 Riddle with numbers.

294 Find 10 differences.

295 Decode the 3-letter word.

2 E	3 D	1 R
1	2	3

298 Riddle with numbers.

296 Trace and colour.

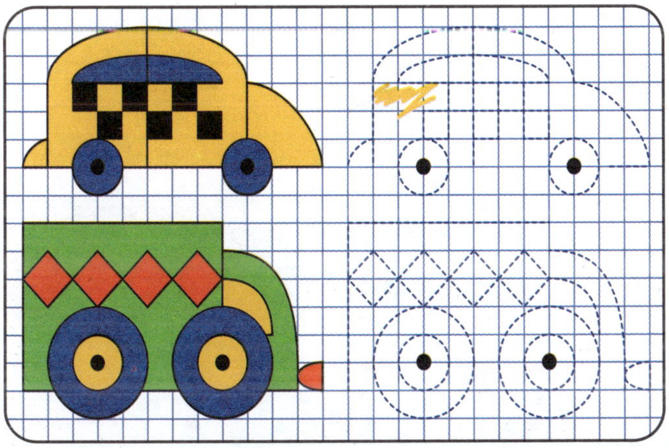

299 Pick the balls.

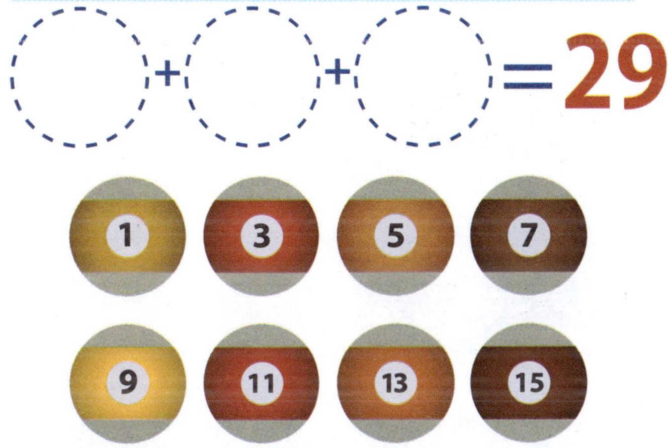

297 Number the birdhouses in sequence.

300 Write its name.

301 What is it used for?

302 What letter does this penguin look like?

303 How many?

304 Draw the remaining shapes.

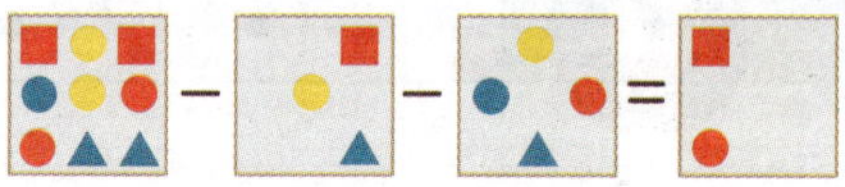

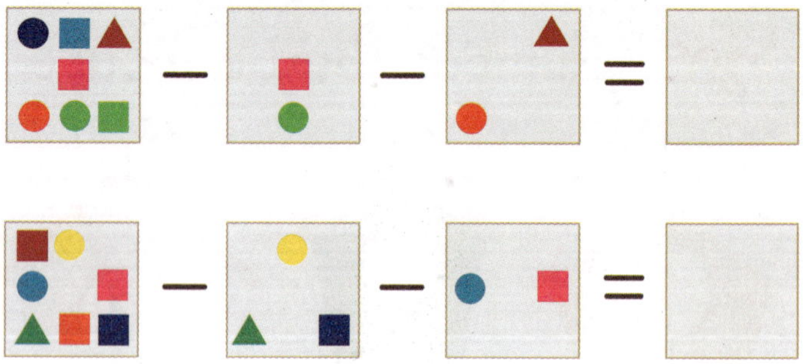

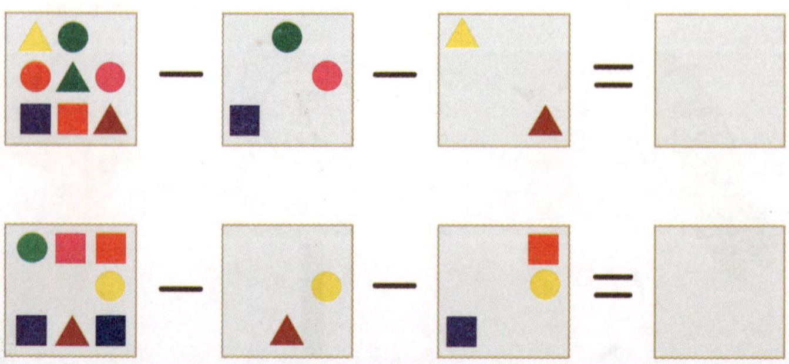

305 Find the identical two.

306 Dot to dot, then colour.

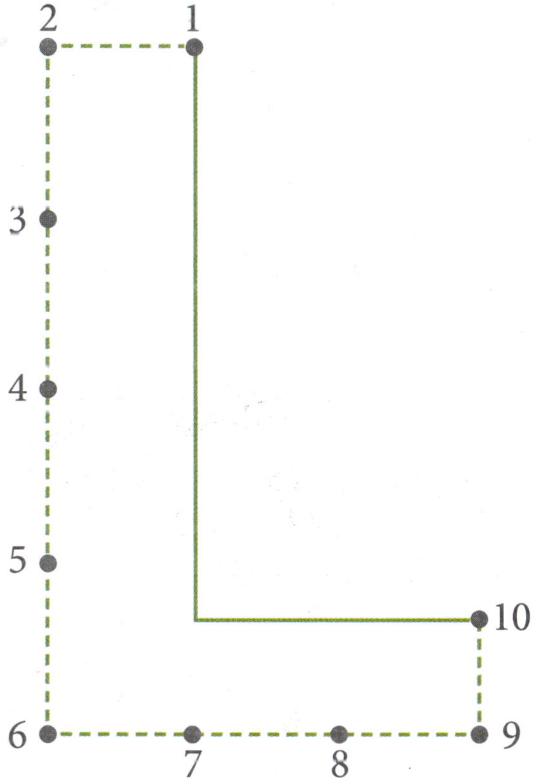

307 Find 5 differences.

308 How many?

309 Cross out W, 4 and question mark in the group.

A B C D E F G H I J K L M N O P

Q R S T U V W X Y Z ≠ ✓ ✗ ✱ @

1 2 3 4 5 6 7 8 9 0 − + × ÷ = ?

310 Find their values.

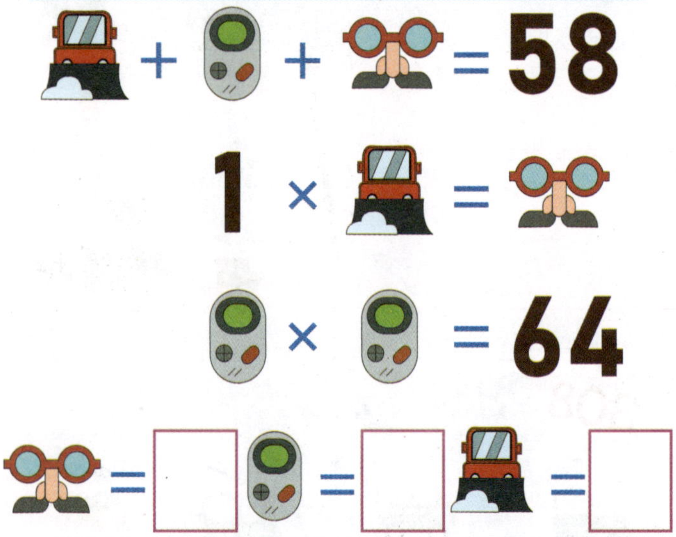

312 Which goes in?

311 Find 8 differences.

313 Write their count.

314 Trace and colour.

316 Can the bee reach the nectar?

315 Add and match.

317 Add and write.

+	6	7	8
5	11		
6			
7			
8			

318 Dot to dot, then colour.

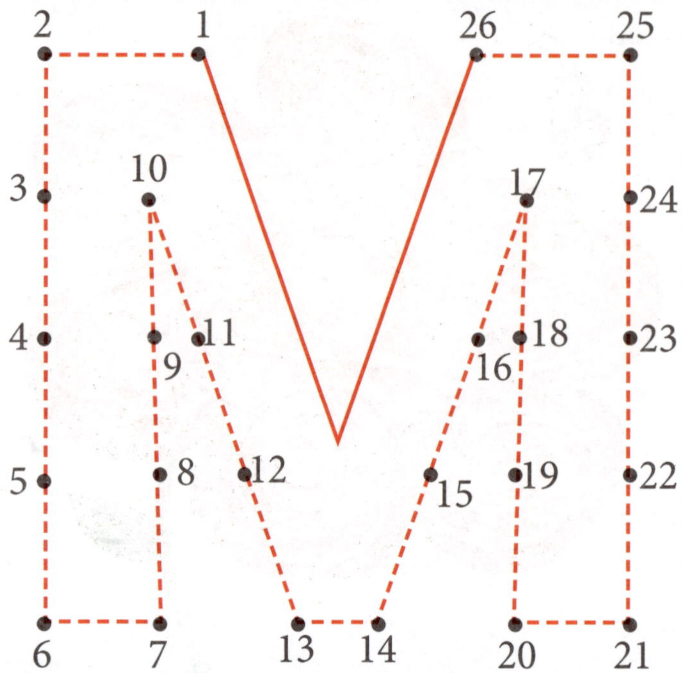

319 Trace and match the hats.

320 Write the fractions.

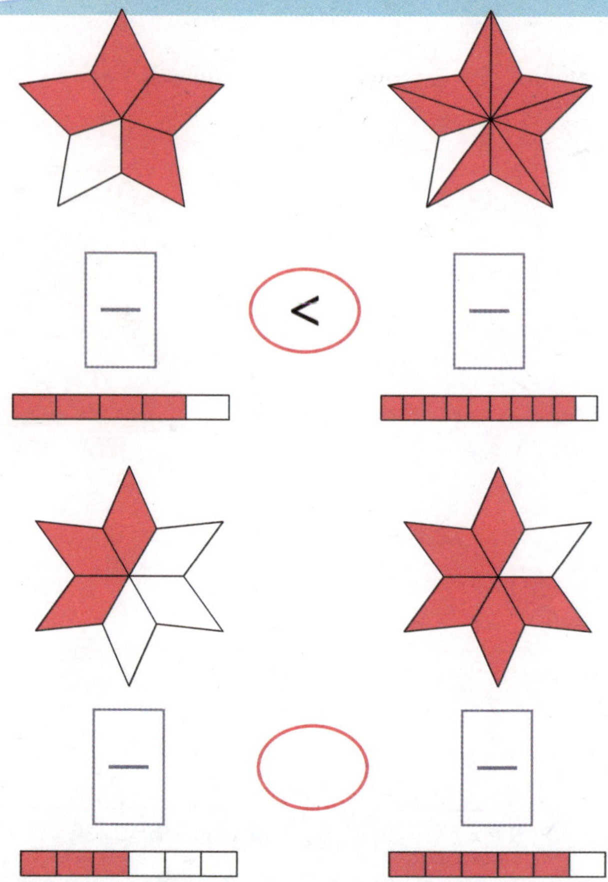

321 Find one balloon without a copy.

322 Which will come next?

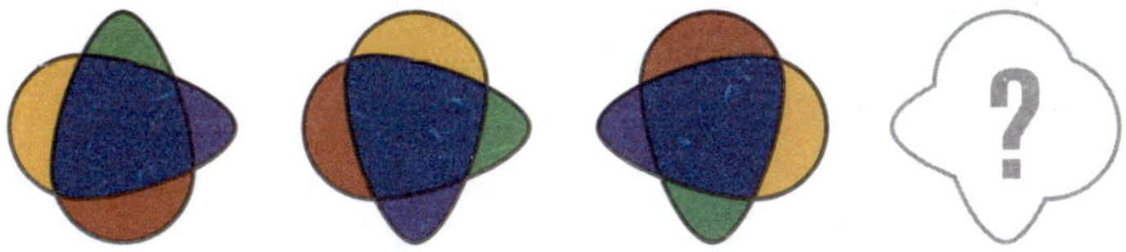

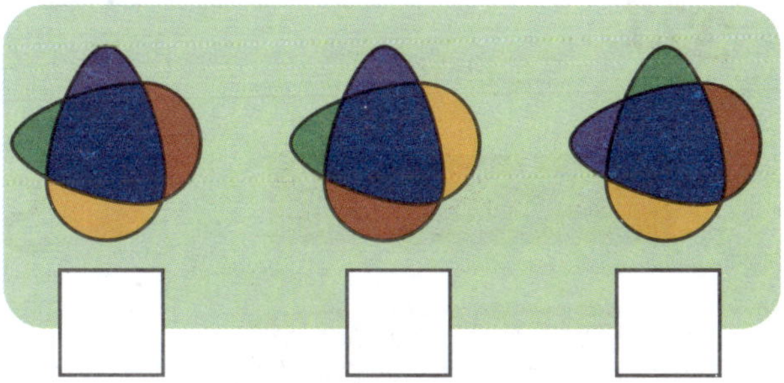

323 What is it used for?

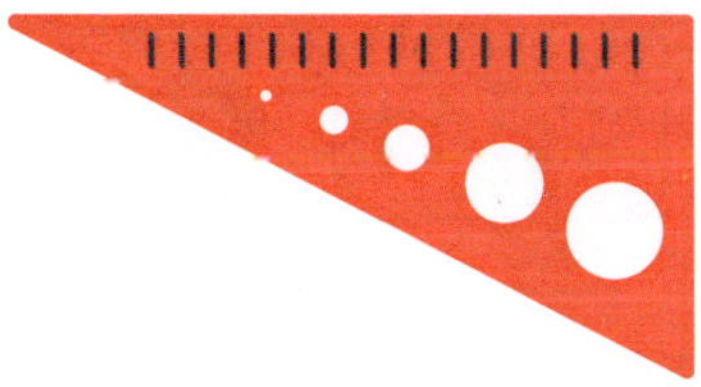

324 Guess the shape?

P___t_g___

325 Match with their names.

 • Quiver

 • Quince

 • Quail

 • Quill

326 Which is the cow's home?

Answer: ☐

327 Find the beginning sound.

S

H

T

_oney

330 Match by their use.

328 Trace and colour.

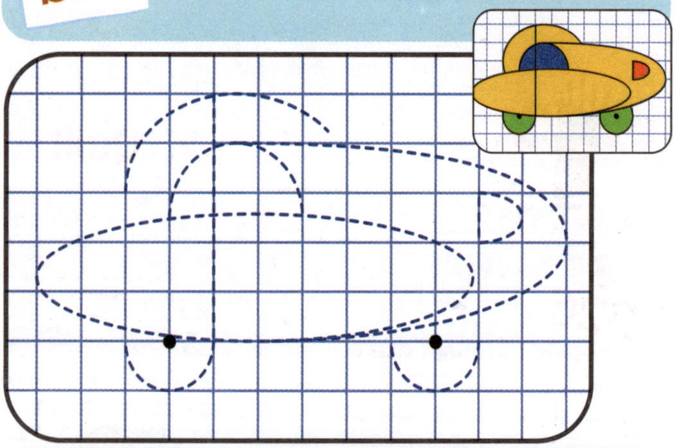

331 Find the value.

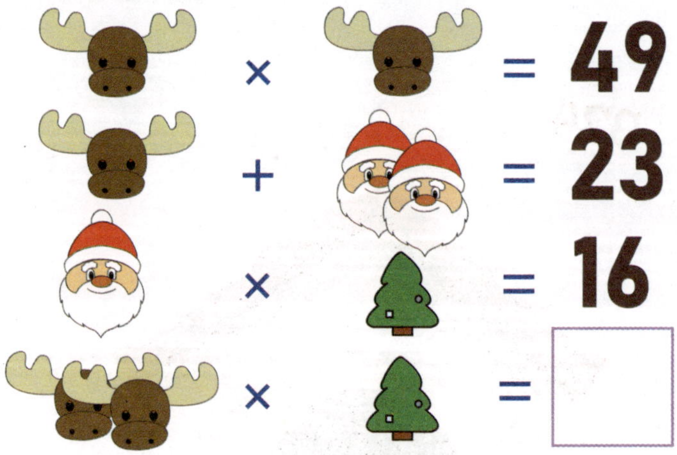

× = 49

\+ = 23

× = 16

× =

329 Decode the 3-letter words.

1 J	3 M	2 A	2 A	1 M	3 P	3 T	1 A	2 N
1	2	3	1	2	3	1	2	3

332 What comes next?

1 → 5 → 9 → ___ → ___ (+4 each step)

2 → ___ → ___ → ___ → ___ (+4 each step)

3 → ___ → ___ → ___ → ___ (+4 each step)

4 → ___ → ___ → ___ → ___ (+4 each step)

333 Circle the pictures with the same beginning sounds.

E... 

F... 

G... 

H... 

334 How many squares?

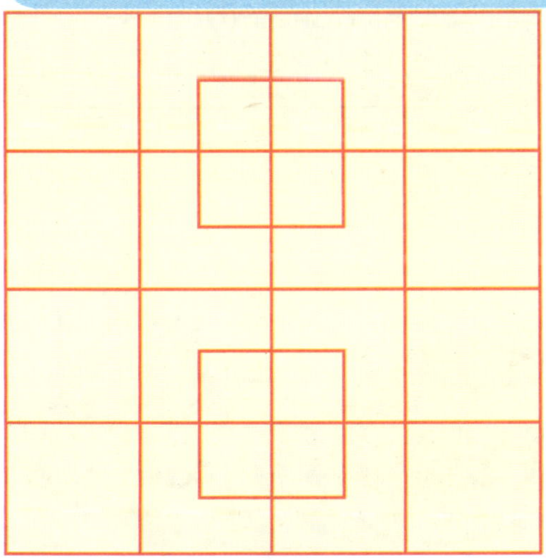

335 What is it used for?

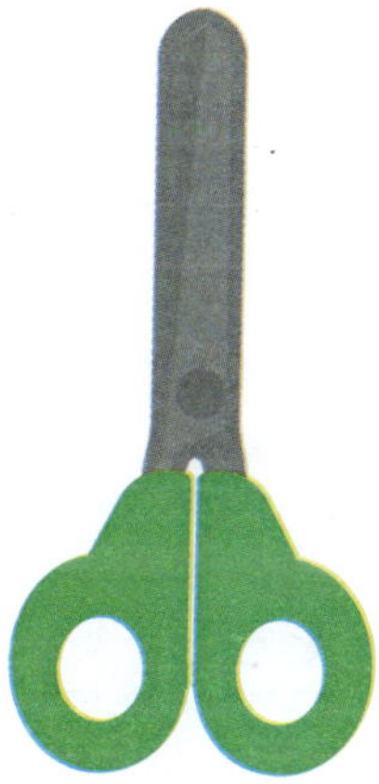

336 Count the squares.

= 5

= ___

337 Count, add and write the sum in the box.

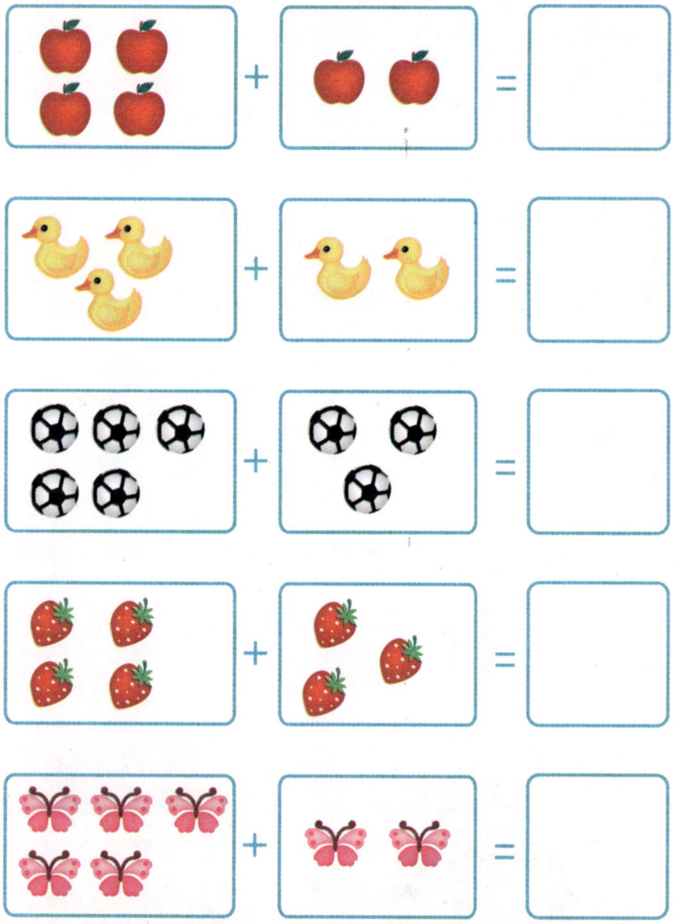

340 Mark the odd in each row.

338 Letter writing practice

iguana

339 Odd one out

341 Colour by number.

342 Trace the cursive alphabet.

343 Find the right top.

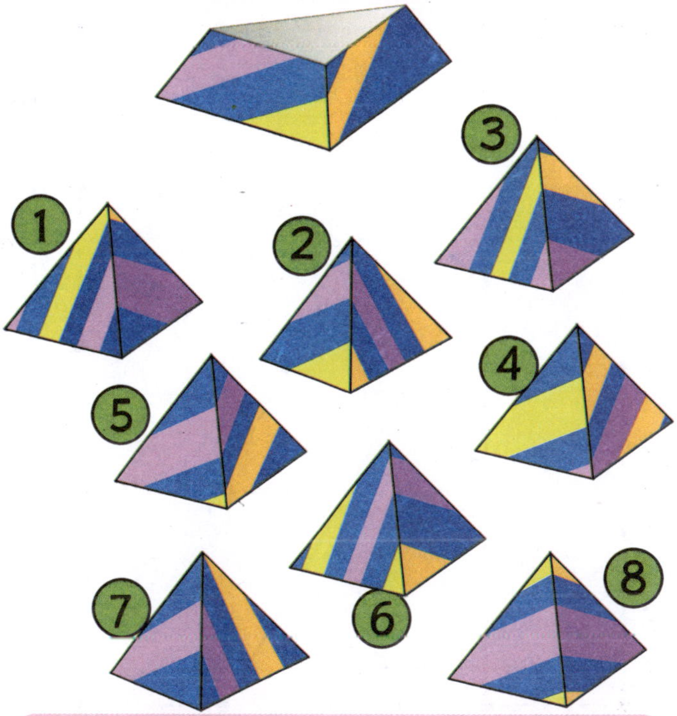

344 Colour by letter.

D e e R

brown green yellow blue

345 Dot to dot, then colour.

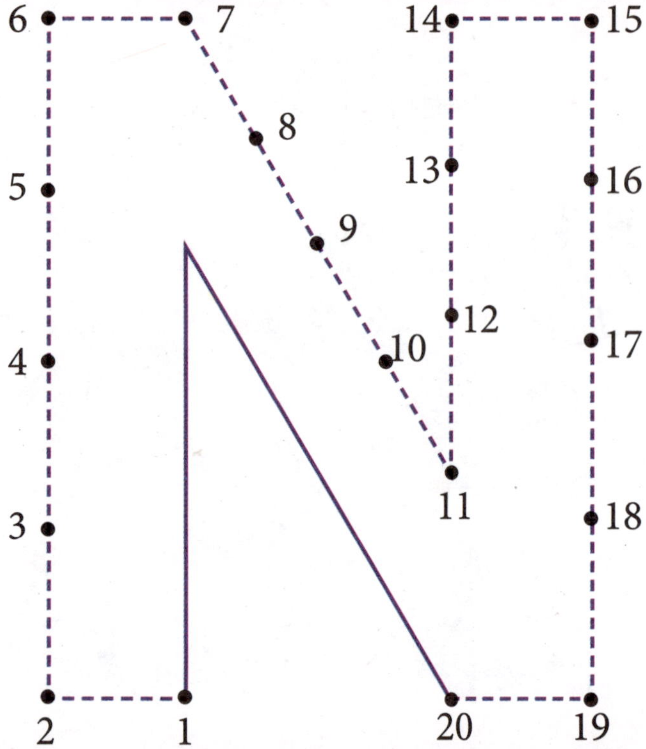

346 How many?

347 Write the fractions.

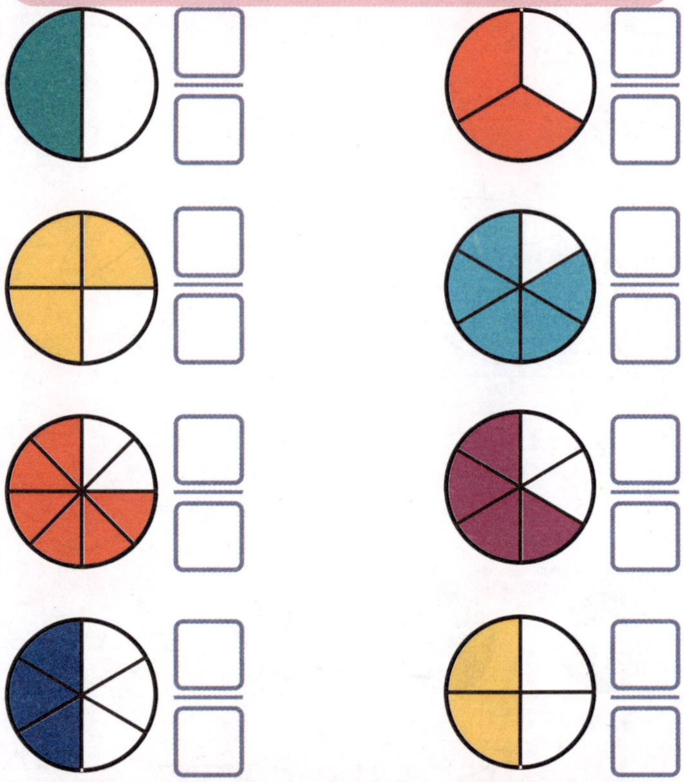

348 What is different?

349 Find the beginning sound.

_eehive

B

S

K

352 Match by shadow.

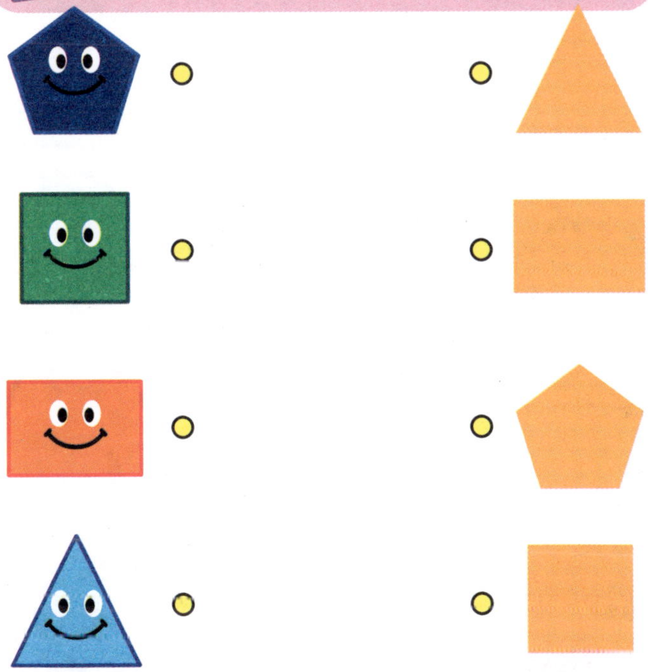

350 How many dollars in the purse?

353 Counting game

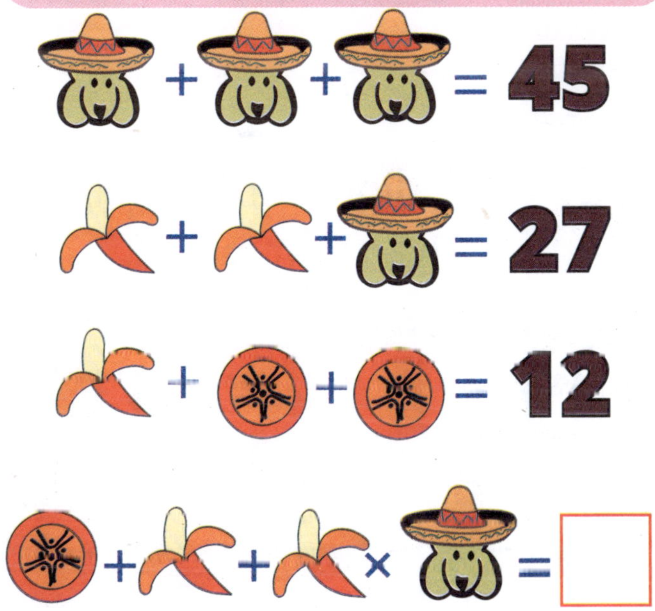

351 Solve the task.

6 7 9

4 2 ☐ ☐

4 5 7

4 0 ☐ ☐

354 Join the dots and colour the picture.

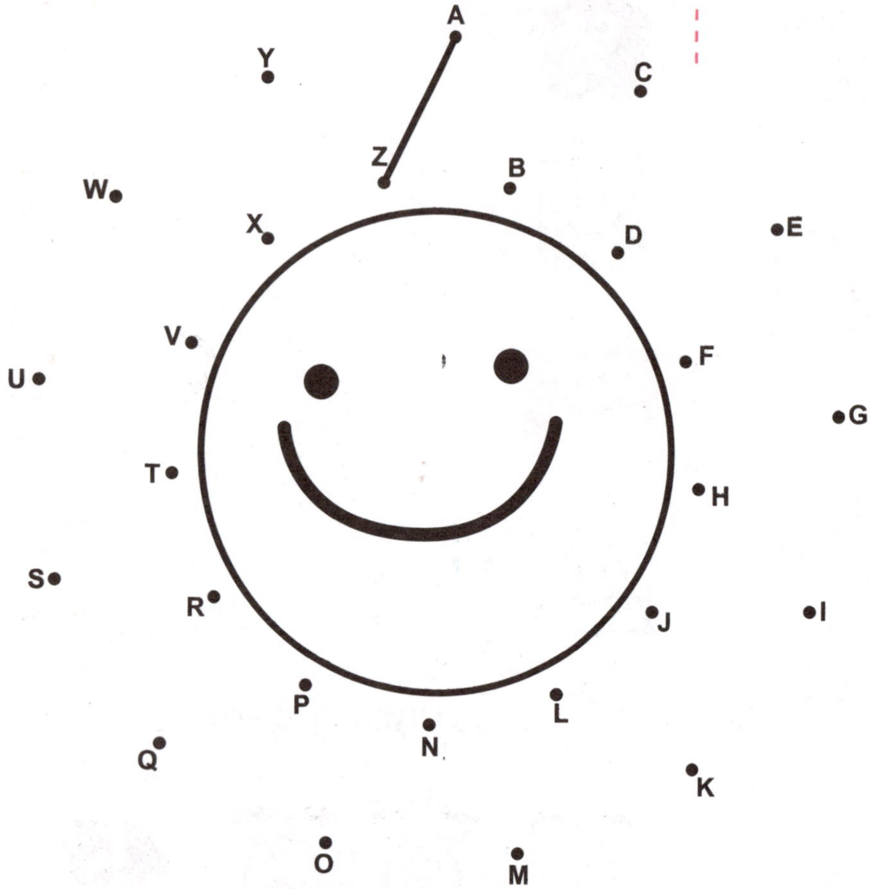

356 Find 10 differences.

355 Put digits and symbols in the right place.

1 + ☐ = 4

2 ☐ 6 = ☐

5 + ☐ ☐ 9

6 + ☐ = 7

= 1 4 + 3 8

357 Finish the pattern.

358 Which will go into the fourth cell?

359 Solve the rebus.

360 Letter writing practice

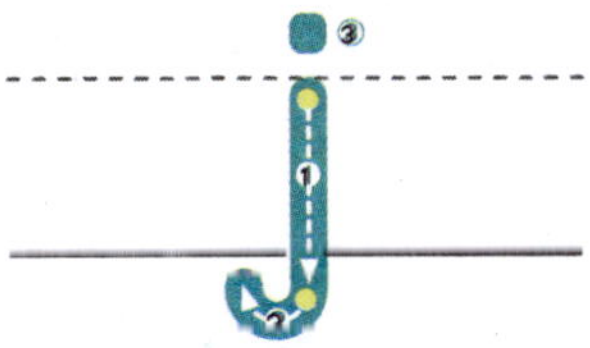

jacket

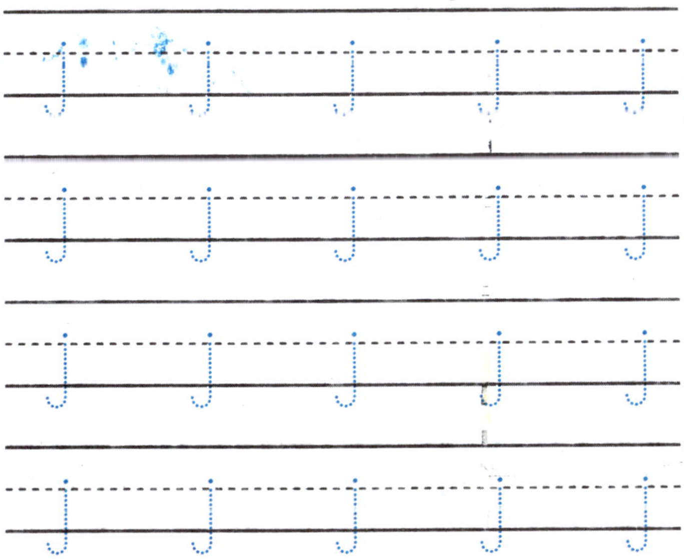

361 Counting game

362 What is it used for?

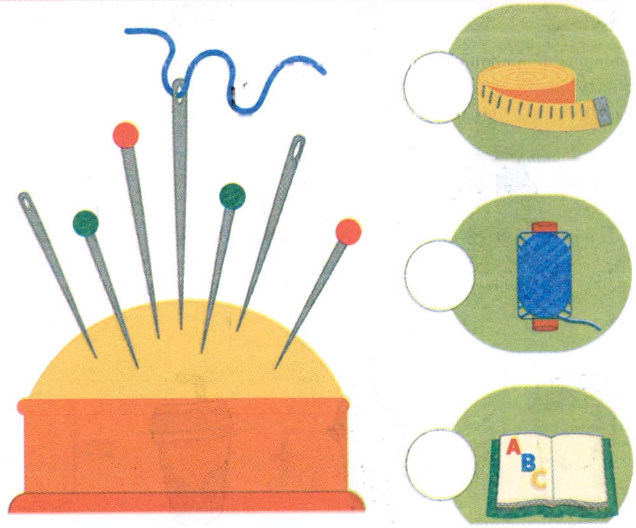

363 Colour as dotted.

365 Tick (✓) the correct shadow.

364 Find the value.

366 Match by shadow.

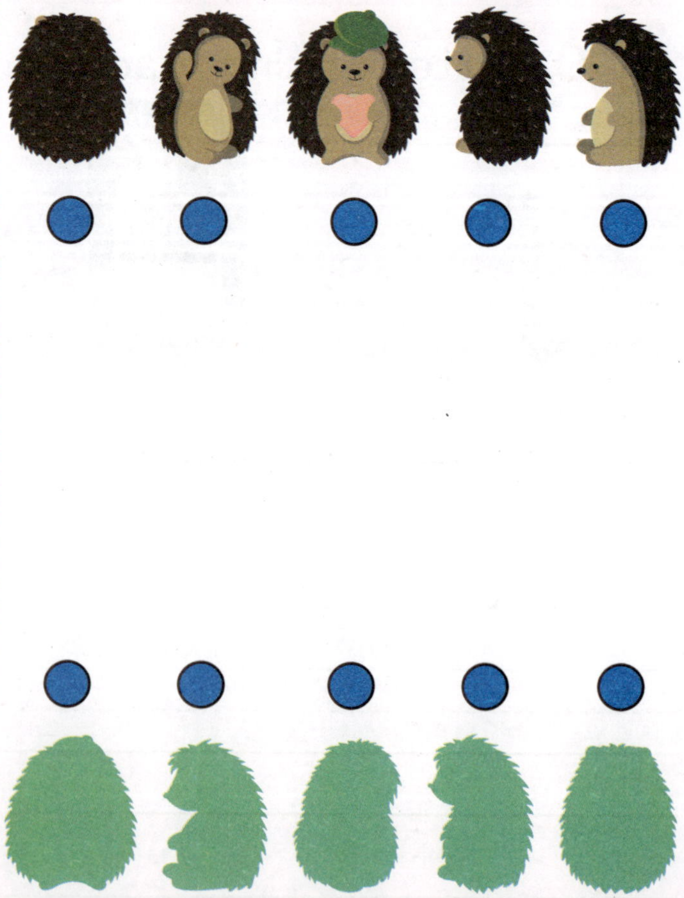

367 Subtract and write.

-	6	7	8
2	4		
3			
4			
5			

369 Help the kids reach the candy house.

368 What comes next?

+1 +1 +1 +1

9 → 10 → 11 → ___ → ___

+1 +1 +1 +1

6 → ___ → ___ → ___ → ___

+1 +1 +1 +1

2 → ___ → ___ → ___ → ___

+1 +1 +1 +1

13 → ___ → ___ → ___ → ___

370 Find the other half.

371 Find the beginning sound.

H

B

R

_ee

372 Count how many flowers?

373 Finish the pattern.

374 Help the gardener water the flower bed.

375 Dot to dot, then colour.

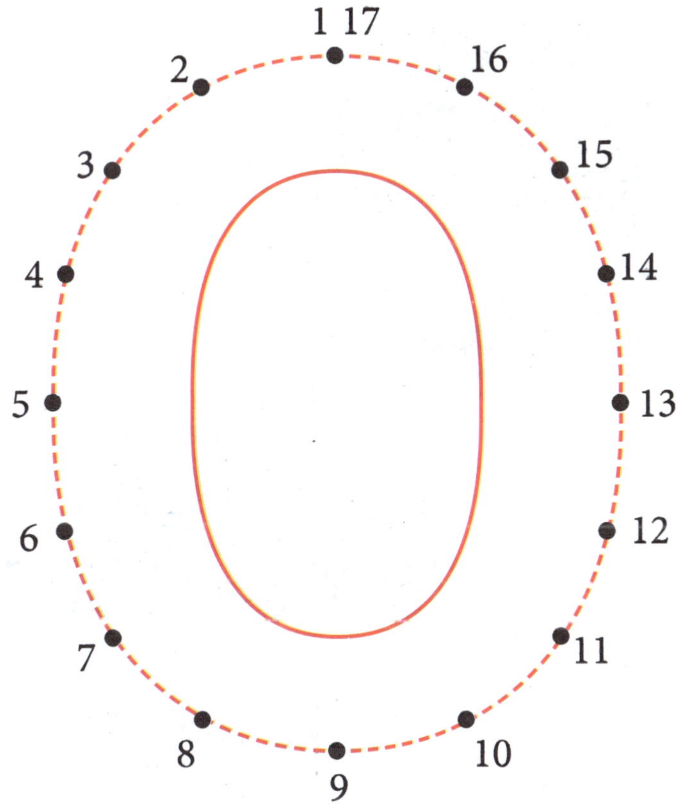

376 Find the sum.

377 Match the pieces.

378 Number sudoku

	5		3	1	4		6	
8	7				9	4		3
6	4	3	5		7	1	9	2
		7	8		5	2	1	
4	1		9					
	2	5		6	1	9		7
7	9		2	5		8	4	
		4		9	6			5
	3		1		8	6	7	

379 What do the letters say?

381 Find 9 differences.

380 Letter writing practice

382 Count how many shapes?

383 What comes next?

6, 12, 18, ___, ___ (+6 each step)

5, ___, ___, ___, ___ (+6 each step)

10, ___, ___, ___, ___ (+6 each step)

11, ___, ___, ___, ___ (+6 each step)

385 Mark the correct top view.

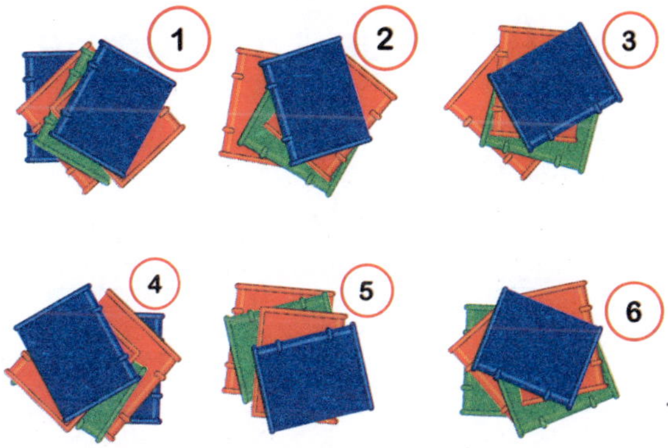

384 Find the way.

386 Match by shape.

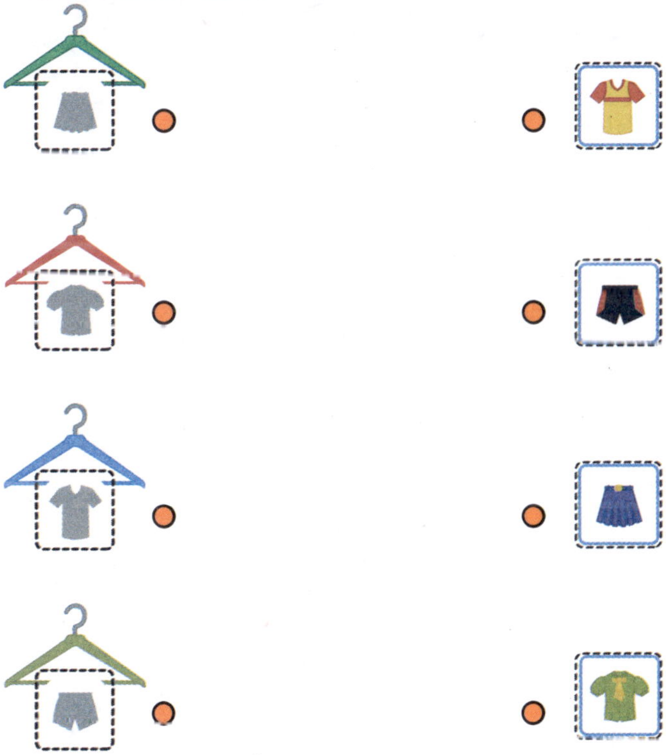

387 Match and colour the shapes.

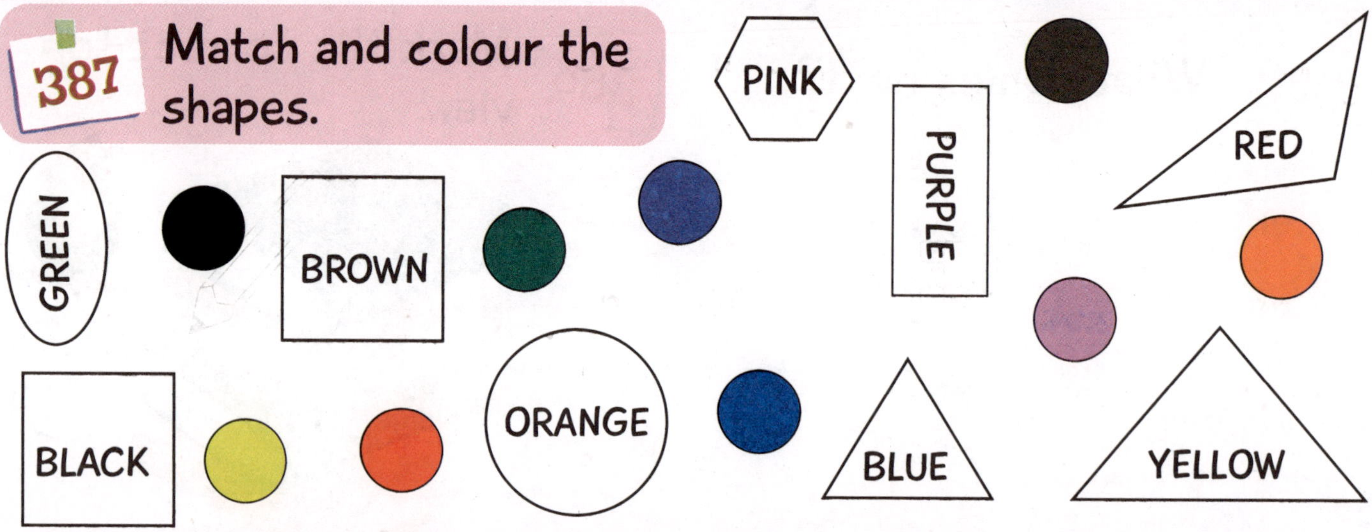

388 Arrange the numbers from greatest to smallest.

7	6	10	2	4					
10	8	1	5	9					

389 Dot to dot, then colour.

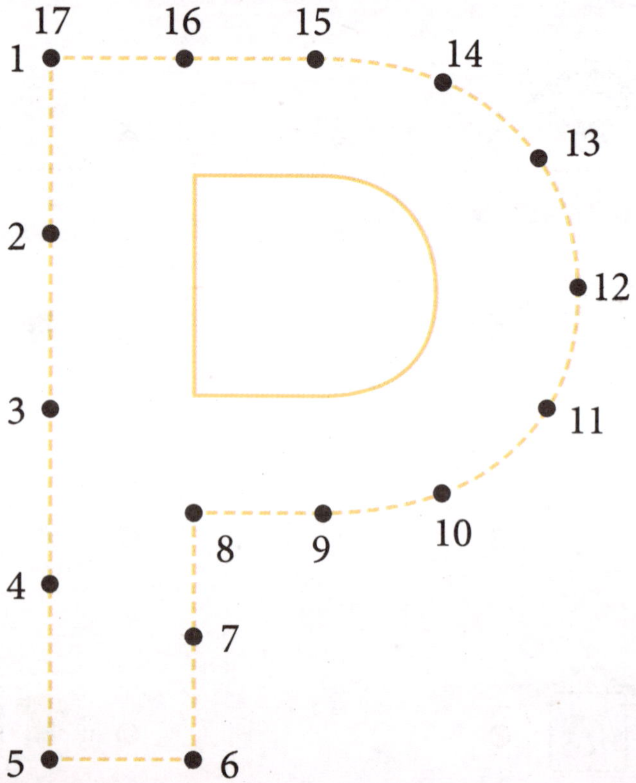

390 Mark the correct top view.

391 A or an?

○ a
○ an
pencil

○ a
○ an
house

○ a
○ an
apple

○ a
○ an
book

392 Write their count.

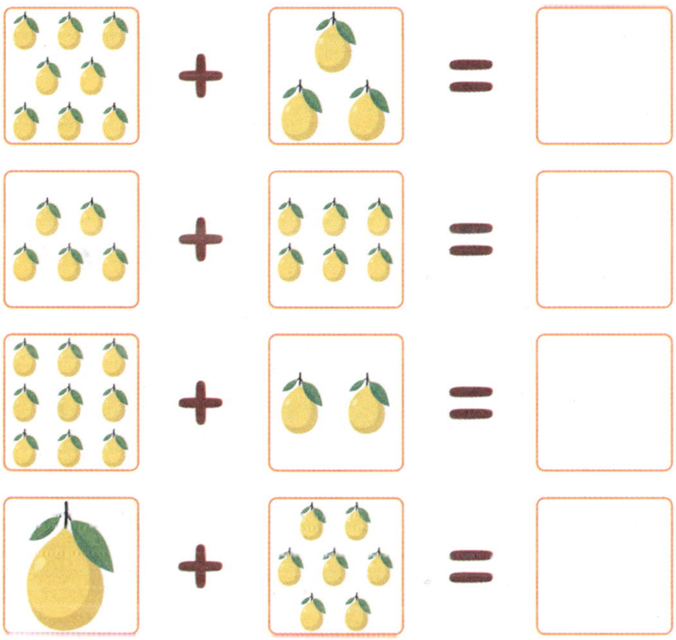

394 Guess the shape.

_ _t_ _o_

393 Odd one out

395 Write the numbers in the ascending order.

8 – 5 – 2 – 10 – 7

8 – 1 – 10 – 4 – 2
....

3 – 5 – 1 – 6 – 10
....

9 – 10 – 5 – 3 – 6
....

6 – 8 – 2 – 10 – 3
....

7 – 0 – 1 – 6 – 4
....

5 – 2 – 9 – 10 – 7
....

396 Circle the pictures with the same beginning sounds.

A... 

B... 

C... 

D... 

397 Colour according to the sum.

1 7 1+7 =

2 4 2+4 =

6 1 6+1 =

1 3 1+3 =

398 How many?

399 Match with their names.

X-mas

Xiphias

Xylophone

X-ray

400 Substitute numbers for fruits and solve.

 =21  =18  =15  =9

 = ☐

 = ☐

 = ☐

401 Write the missing numbers.

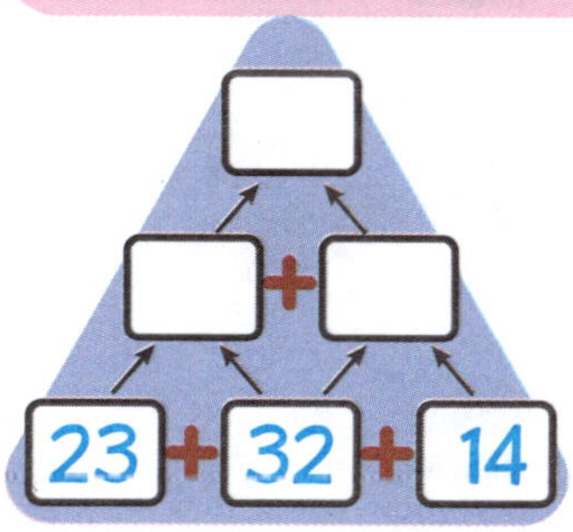

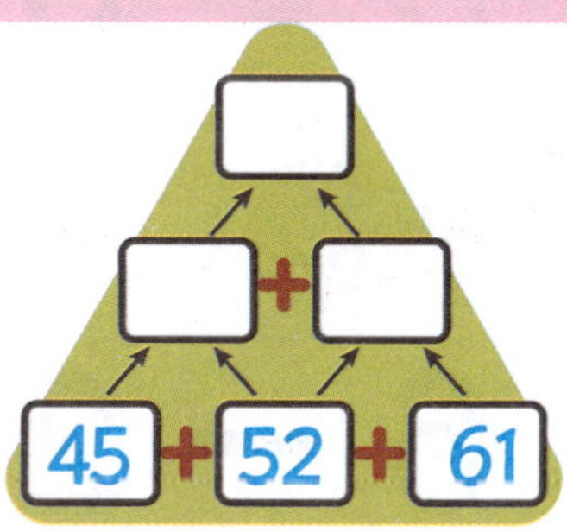

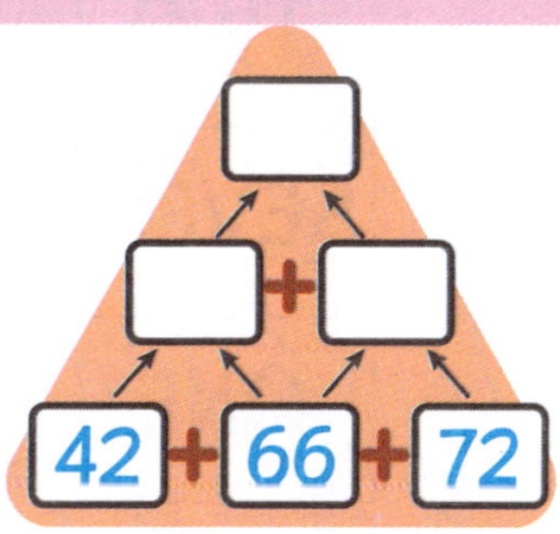

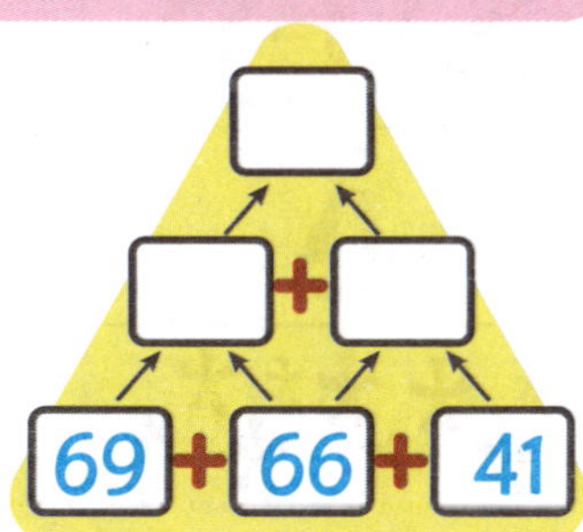

402 Letter writing practice

lion

403 Solve the rebus.

404 Trace and colour.

405 Count and match.

FIVE
SIX
THREE
TEN
EIGHT
FOUR
NINE
TWO
SEVEN
ONE

406 Find the identical two.

407 Solve the puzzle.

3 – 2 = ☐

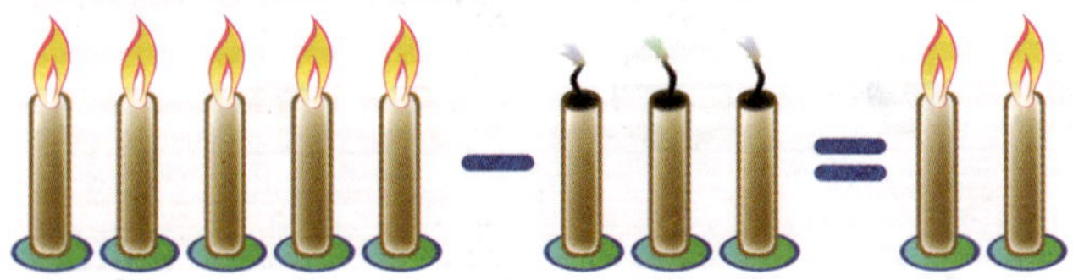

5 – 3 = ☐

6 – 2 = ☐

408 A or an?

- ◯ a / ◯ an **truck**

- ◯ a / ◯ an **egg**

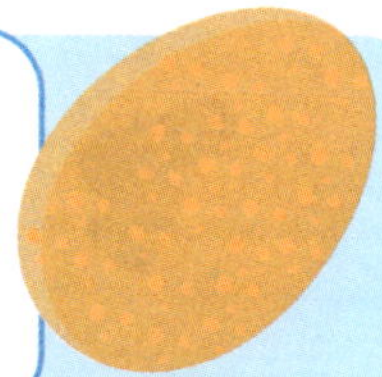

- ◯ a / ◯ an **bag**

- ◯ a / ◯ an **scissors**

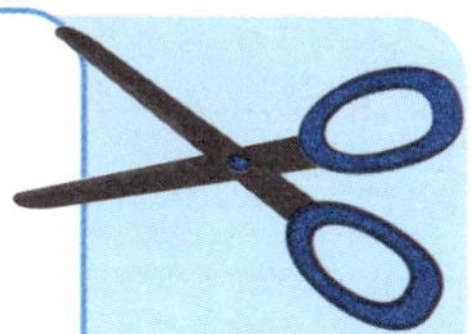

409 Find the values.

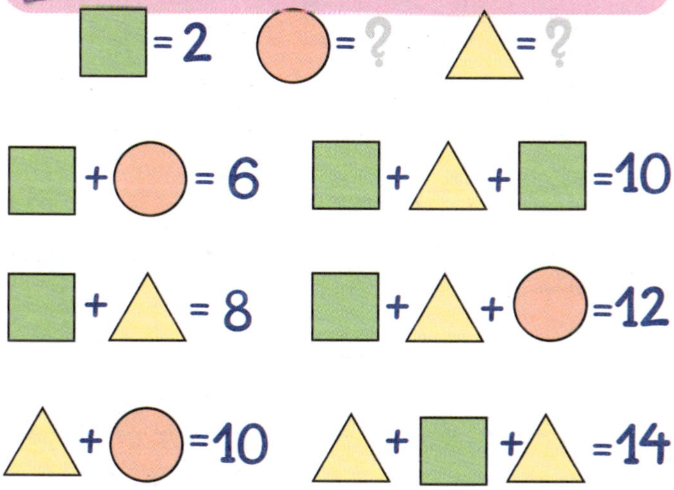

0 1 2 3 4 5 6 7 8 9 + – =

0 1 2 3 4 5 6 7 8 9 + –

10 11 12 13 14 15 16 17 18 19 20 =

410 Write in the number form.

Twenty-two =

Thirty-seven =

Forty-two =

Thirty-eight =

411 Solve the rebus.

412 Count and write.

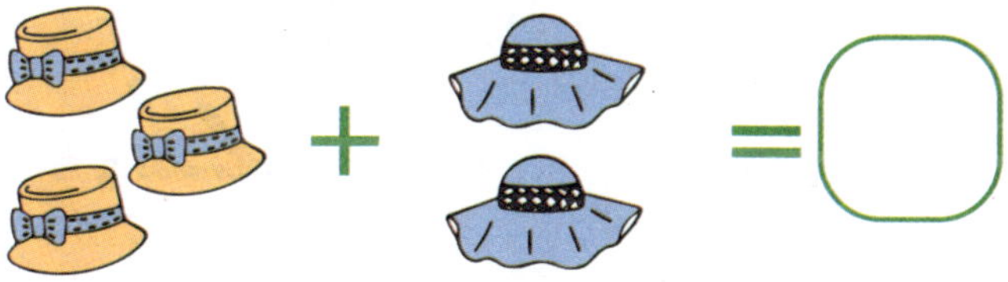

413 Colour the picture by addition and subtraction.

1 =
2 =
3 =
4 =
5 =
6 =
7 =
8 =

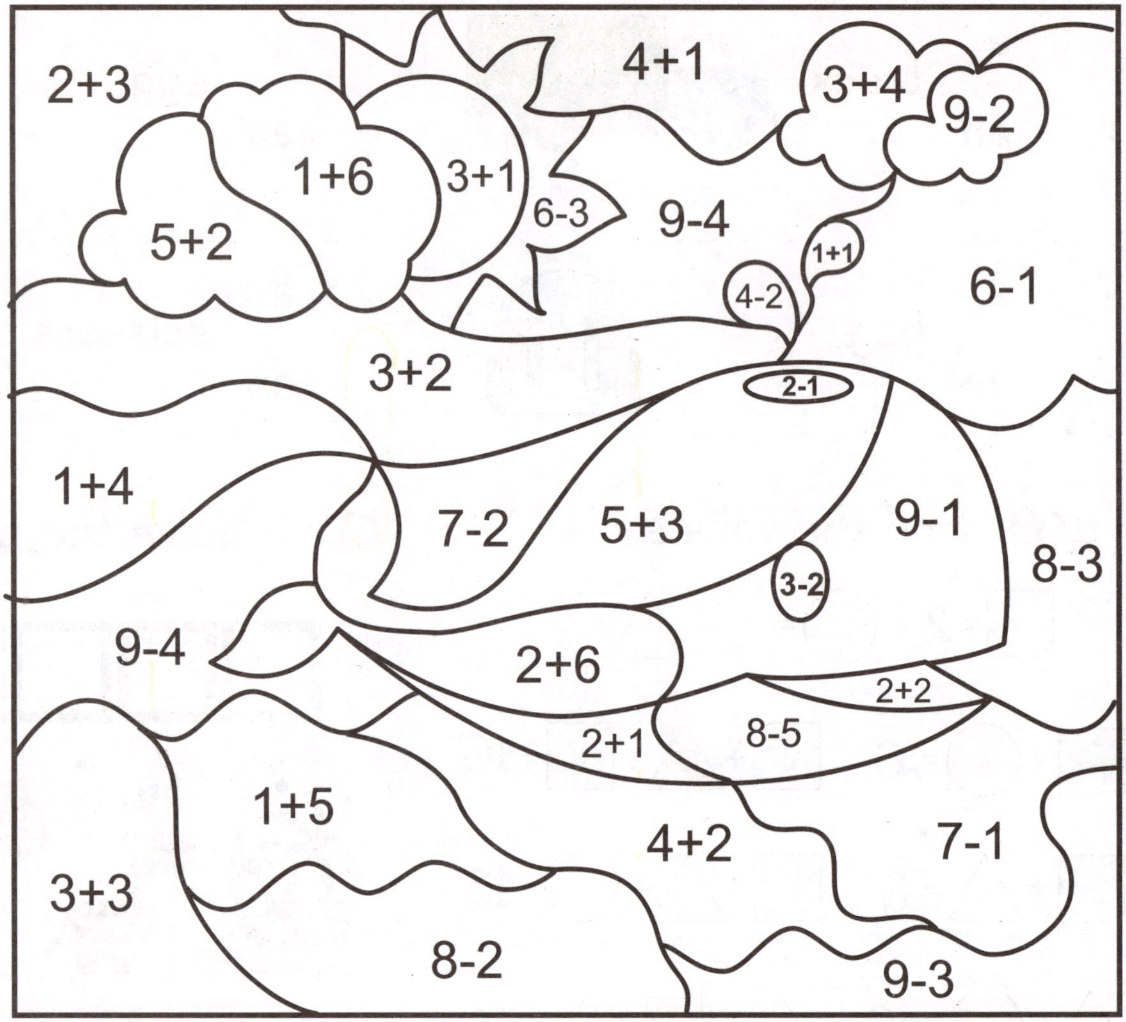

414 Write the time.

415 Match by the use of senses.

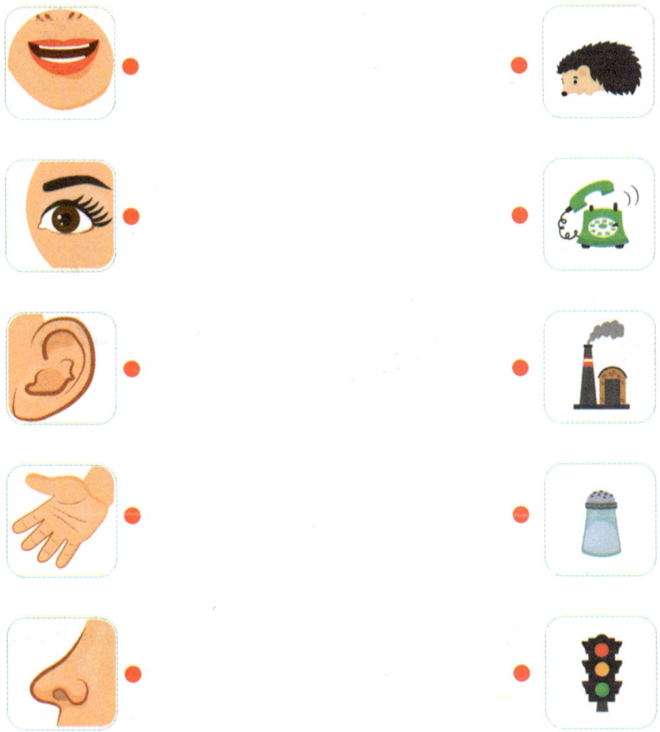

416 Dot to dot, then colour.

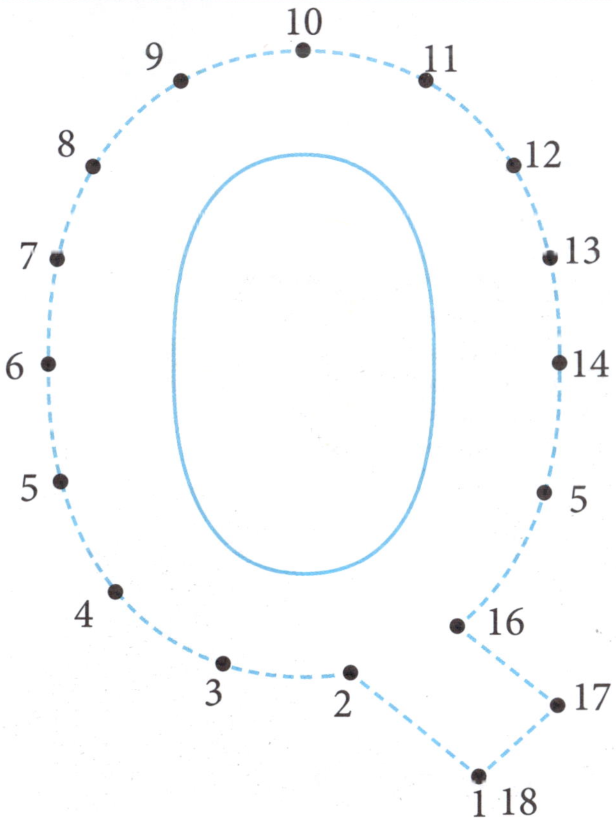

417 Count how many birds?

418 Count with the clue.

419 Match the number names.

420 A or an?

○ a / ○ an **ball**

○ a / ○ an **orange**

○ a / ○ an **mushroom**

○ a / ○ an **bird**

421 Help the ant return to her anthill.

422 Letter writing practice

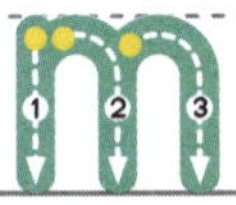

mouse

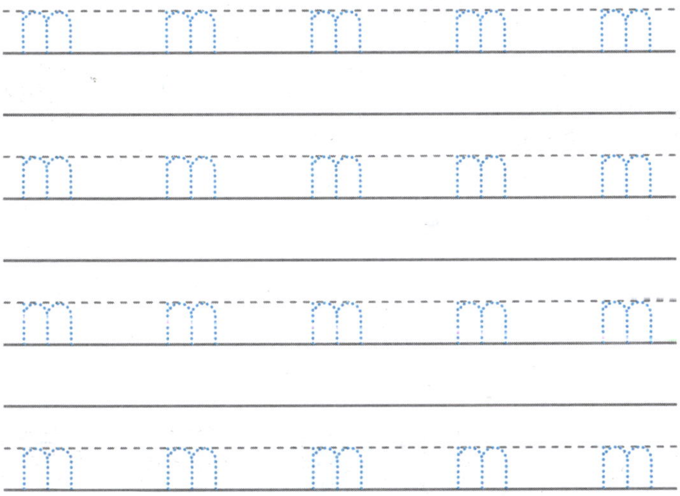

424 None should repeat in the row and the column.

1 2 3 4

423 Find two same potted plants.

425 Send each back home.

426 How many?

427 What come next?

428 Find the product.

9 × 3 = ☐

7 × 3 = ☐

8 × 2 = ☐

20 × 1 = ☐

10 × 5 = ☐

4 × 4 = ☐

8 × 1 = ☐

4 × 8 = ☐

429 Find the correct shadow.

430 Handwriting practice

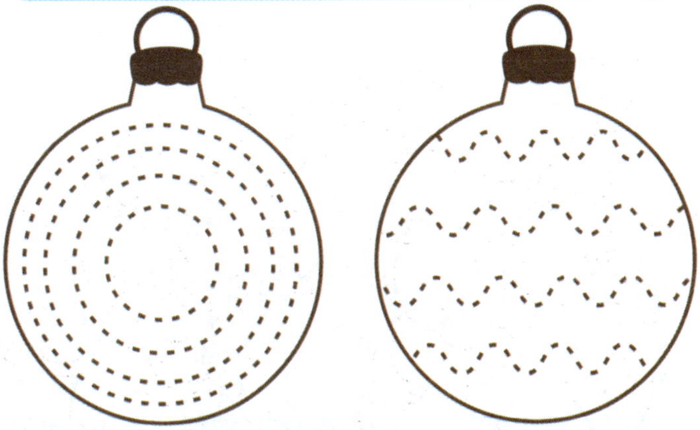

431 Use logic.

111 = 13

112 = 24

113 = 35

114 = 46

115 = 57

117 = ☐

432 Guess the name.

19	20	5	23	16	1	14

a	b	c	d	e	f	g	h	i	j	k	l	m
1	2	3	4	5	6	7	8	9	10	11	12	13

n	o	p	q	r	s	t	u	v	w	x	y	z
14	15	16	17	18	19	20	21	22	23	24	25	26

433 Choose and label right.

Sunlight

Oxygen

Carborn Dioxide

Water

434 Match the opposites.

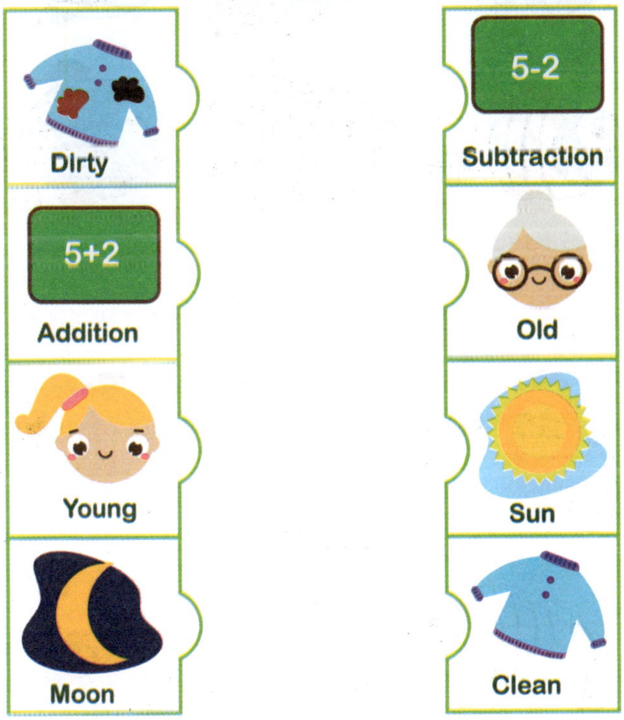

435 Pair matching

436 Draw similar.

437 Find 7 differences.

438 What is it used for?

439 Growing patterns

440 Draw by square.

441 Dot to dot, then colour.

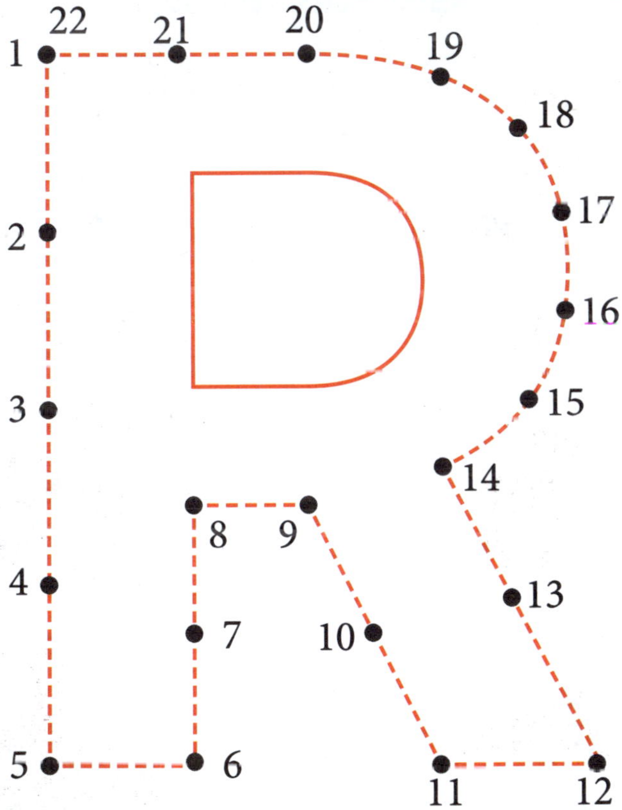

442 Add and write.

+	5	6	7
4	9		
5			
6			
7			

443 What comes next?

+2 +2 +2 +2

3, 5, 7, ___, ___

+2 +2 +2 +2

4, ___, ___, ___, ___

+2 +2 +2 +2

2, ___, ___, ___, ___

+2 +2 +2 +2

11, ___, ___, ___, ___

444 Letter writing practice

n

nest

n n n n n

n n n n n

n n n n n

n n n n n

445 Find the next number.

21, 18, 15, 12

9, 6, 3, ___

446 What number comes next?

2	7	12	17	➜ ___
1	4	7	10	➜ ___
2	5	8	11	➜ ___

447 Match with their homes.

448 Addition

5 + 1 = ☐ | 2 + 2 = ☐

4 + 1 = ☐ | 4 + 2 = ☐

449 Subtraction

65	49	92	75
− 55	− 37	− 51	− 54
◯◯	◯◯	◯◯	◯◯

450 A or an?

◯ a
◯ an
eye

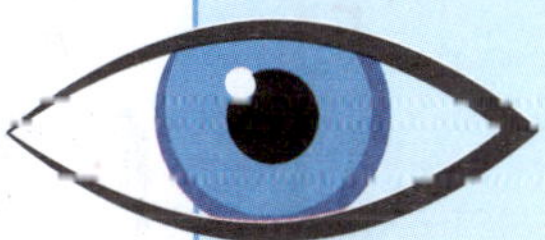

◯ a
◯ an
fish

◯ a
◯ an
car

451 Write the correct time.

11:00 8:00 6:00 7:00
5:00 9:00 3:00 2:00
10:00 12:00 4:00 1:00

452 Find the right piece.

A)

B)

C)

453 How many?

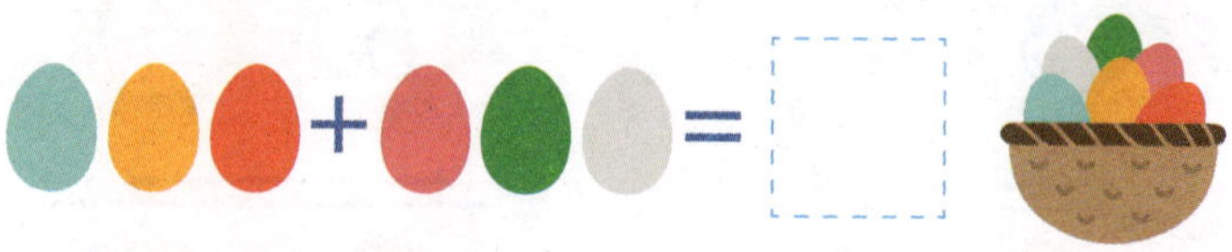

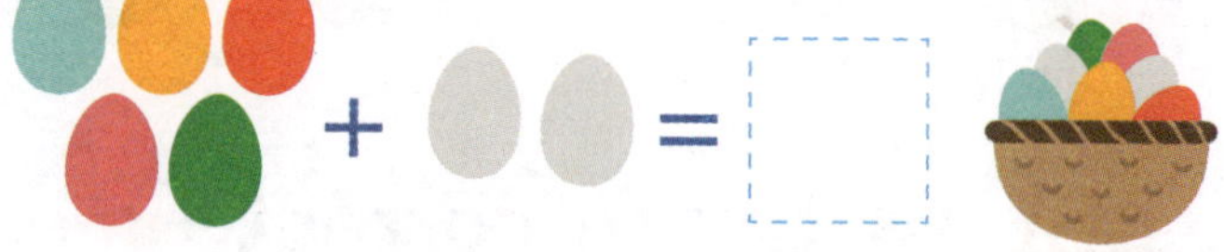

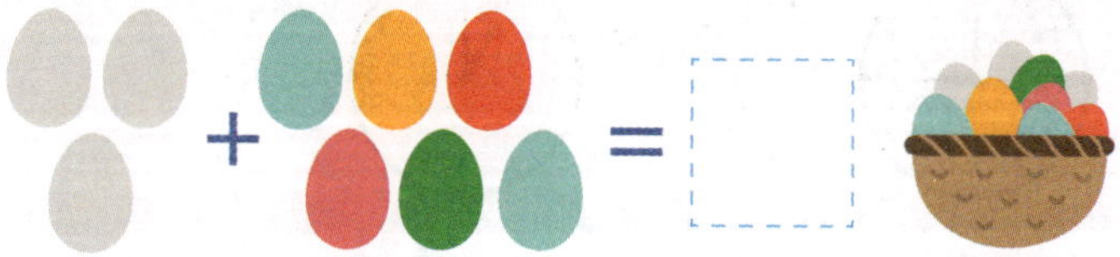

454 Solve the rebus.

455 Sort by type.

WOOD		METAL	
?	?	?	?
?	?	?	?

456 Which is the missing letter?

A

E

I

L ◯ M O N

457 Trace the beelines.

460 Draw to complete the sudoku.

458 Addition

	1 4		2 4		3 2		4 4
+	2 1	+	1 3	+	2 1	+	1 1
	◯ ◯		◯ ◯		◯ ◯		◯ ◯

459 After and before.

1 ◯ 3 — 7 8 ◯

◯ 6 ◯ — ◯ 4 5

◯ 14 ◯ — 6 ◯ 8

◯ ◯ 8 — ◯ 10 ◯

461 What should be added?

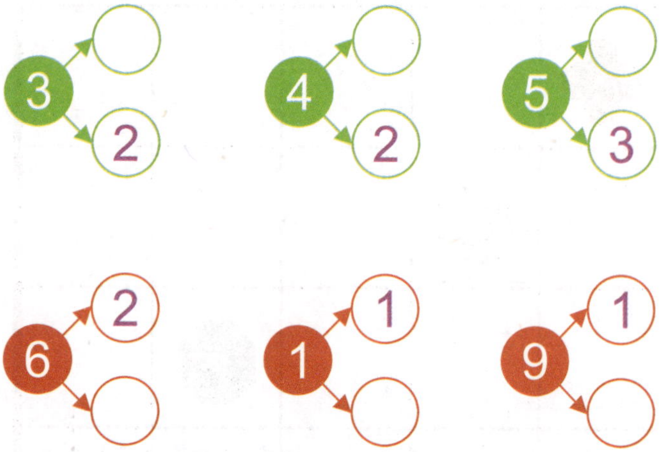

462 What is this place called?

463 Multiplication

7 × 7 =	9 × 1 =
5 × 6 =	2 × 9 =
9 × 2 =	3 × 7 =
4 × 2 =	5 × 7 =

464 Which one is missing?

465 Fit the pieces.

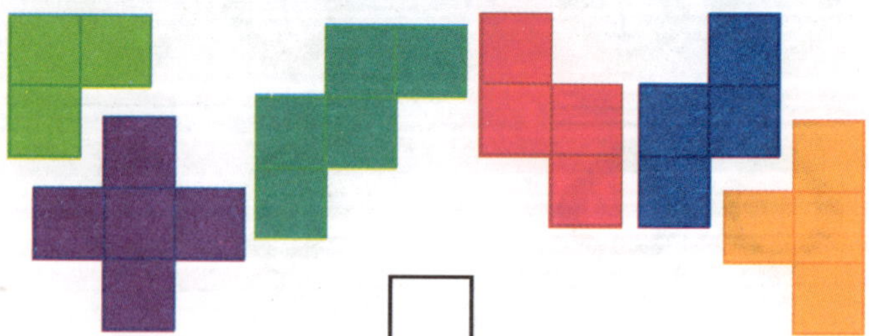

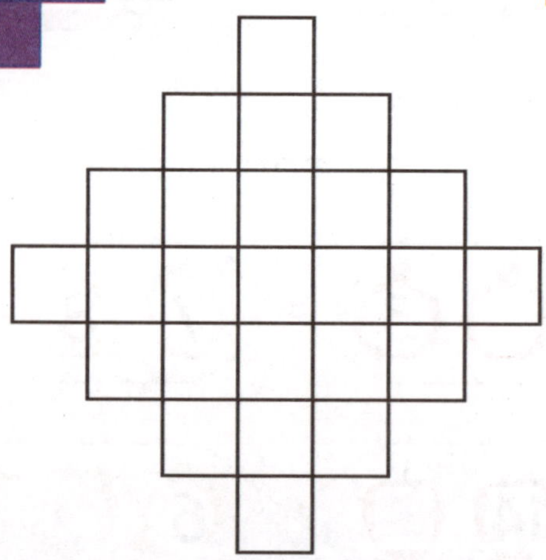

466 Match with their homes.

468 Find two same toys.

467 Maths puzzle

469 Letter writing practice

orange

470 Join equal groups of dots.

473 Outline from 1 to 30, calling them out loud.

471 Find the right piece.

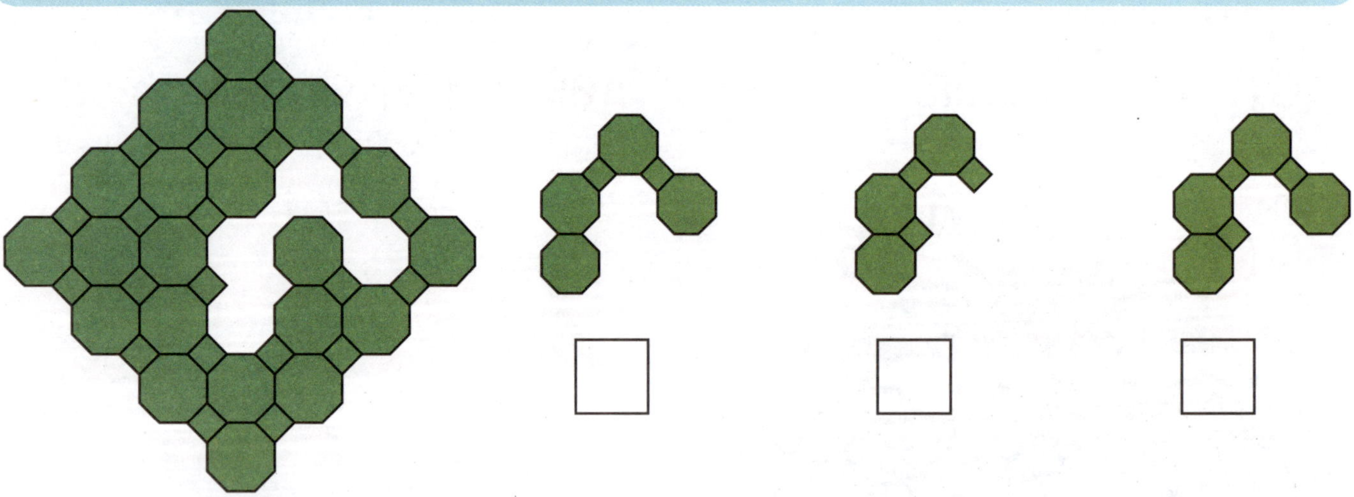

472 Odd one out

474 Dot to dot, then colour.

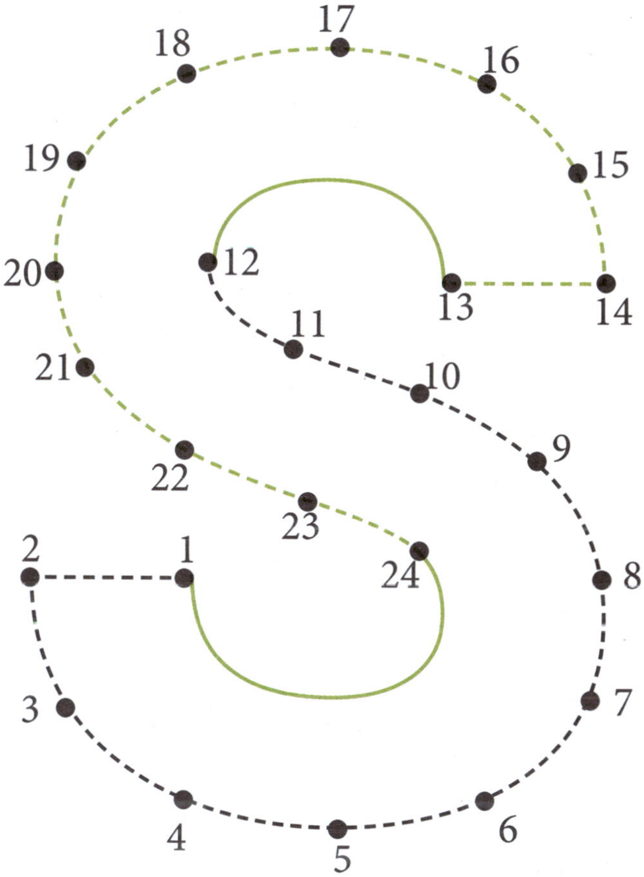

476 Count and write.

475 Find 5 differences.

477 Join the dots and colour.

478 Trace and colour.

479 Find their compartments.

480 Draw to complete the sudoku.

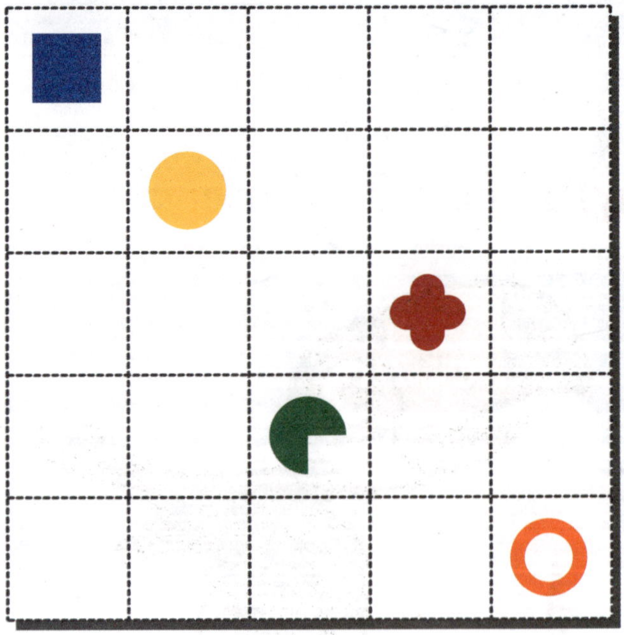

481 Let him eat the muffin.

482 Find 10 differences.

483 Match houses and shadows.

484 A or an?

○ a
turtle
○ an

○ a
owl
○ an

○ a
hat
○ an

485 Which ones are missing?

486 Draw by square.

487 Trace and colour.

488 Find 7 differences.

490 Find 5 differences.

489 Match pictures and numbers.

2 6 4 5 3

491 Match pictures and numbers.

1 3 4 2

494 Find two same pictures.

492 What replaces the question mark?

493 Find the same shape.

495 Letter writing practice

p

parrot

p p p p p

p p p p p

p p p p p

p p p p p

496 Count the ladybird dots and match.

3

5

1

4

2

497 How many to the left and how many to the right?

LEFT

RIGHT

498 Match the halves.

499 Count by shape.

500 A or an?

a
an
mouse

a
an
board

a
an
eraser

502 Colour the mandala.

501 Colour according to the sum.

4 2 $4 + 2 =$ ○

2 5 $2 + 5 =$ ○

7 1 $7 + 1 =$ ○

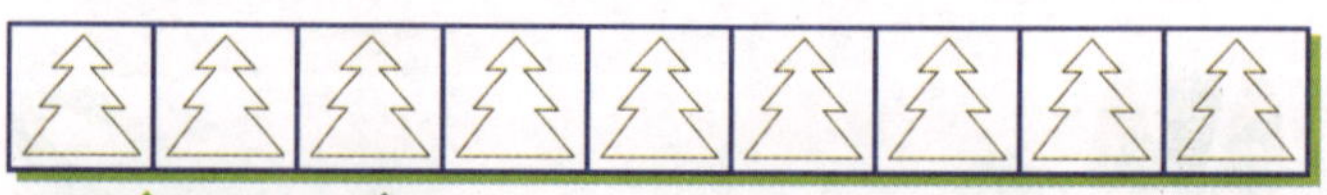

1 6 $1 + 6 =$ ○

503 Dot to dot, then colour.

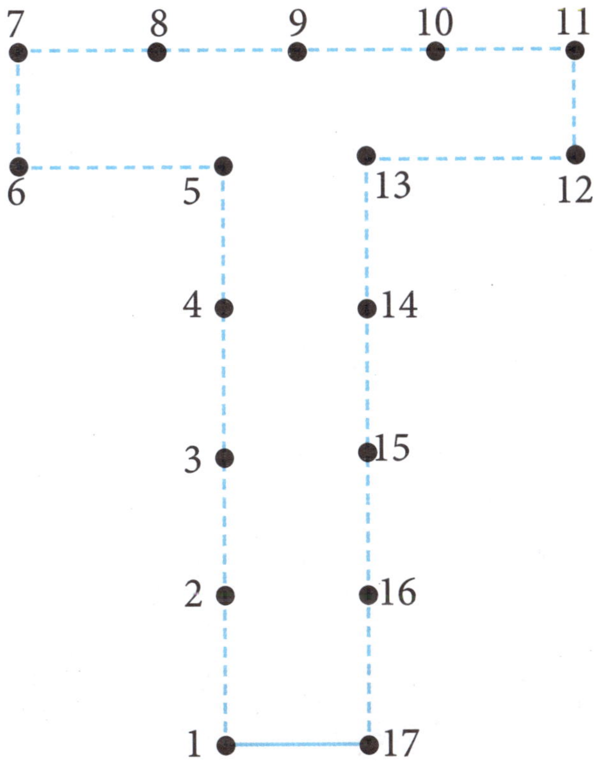

504 Help the cat find the way up.

505 How many circles?

506 Add the symbols.

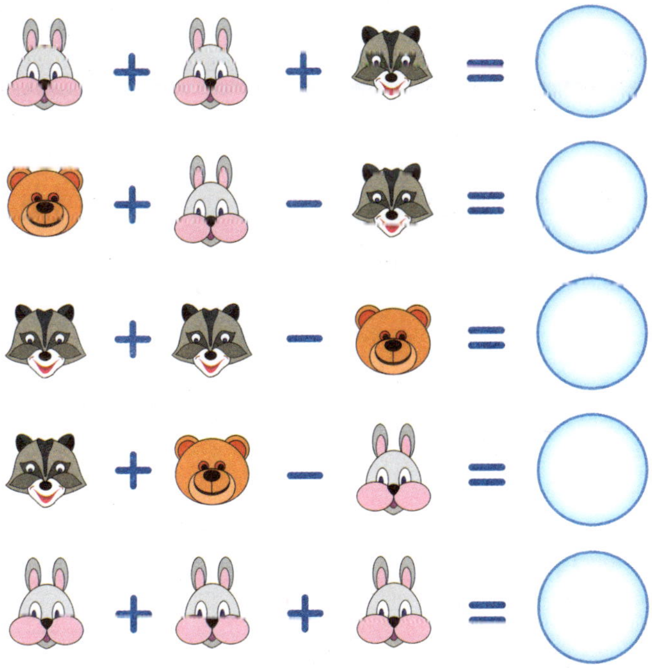

507 True or false?

True False

$0 < 1$		$3 < 6$		$5 > 4$	
$1 > 5$		$7 > 4$		$4 = 4$	
$9 > 2$		$7 < 10$		$8 > 3$	

508 Find the beginning sound.

_nt

A

V

C

510 Find their values.

509 Identify and colour the mentioned shape.

Circle

Ellipse

511 Trace the clown's hair.

512 Draw by square.

513 Find 10 differences.

514 Draw to complete the sudoku.

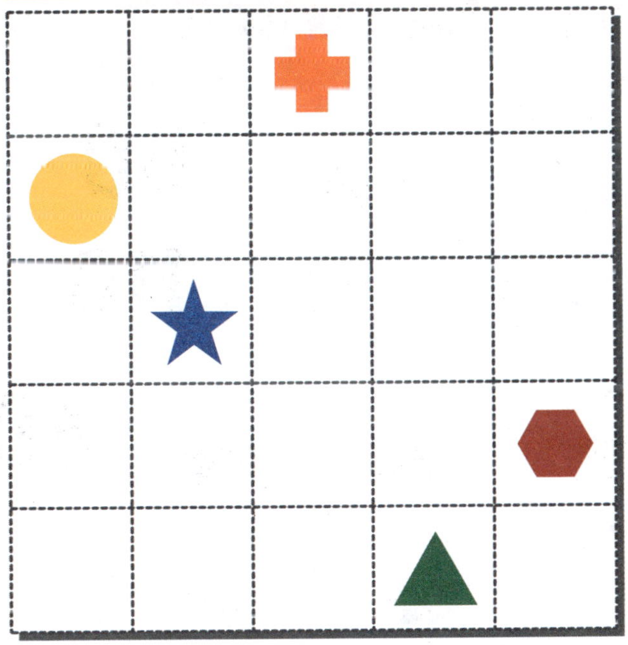

515 Write the missing numbers.

4	
3	1
	4
2	

8	
	7
4	
	3

6	
2	
	5
3	

7	
	4
2	
	6

516 Trace and colour.

517 Find the value.

518 What follows next?

519 A or an?

a
an
bed

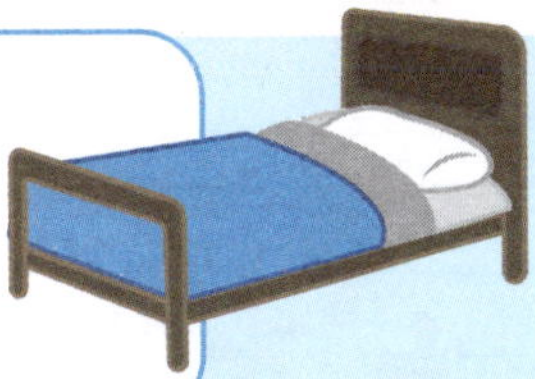

a
an
table

a
an
cat

520 Which one is missing?

521 How many?

522 Trace and colour.

523 Write the number names.

Four ....

....

....

....

524 Choose and complete.

A)

C)

B)

D)

525 Find the pair.

526 Finish the pattern.

527 Copy the picture.

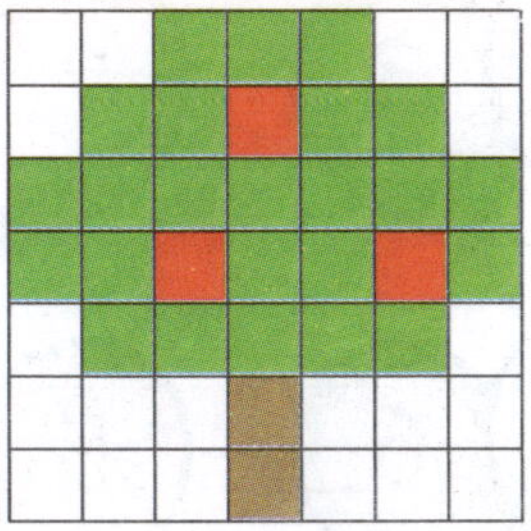

529 Dot to dot, then colour.

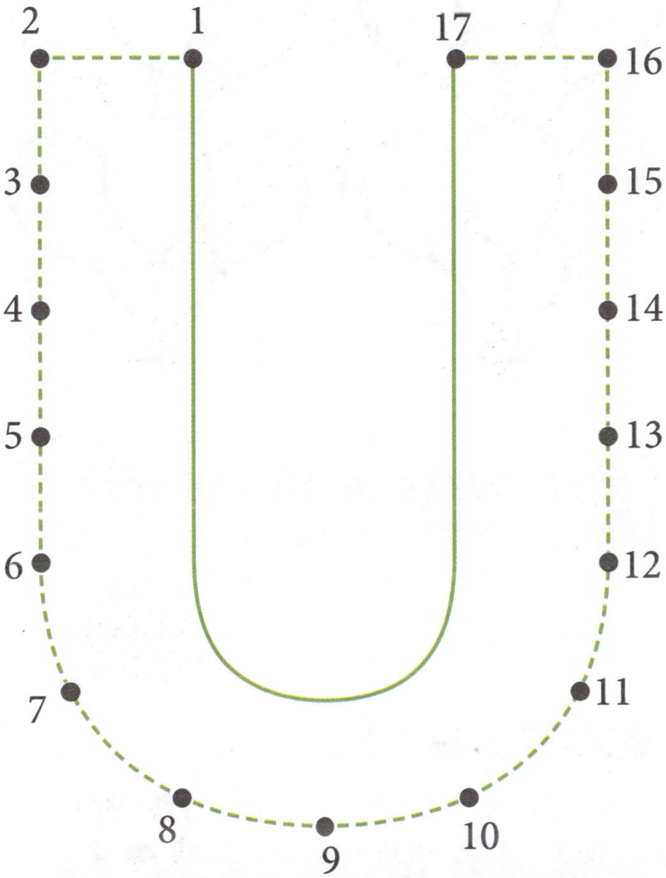

528 Sort by type.

530 Match pictures and numbers.

 4

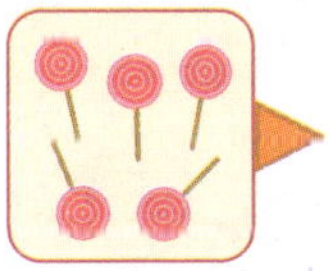 3

 5

 2

531 Compare the numbers.

532 What is it used for?

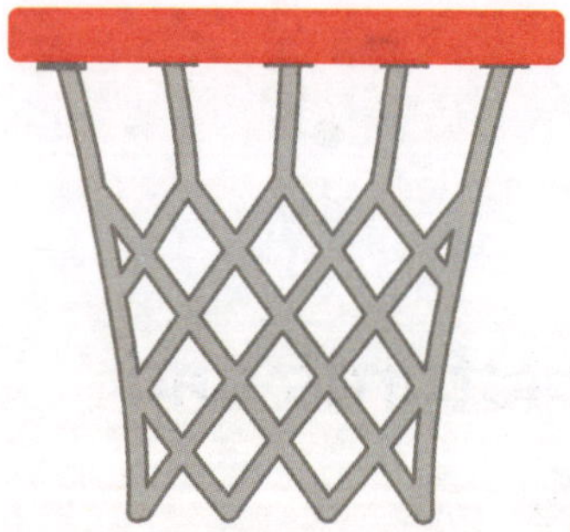

534 Find the values.

533 Find two identical geese.

535 Letter writing practice

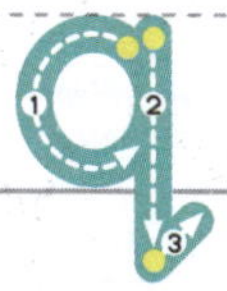

536 How many trapeziums?

537 Finish the pattern.

538 Follow to colour.

539 How many?

541 Trace and colour.

540 Find 10 differences.

542 Count, track and write.

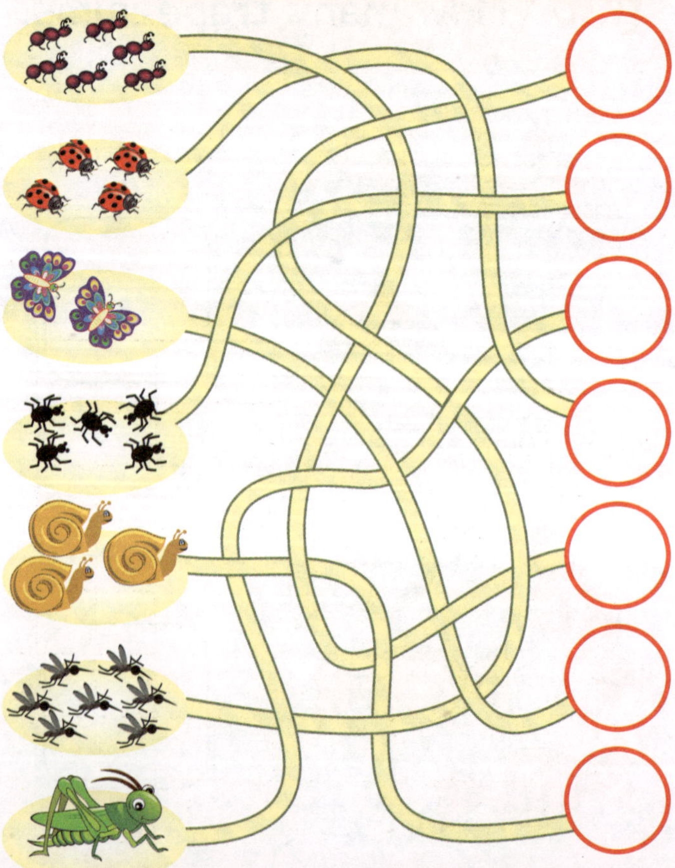

543 Colour, count and fill the grid.

☆										
○										
□										
△										

545 Find 7 differences.

544 Crossword

546 Mirror symmetry drawing

547 Find the beginning sound.

548 Choose and complete.

549 Dot to dot, then colour.

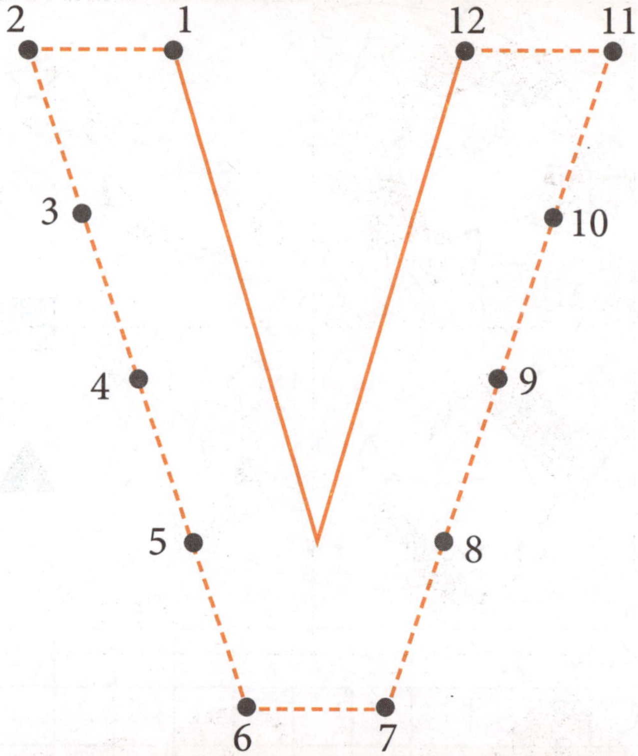

550 What is it used for?

551 Match the missing parts.

553 Circle all ovals.

552 What fills the yellow space?

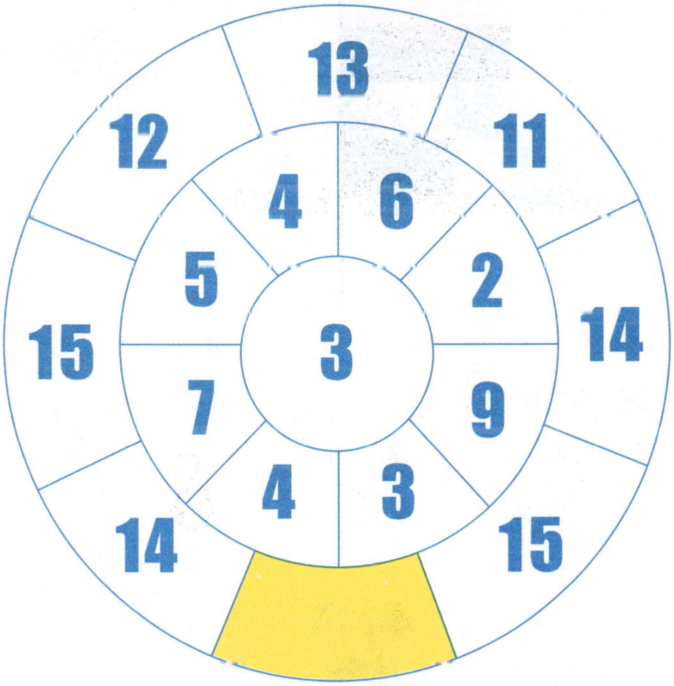

554 How many?

5 11 3

555 Before and after.

	33			55			80	
	19			29			41	
	83			68			71	

556 Match with their homes

558 Mirror Symmetry Drawing

557 What replaces the question mark?

559 How many?

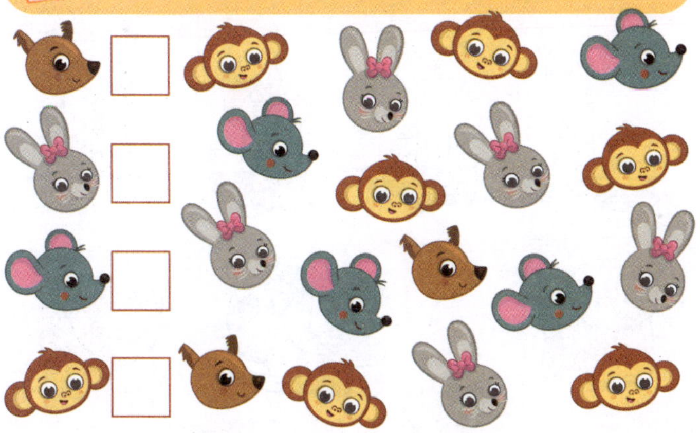

562 What is it used for?

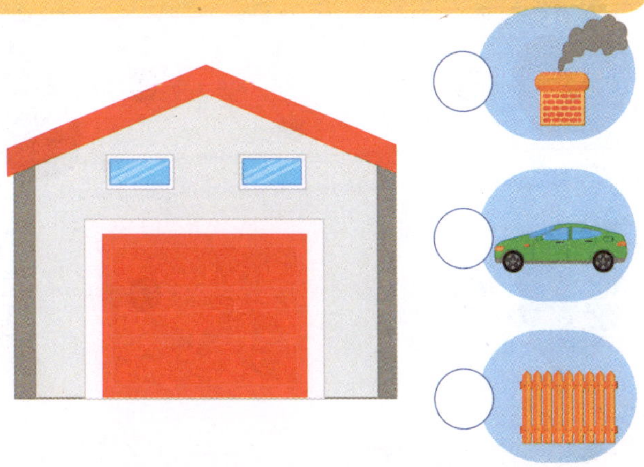

560 Crack the maze.

563 Follow to colour.

561 Letter writing practice

rainbow

r r r r r

r r r r r r r r r r

r r r r r r r r r r

564 Match fruits and vegetables by colour.

566 Find two same pictures.

565 Count how many shapes?

567 Riddle with numbers.

568 Dot to dot, then colour.

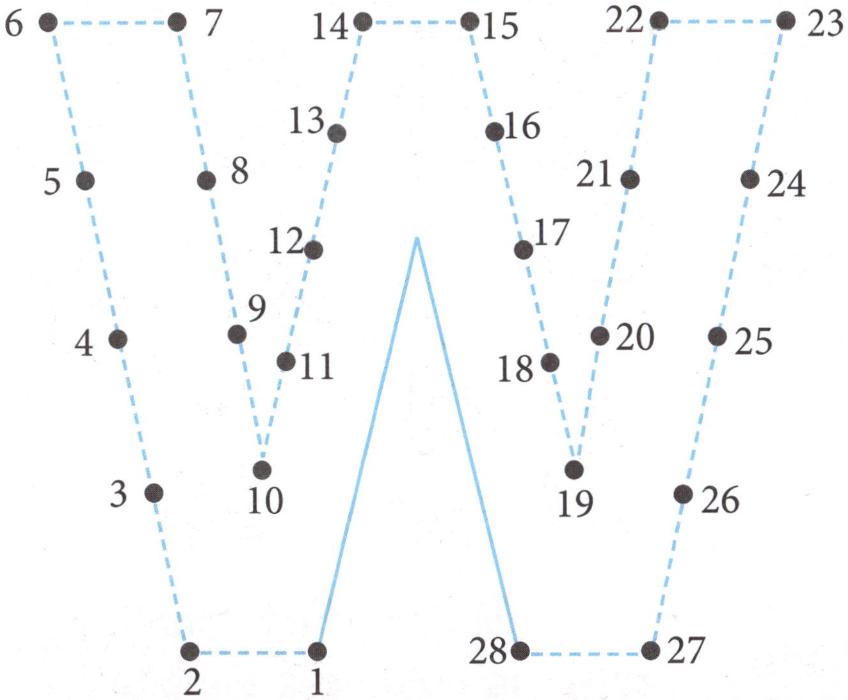

571 Add and write.

569 Double-digit addition

	1	5
+	2	1

	1	7
+	6	1

	4	6
+	1	2

	5	8
+	2	1

570 Trace rhombuses and colour.

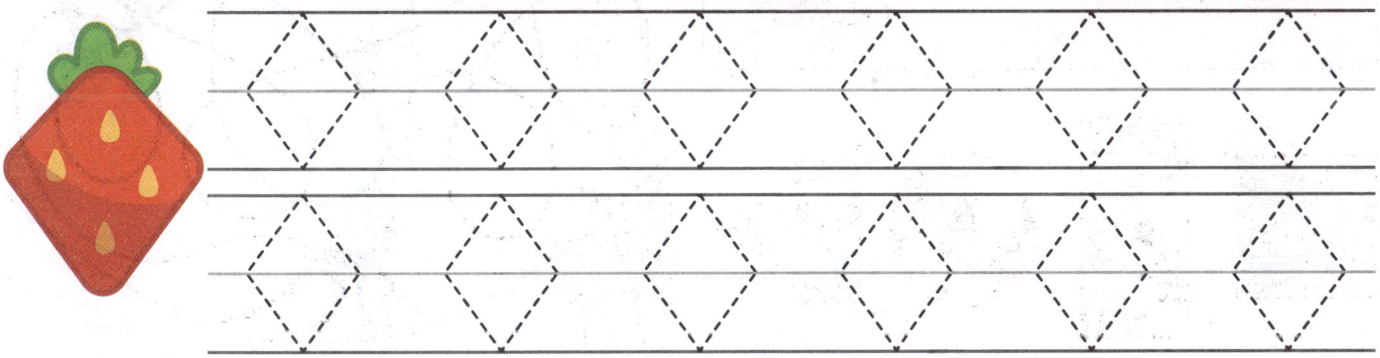

572 Trace the lines.

573 Match parts by shape.

574 Guess which monkey is holding a banana with its tail?

575 Connect the dots and colour.

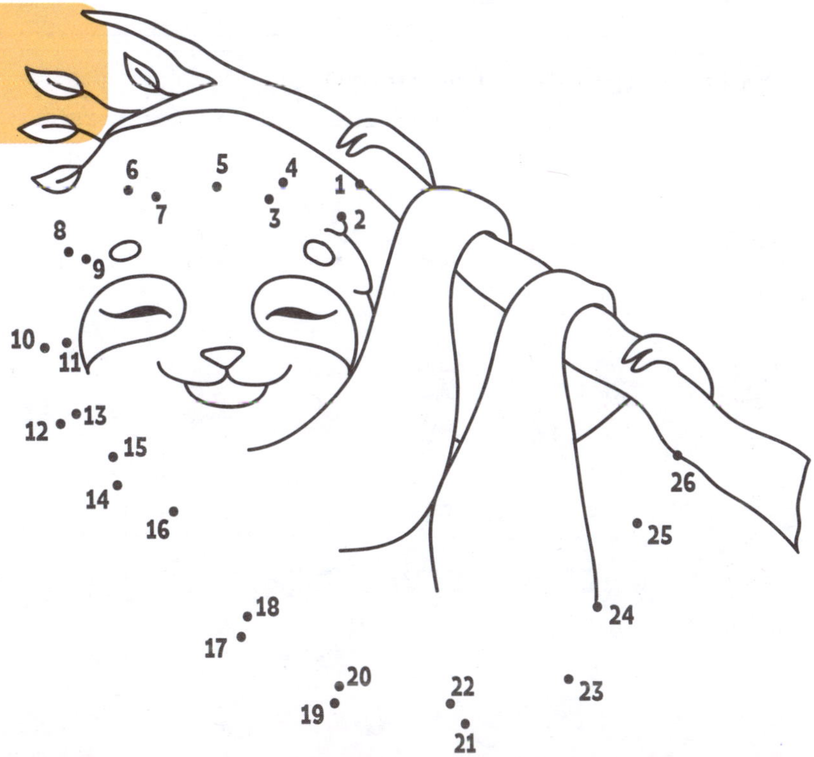

576 How many?

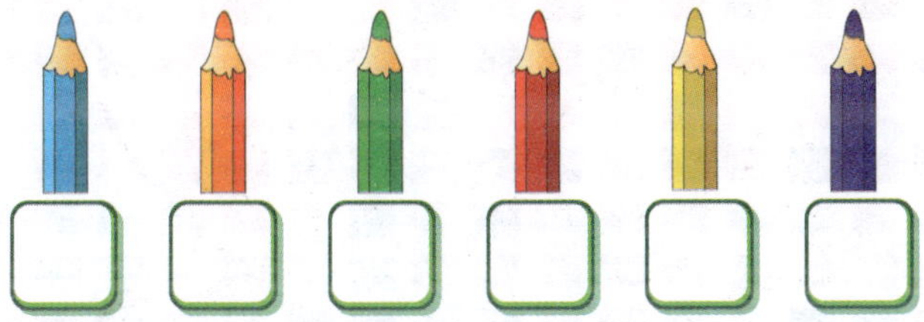

577 Word search

L	I	S	D	A	R	T	R
H	O	T	E	C	I	C	E
S	L	I	D	C	H	E	E
A	A	Y	A	R	R	I	S
N	T	W	J	E	I	N	T
S	N	O	E	S	U	D	M
N	D	Y	P	U	S	E	A
A	C	H	C	N	R	E	S

candy cedar christmas

holiday ice Jesus

list punch reindeer

Santa snow tree

578 Count and circle.

 3 5 2

 3 1 2

 5 2 4

 7 6 4

579 Letter writing practice

S

square

S S S S S

S S S S S

S S S S S

S S S S S

580 Handwriting practice

581 This fragment is repeated 12 times. Find and mark them.

582 Copy the lines.

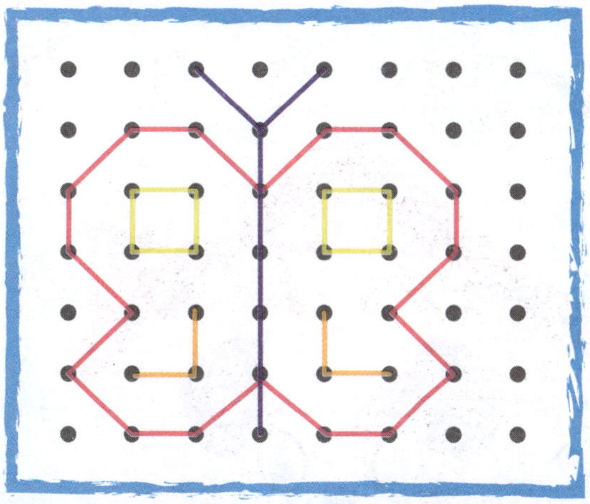

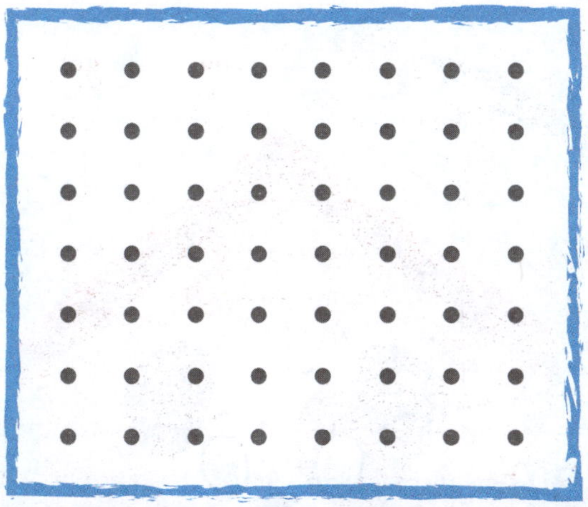

583 Find the value.

+

= 18

×

= 49

+

+

= 24

+

×

= ?

584 Choose the next in the series.

?

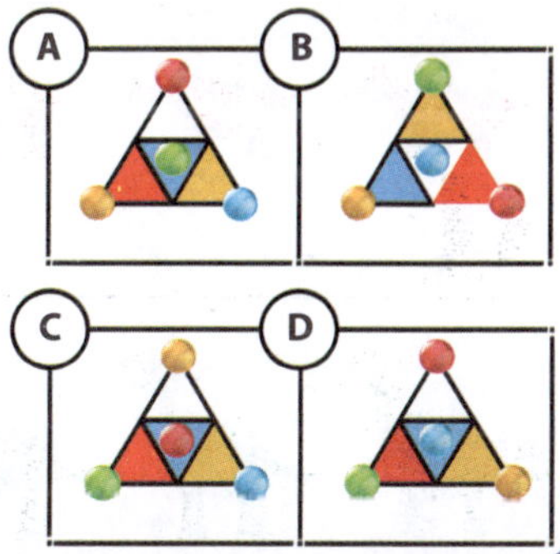

585 Repeat the pattern.

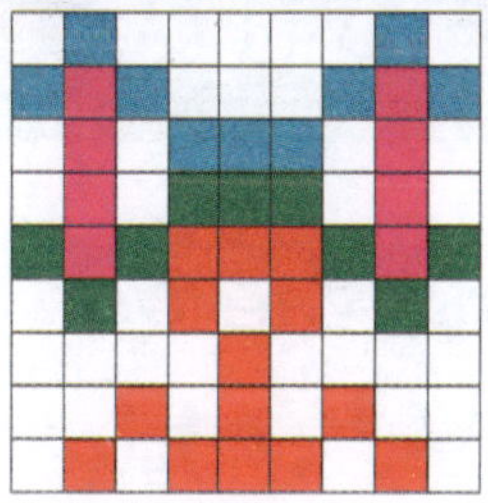

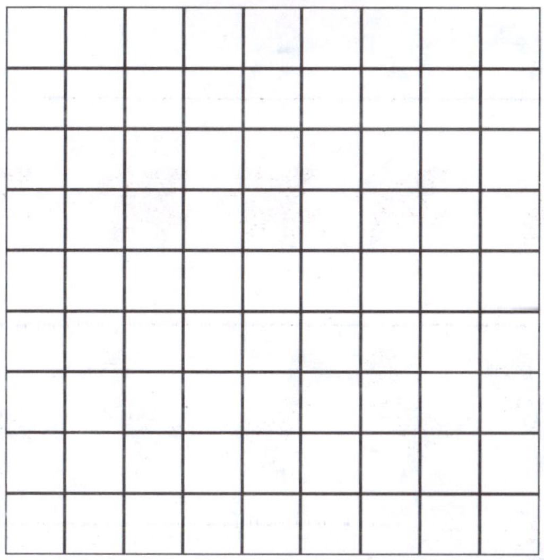

586 Find 5 differences.

587 Find the odd in each row.

588 Count and number the boxes below.

589 Dot to dot, then colour.

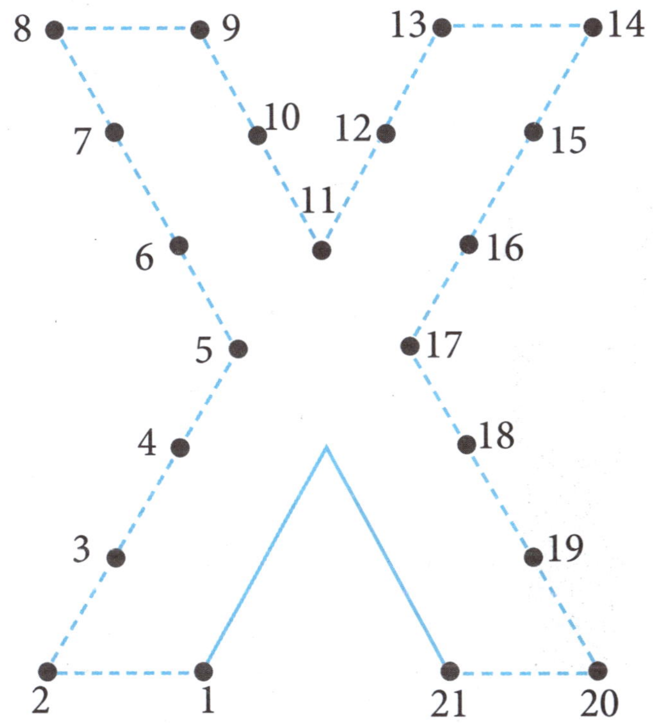

590 Finish the pattern.

591 Yes or no?

592 Track and number the cars.

593 Count and write.

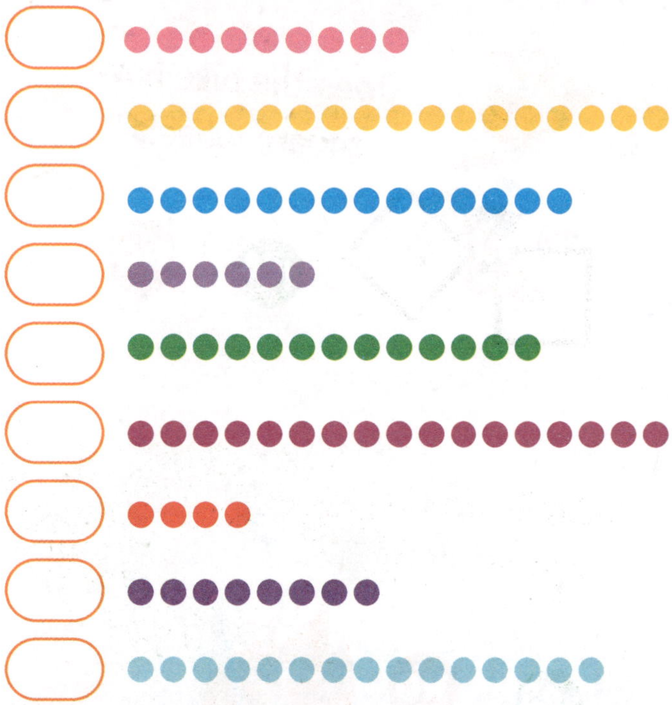

595 Match, trace and colour their caps.

594 Sort by type.

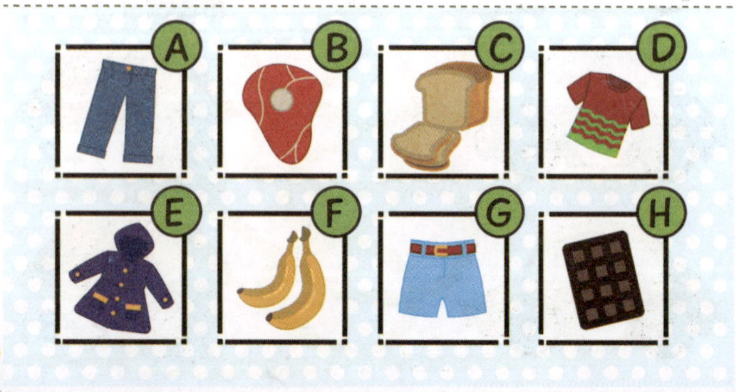

596 How many?

597 Trace the balloons. Colour each new shape different.

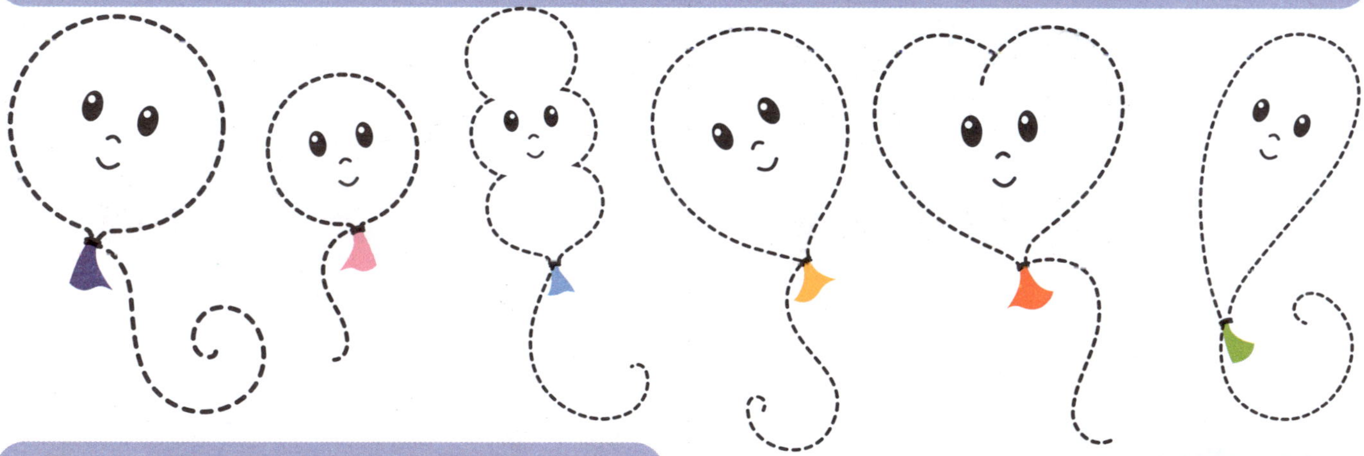

598 Draw with the fingers and palm.

599 Add or subtract.

5 ☐ 3 = 2	8 ☐ 3 = 5	10 ☐ 6 = 4
4 ☐ 4 = 8	3 ☐ 6 = 9	9 ☐ 8 = 1
7 ☐ 2 = 9	2 ☐ 3 = 5	1 ☐ 6 = 7

600 Count and match.

6

7

8

9

10

602 Trace and colour.

601 Crossword

603 Letter writing practice

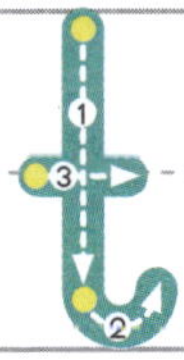

604 Guess the shape.

605 <, > or = ?

14 = 14	32 ○ 30	18 ○ 28
56 ○ 55	46 ○ 16	19 ○ 29

606 Decode the 5-letter words.

5	3	4	1	2
R	G	A	S	U
1	2	3	4	5

4	1	2	5	3
S	G	U	T	E
1	2	3	4	5

607 Find the beginning sound.

R B P

_abbit

608 Maze game

609 Find a pair for each crocodile.

610 Dot to dot, then colour.

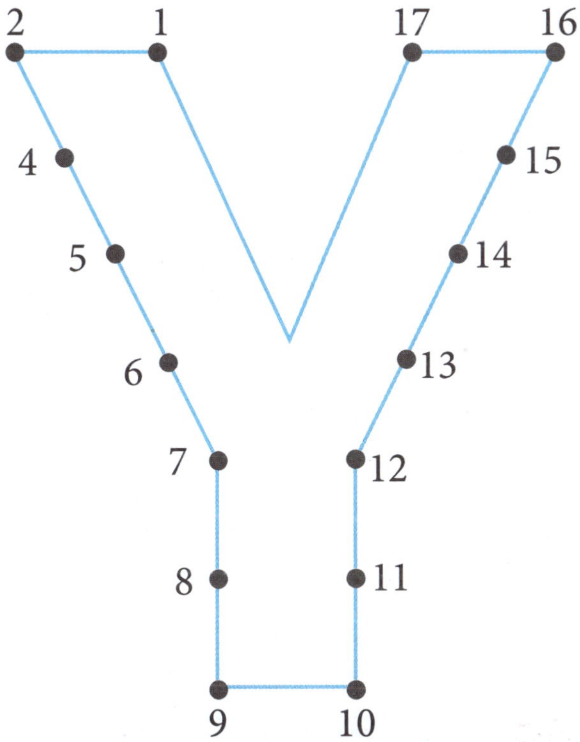

612 <, >, or =?

23 = 23

17 ○ 17

18 ○ 14

10 ○ 11

22 ○ 35

27 ○ 27

42 ○ 14

34 ○ 40

31 ○ 31

47 ○ 46

611 Finish the other half.

613 How many?

614 Join the dots and colour.

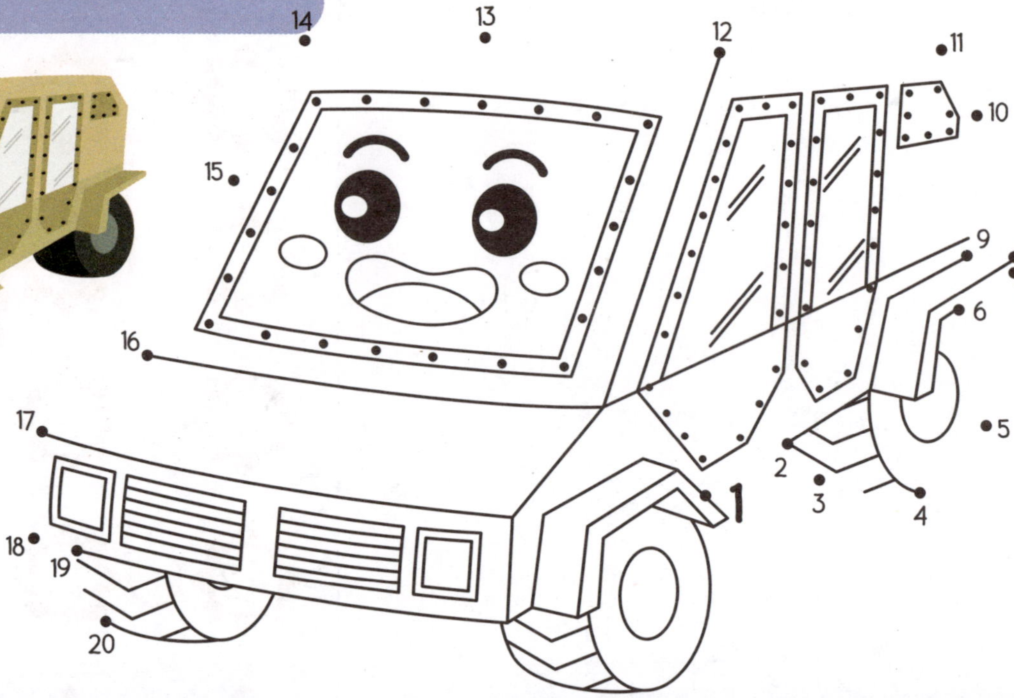

615 Count and trace.

616 Finish the other half.

617 Count and match.

9 + 3	10
1 + 18	12
2 + 6	15
5 + 5	8
4 + 11	19

619 Write the fractions.

$\frac{4}{7}$

$\frac{\square}{\square}$

$\frac{\square}{\square}$

$\frac{\square}{\square}$

618 Decode the 5-letter words.

2	4	5	1	3
R	A	M	D	E
1	2	3	4	5

4	1	2	5	3
O	C	A	L	R
1	2	3	4	5

620 Draw to complete the sudoku.

621 Find the path from 1 to 10.

		1	5	4	3	8	9
		4	8	7	1	5	9
1	2	3	2	6	4	7	2
6	5	4	5	5	6	9	8
4	7	3	6	4	10		
5	8	7	7	8	9		

622 Draw and find each dinosaur a pair.

623 Divide, trace and write.

624 Find 5 differences.

626 Match by use.

625 How many?

627 Letter writing practice

umbrella

628 Count and match.

2 5 1

630 Help the mermaid have that pearl.

629 Find the value.

 = 18

 = 14

 = 9

 = ☐

631 Colour, count and write.

632 Crossword

633 Compare the fractions.

$\frac{1}{8} = \frac{1}{8}$

$\frac{2}{4} \;\bigcirc\; \frac{3}{4}$

$\frac{1}{3} \;\bigcirc\; \frac{1}{4}$

$\frac{1}{9} \;\bigcirc\; \frac{1}{4}$

$\frac{2}{3} \;\bigcirc\; \frac{1}{3}$

$\frac{7}{11} \;\bigcirc\; \frac{10}{11}$

634 Find pairs of fishes.

635 Join the dots and colour.

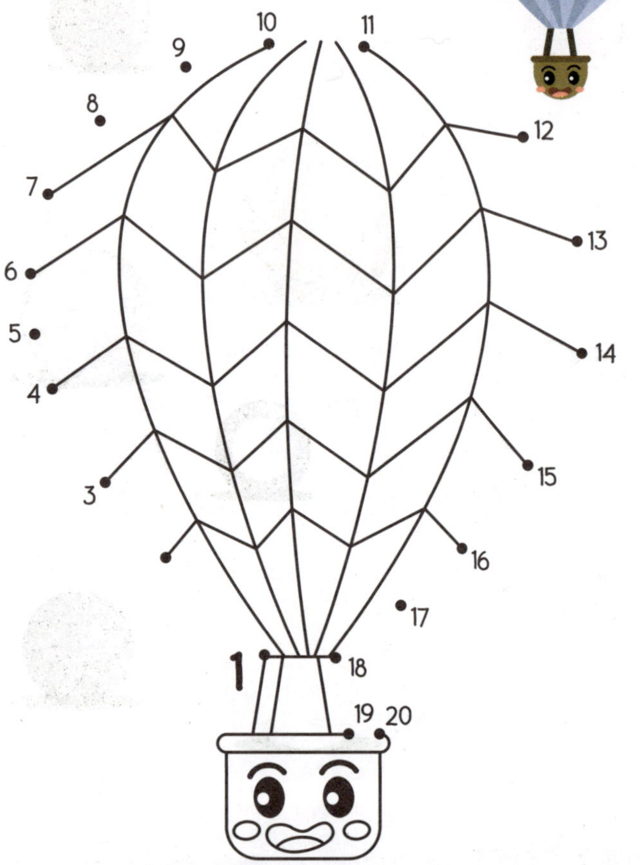

637 Name them.

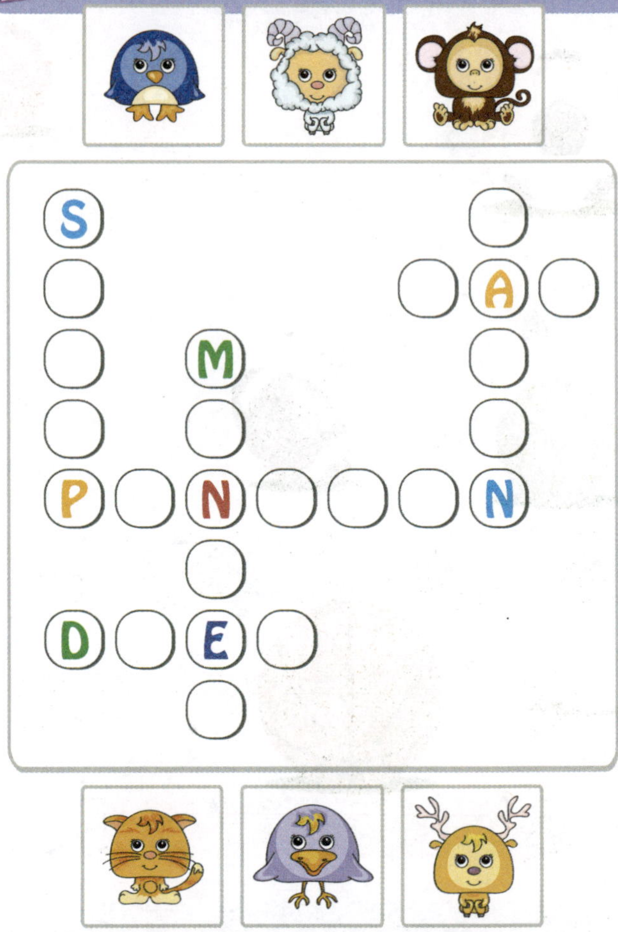

636 Colour by square.

638 What replaces the question mark?

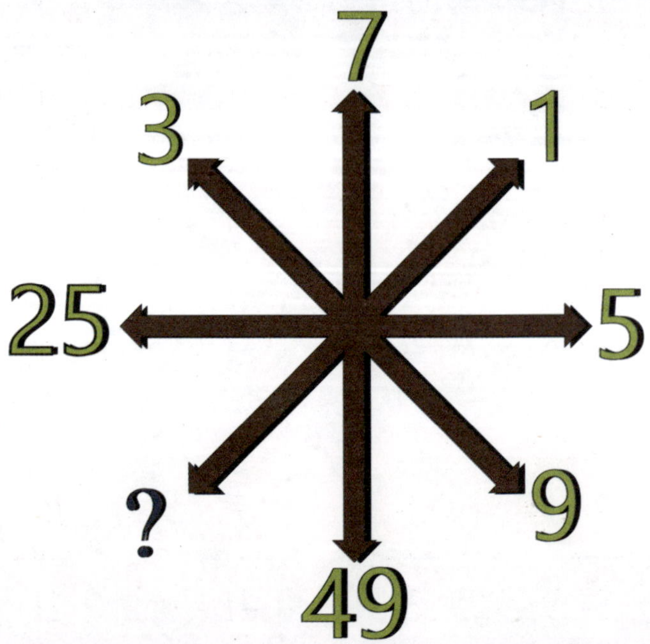

639 Trace and colour.

640 Find the value.

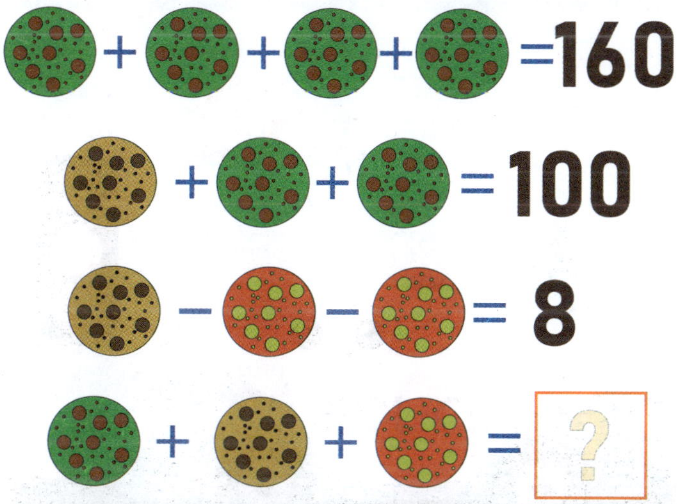

641 Tick (✓) with the missing part.

642 Can you find any twin foxes?

643 Arrange the numbers from largest to least.

644 Find 7 differences.

645 The witch wants to brew a potion. Find the jar or sack with the right ingredients.

646 Help the skier get down the mountain.

647 Group 4 different directions.

↓	←	↑	↓	→	→	→	↑
→	→	→	↑	←	←	←	↑
←	↓	←	↑	↓	↓	↓	↓
↓	↑	↑	↓	↑	↑	←	←
→	←	↓	↑	←	→	→	→
→	←	↓	←	→	↓	↑	↓
↓	↑	↑	→	←	←	↑	→

648 Yes or no?

649 How many to the left and how many to the right?

650 Find 5 differences.

651 What replaces the question mark?

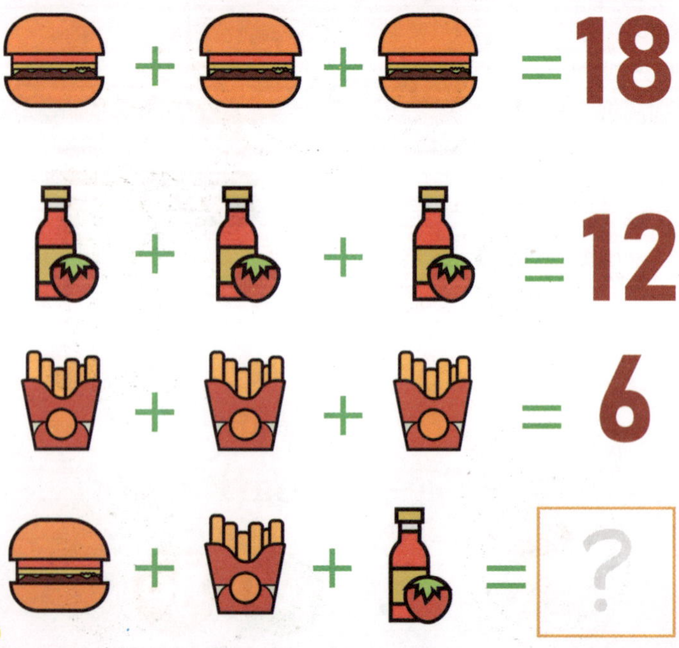

652 What's wrong with the picture?

653 Dot to dot, then colour.

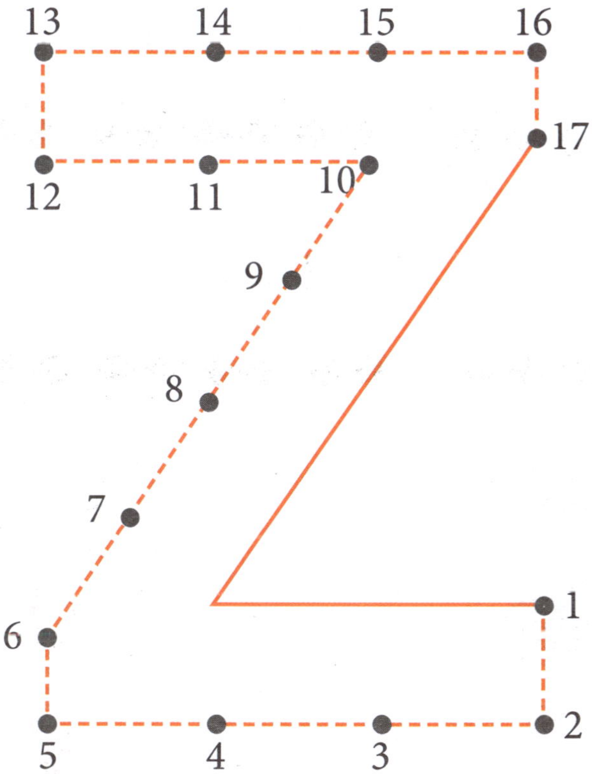

655 Colour by number.

654 Match ducklings and shadows.

656 Where is the hourglass?

657 Compare.

658 Letter writing practice

v

van

v v v v v

v v v v v

v v v v v

v v v v v

660 Match by the first letter.

U

V

W

X

Y

Z

659 Write the missing numbers.

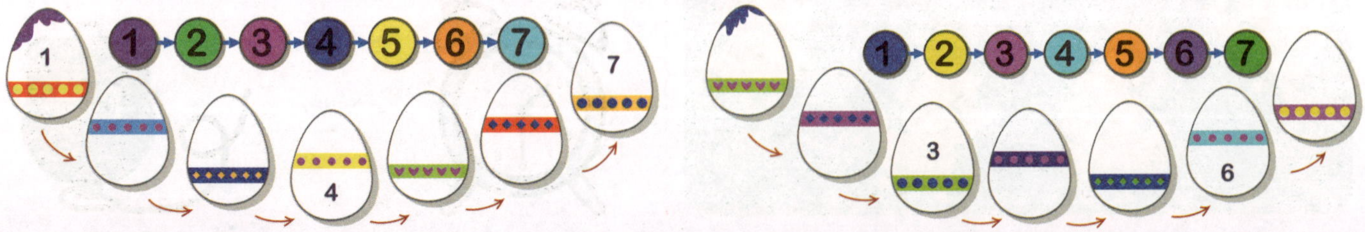

661 Compare the fractions.

$\frac{7}{7} = \frac{8}{8}$

$\frac{5}{11} \bigcirc \frac{1}{2}$

$\frac{1}{11} \bigcirc \frac{6}{11}$

$\frac{3}{3} \bigcirc \frac{3}{6}$

$\frac{1}{1} \bigcirc \frac{9}{9}$

$\frac{5}{5} \bigcirc \frac{10}{12}$

662 Find the correct shadow.

663 Colour by number.

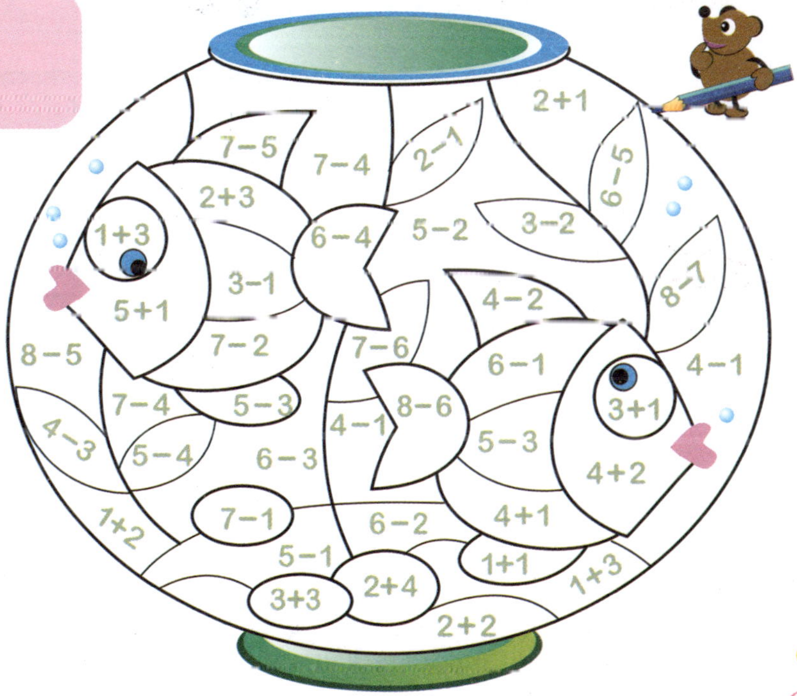

664 Find the beginning sound.

m

c

u

_uckoo clock

665 Which goes together?

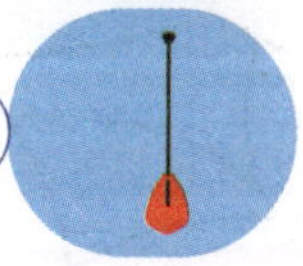

666 Colour odd numbers.

667 Copy and colour.

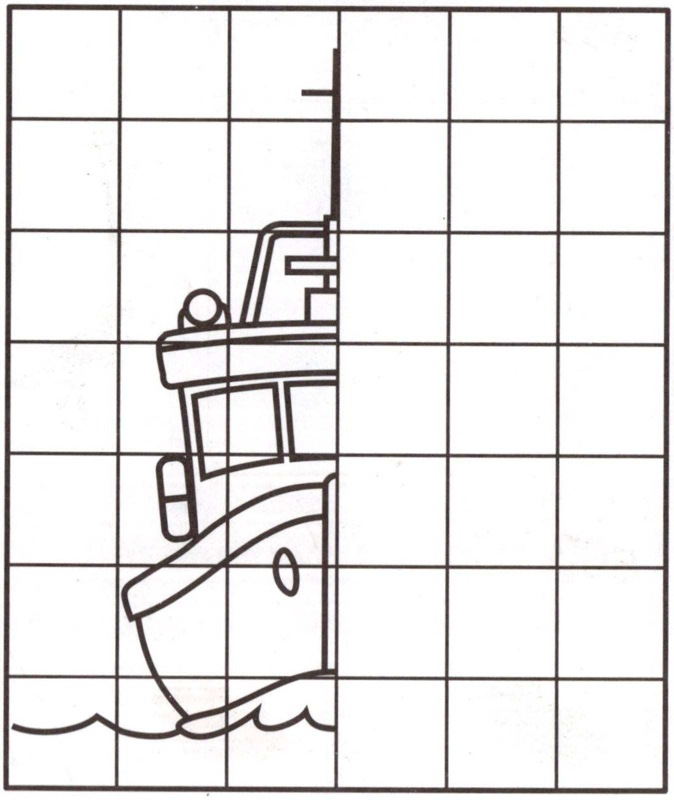

1 2 3 8 0

4 5 6 7 9

668 Follow the pattern.

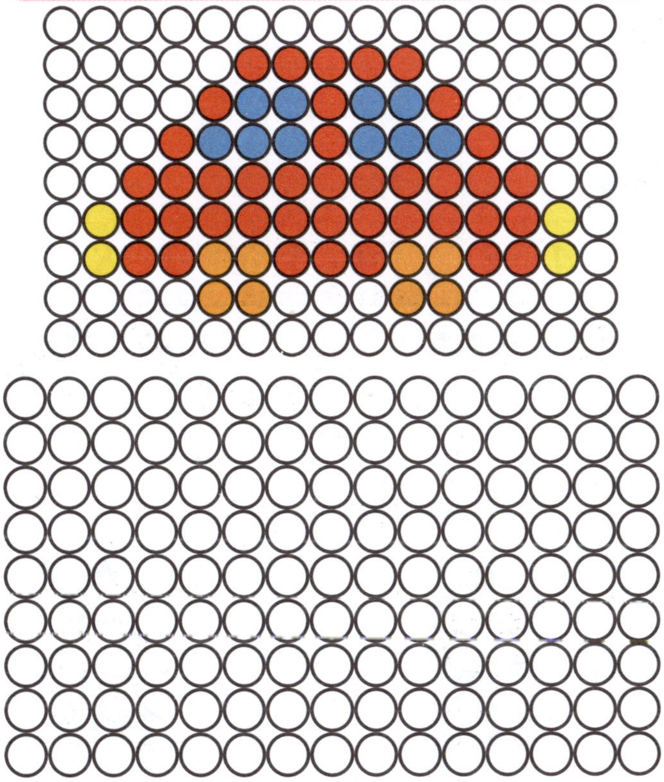

670 How many?

669 Find the hidden.

671 Find the clocks showing the same time.

672 Counting game

673 Find the twin princesses.

674 How many?

675 Find the correct shadow.

677 What comes next?

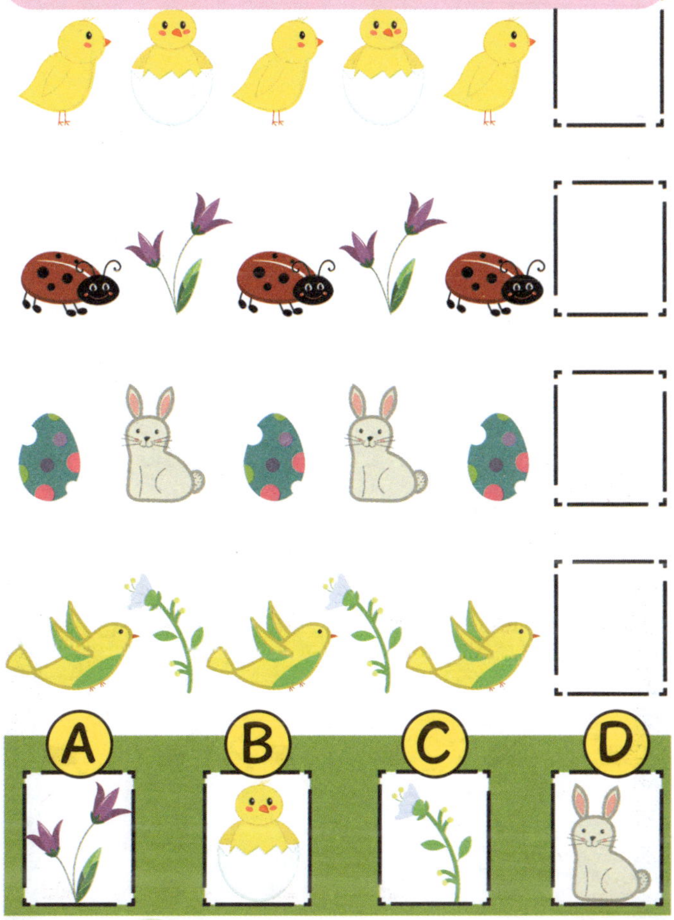

676 Crossword

678 Colour by fraction.

$\frac{2}{4}$

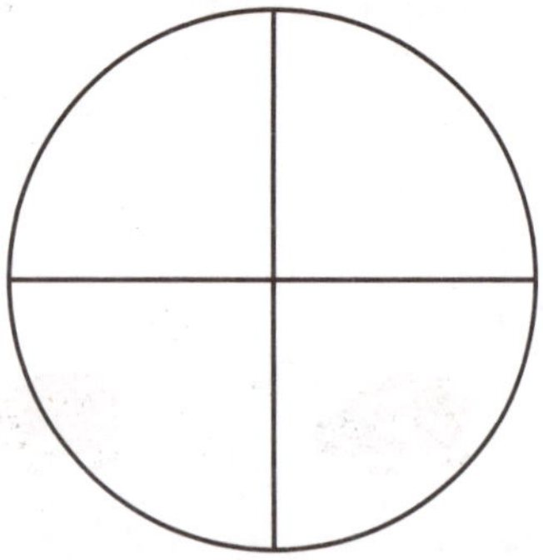

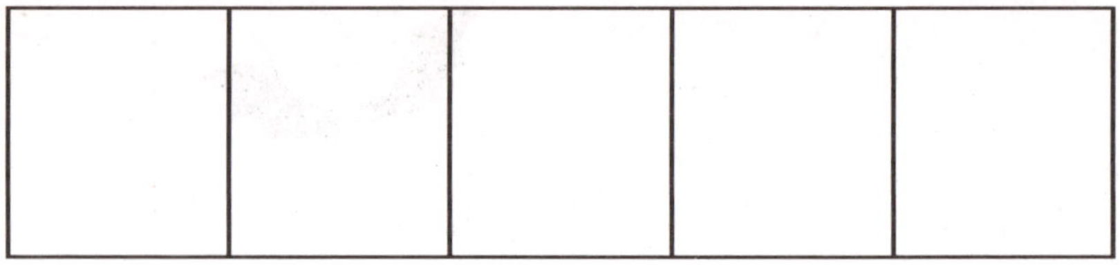

$\frac{3}{5}$

679 Fill in the missing numbers.

681 Find the value.

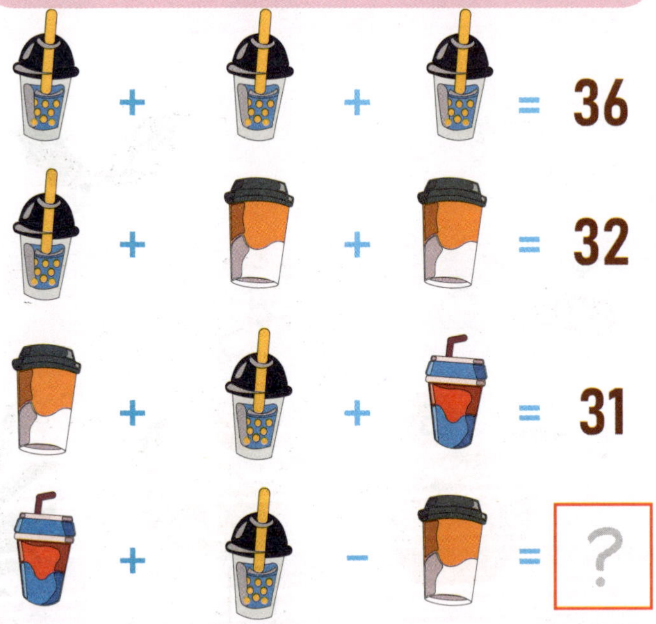

680 What toys are in the box?

682 Colour the pictures beginning with sound 'd'.

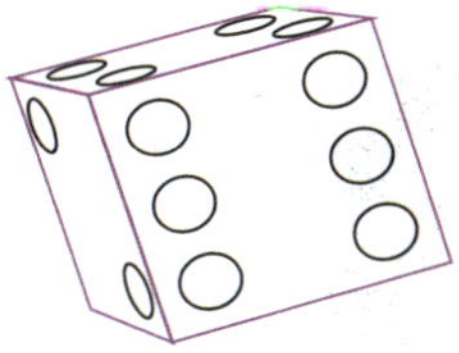

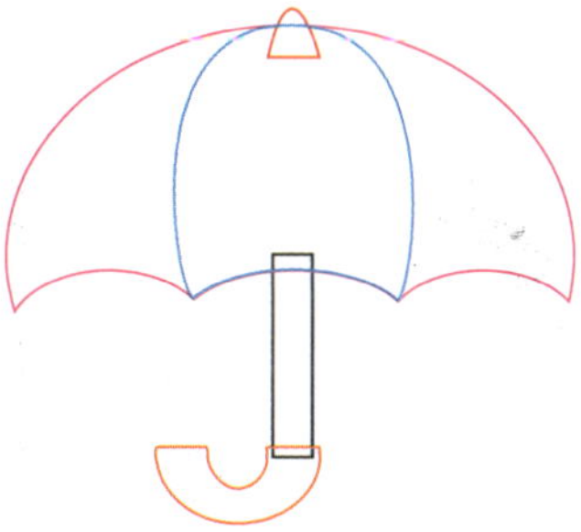

683 Find the way from each insect and join letters so you can read the words.

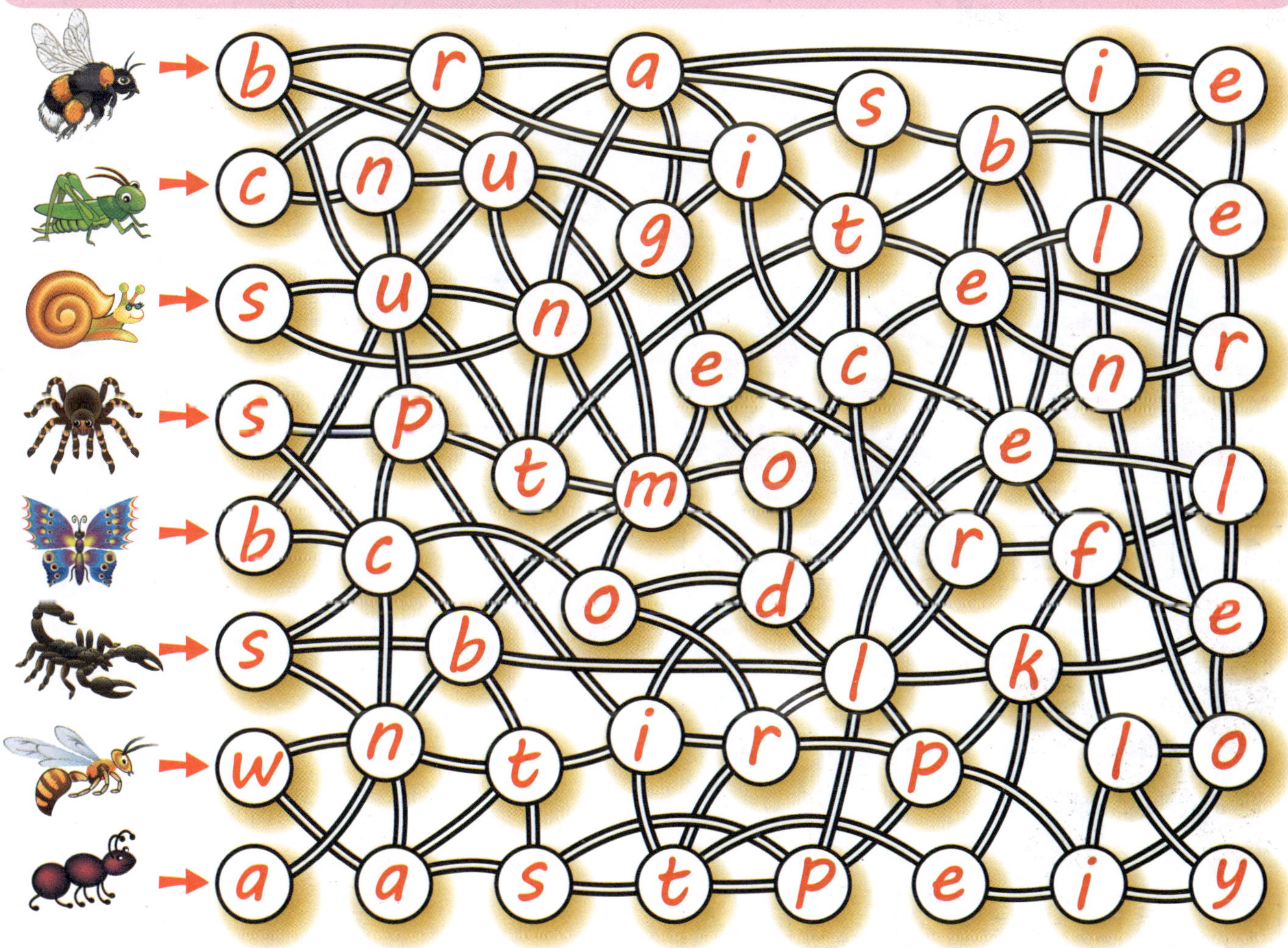

684 Join by letter and colour.

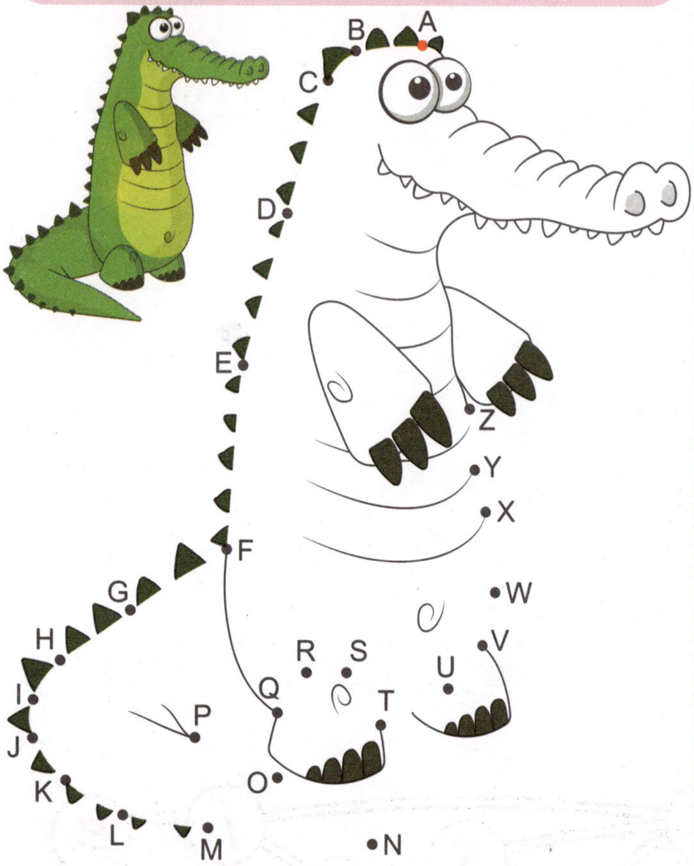

685 Count and circle.

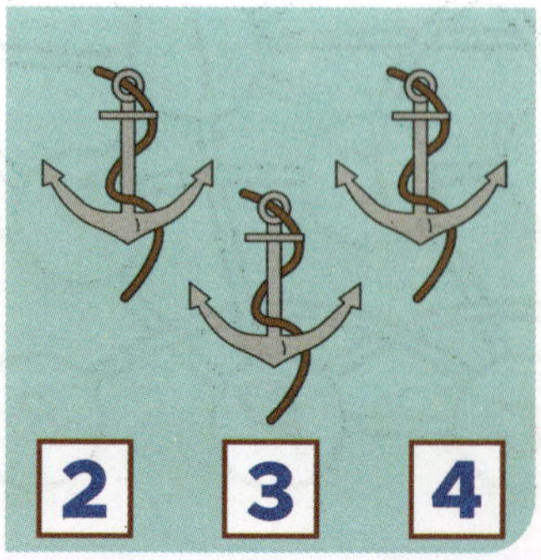

686 Follow the pattern.

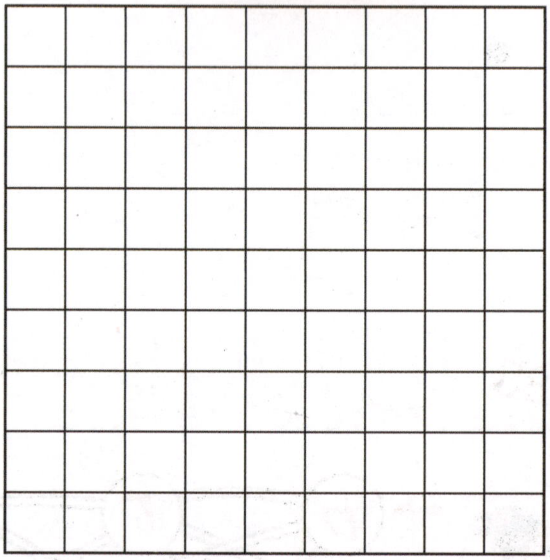

687 Trace the letters.

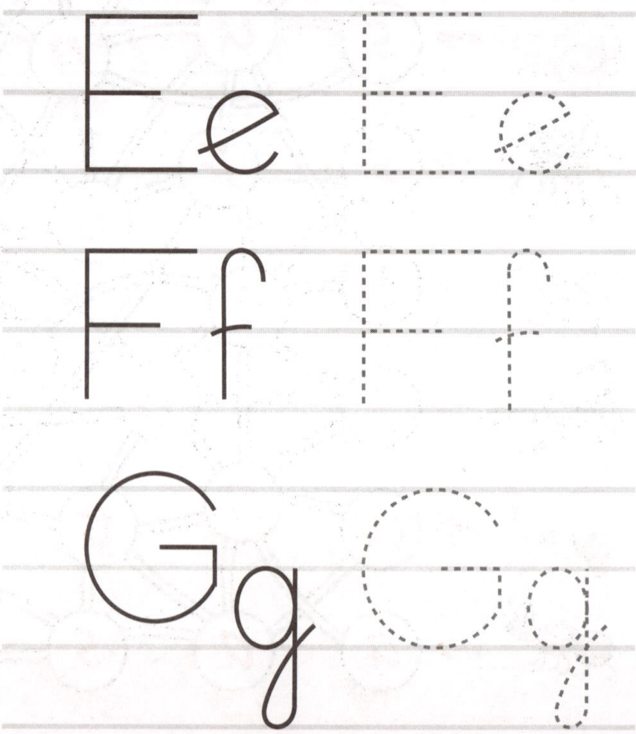

688 Where will the alpaca go?

689 Easter egg maze

690 Find the value.

691 What makes it move?

693 Match by time.

10:00 | 13:45 | 15:00 | 07:30

692 Find the way underground to the hidden treasure chest and draw the line.

694 Write the missing numbers.

695 Find the beginning sound.

696 Reach the exit.

697 Word search

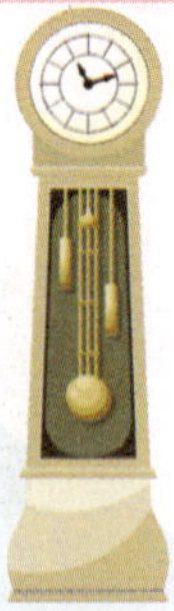

A	R	M	C	H	A	I	R	I	M
F	I	R	E	P	L	A	C	E	T
R	B	O	O	K	M	X	H	J	F
O	P	C	U	P	B	O	A	R	D
C	I	H	W	Y	A	T	B	O	J
L	C	A	Z	B	W	K	X	Z	Z
O	T	I	M	T	A	B	L	E	G
C	U	R	C	U	S	H	I	O	N
K	R	C	N	H	G	Y	C	S	F
S	E	F	C	Z	O	L	S	G	E

698 Complete the puzzle.

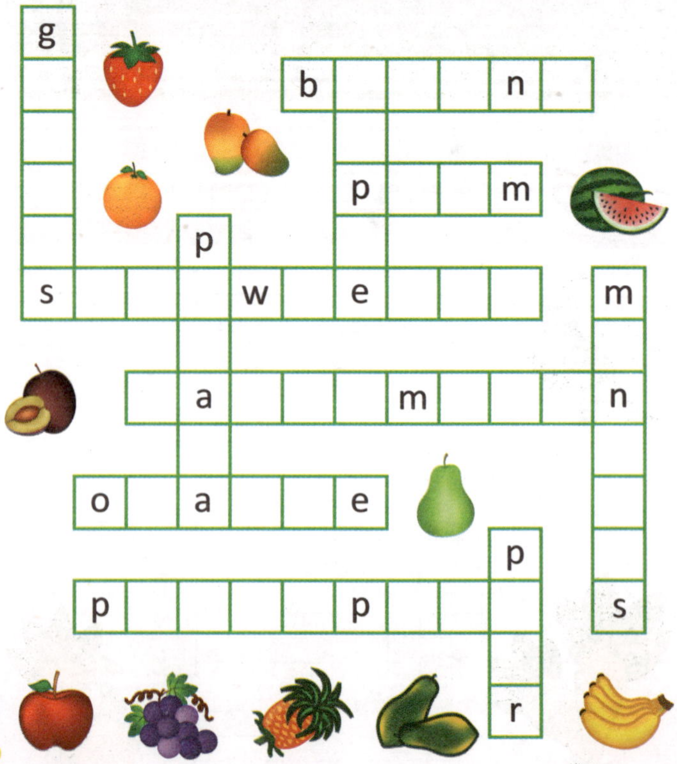

699 Add and match.

1 + 13 ·	· 16
11 + 2 ·	· 11
5 + 6 ·	· 10
3 + 7 ·	· 13
12 + 4 ·	· 14

700 Honeycomb puzzle

701 Colour the pictures beginning with sound 'a'.

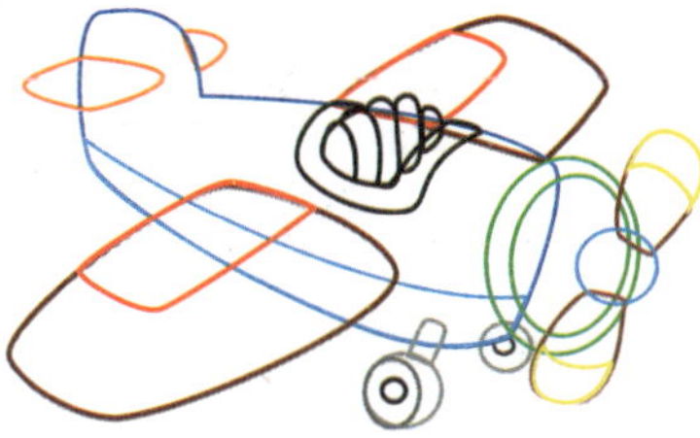

702 How many?

703 Count and trace.

3 2 5

2 3 1

5 4 6

3 1 2

704 < or >?

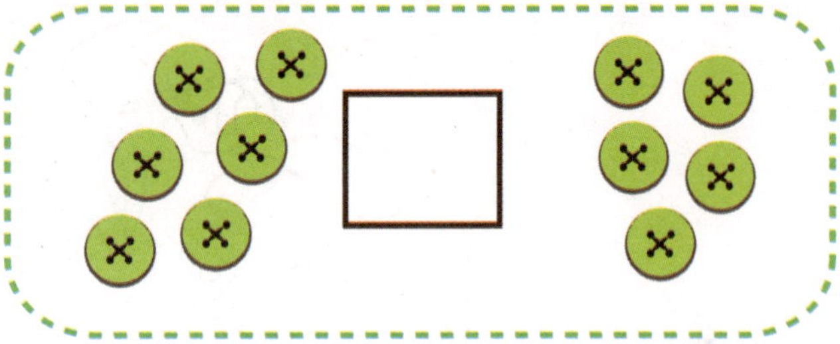

705 How many?

706 List 10 different objects from the picture.

707 Trace and colour.

708 Letter writing practice

xylophone

709 Copy the picture

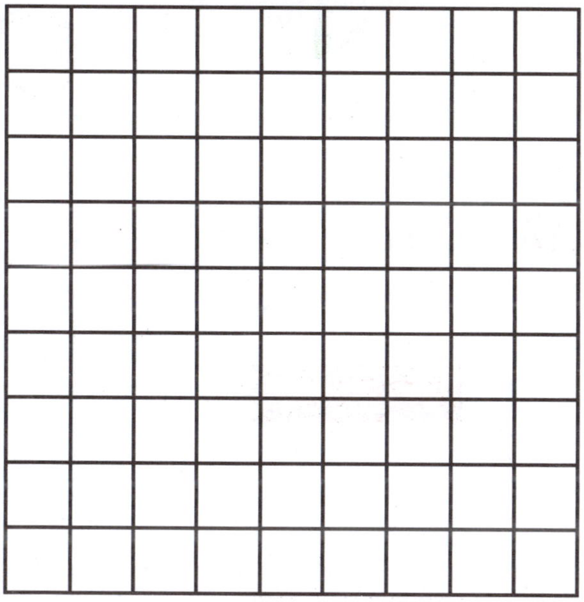

710 Find the value.

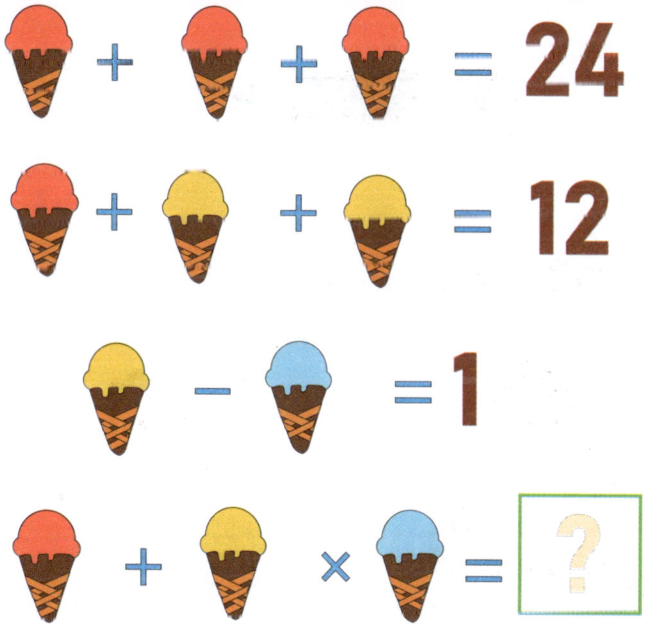

711 Before, between and after

Before

___ ← 54

___ ← 67

___ ← 82

Between

77 ___ 79

48 ___ 50

60 ___ 62

After

49 → ___

20 → ___

71 → ___

712 Colour by fraction.

$\frac{1}{4}$

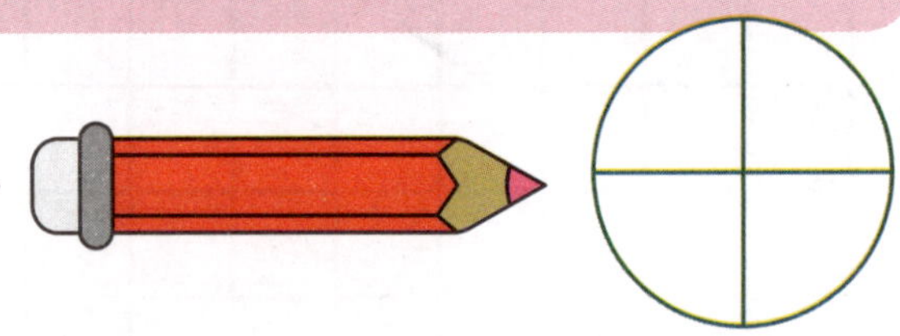

$\frac{10}{12}$

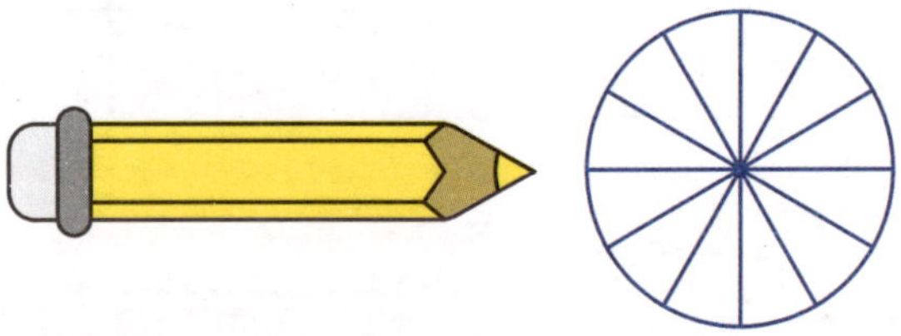

$\frac{7}{9}$

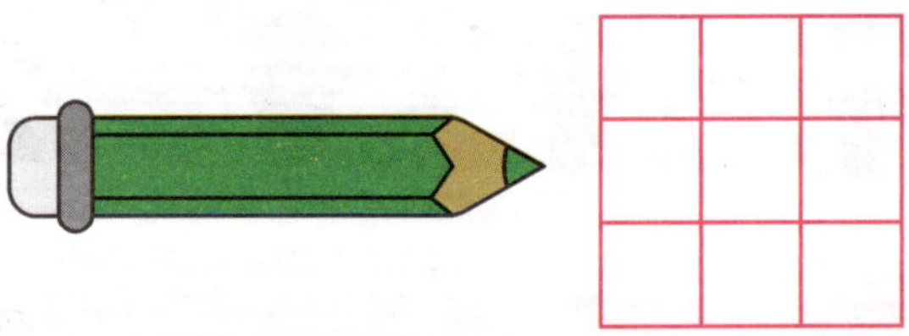

714 Which goes together?

713 Write the action words.

___

___

___

___

715 Colour the fluffy sheep.

718 Whose house is it?

716 Add and write.

 =

 =

 =

 =

717 Measure the capacity.

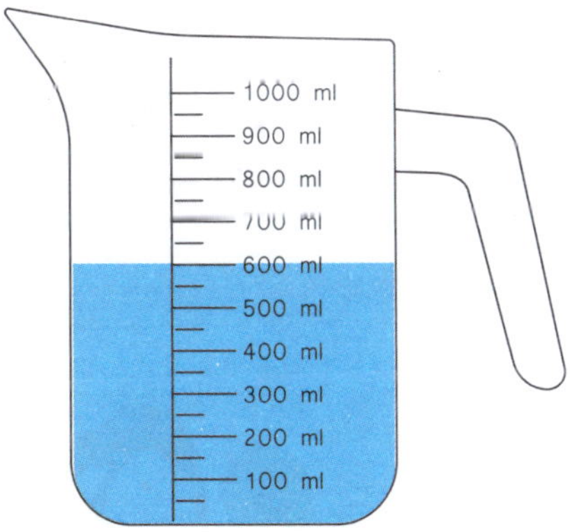

____ ml

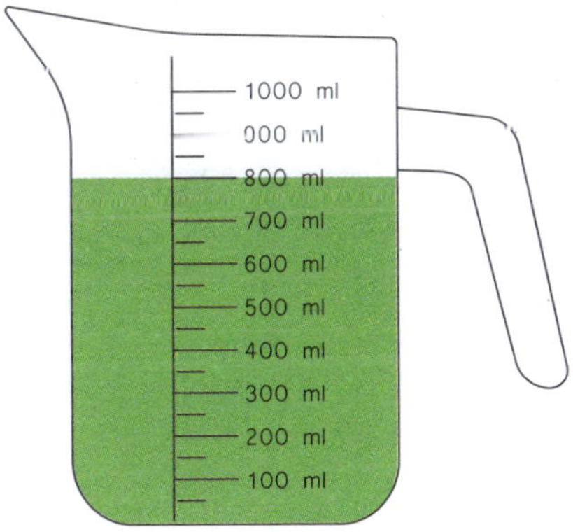

____ ml

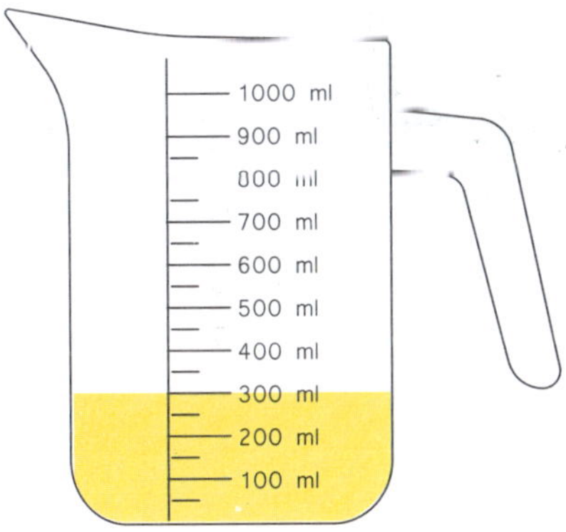

____ ml

719 Cross (×) the balls with only 2 colours.

720 Find 5 differences.

721 Crossword

722 Find the beginning sound.

_ow

K

C

G

723 Find the way between the bear and bees.

724 Match letters and pictures.

 • • P

 • • Q

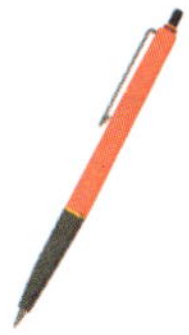 • • R

 • • S

 • • T

725 Find the value.

3 + 2 = 

9 −  = 

 +  = 

 = ? 

726 Fill in the blanks.

Rooster Dog Woof-Woof Moo-Moo
Cow Sheep Baa-Baa Cock-A-Doodle-Do

I am a _____ and I say _____

I am a _____ and I say _____

I am a _____ and I say _____

I am a _____ and I say _____

727 How many?

728 Match letters and pictures.

H •

S •

G •

T •

B •

729 Finish the pattern.

730 Colour using the code.

1		White
2		Yellow
3		Red
4		Blue
5		Grey
6		Green
7		Blue sky

731 Crossword

732 <, > or =?

23 ○ 27	22 ○ 22	59 ○ 35
44 ○ 34	95 ○ 85	67 ○ 88

733 How many differences can you find?

734 Help them get out. Go through all the mazes so as not to wake the animals.

735 Trace and colour the pairs.

736 Find 10 differences.

737 Fill the markers.

2	
1	1
2	

3	
1	2
2	
3	

4	
1	3
2	
3	
4	

5	
1	4
2	
3	
4	
5	

6	
1	5
2	
3	
4	
5	
6	

7	
1	6
2	
3	
4	
5	
6	
7	

8	
1	7
2	
3	
4	
5	
6	
7	
8	

9	
1	8
2	
3	
4	
5	
6	
7	
8	
9	

738 Join and colour.

739 Can you find any differences?

740 Find the given objects in the grid.

R	S	A	G	S	N	U	T	O	R	P
I	G	E	H	R	A	D	I	S	H	S
N	J	K	T	C	R	A	C	K	E	R
G	I	R	A	C	K	E	T	Y	A	U
S	N	S	A	B	L	T	K	N	R	G
R	A	S	P	B	E	R	R	I	E	S
S	S	R	W	K	C	R	A	E	E	N
P	T	O	H	I	K	R	U	D	T	O
G	I	B	S	R	A	C	C	O	O	N
J	I	O	L	E	N	G	I	E	H	E
N	E	T	E	O	G	P	R	A	I	N

Racket

Rain

Raspberries

Raccoon

Robot

Rug

Ring

Radish

741 Riddle with numbers.

 = 27

 = 24

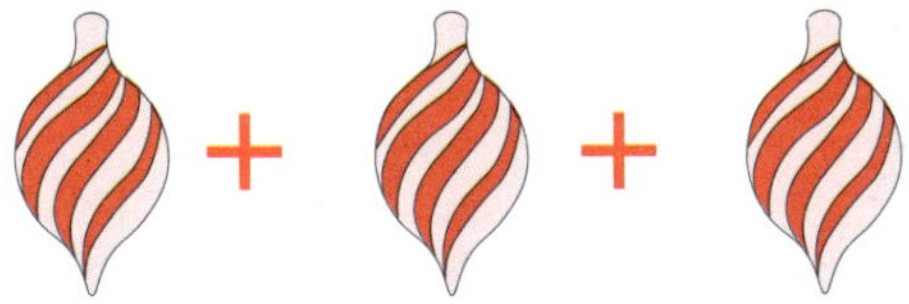 = 21

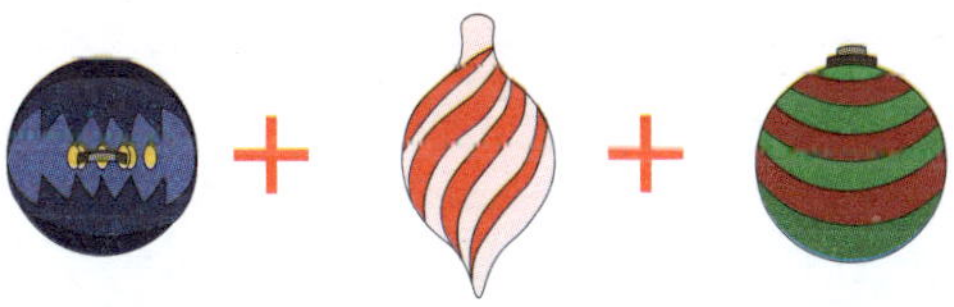 = ?

743 Name the dog's parts.

- ear
- mouth
- paw
- nose
- fur
- tail
- eye
- claw
- tongue

742 Match words according to how they sound.

oo		cheese CHēz
ow		clean klēn
ee		school sko͞ol
ea		snow snō

ue		boat bōt
oa		backhoe ˈbakˌhō
ai	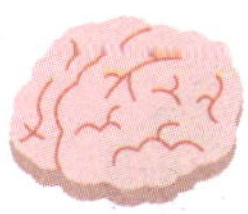	brain brān
oe		blue blo͞o

744 Draw with the fingers and palm.

745 Trace and colour identically.

746 Match to complete the picture.

747 How many?

748 Trace the letters.

749 Colour by fraction.

$\frac{3}{6}$ 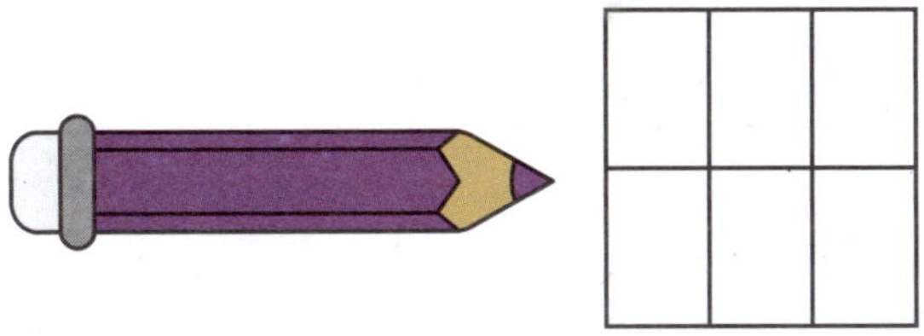

$\frac{6}{8}$ 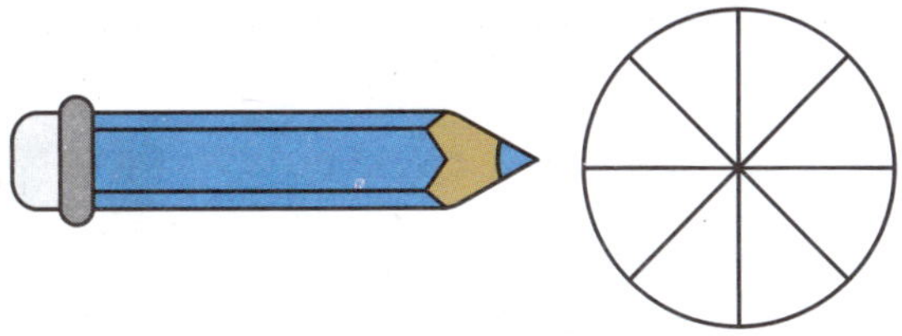

$\frac{8}{10}$ 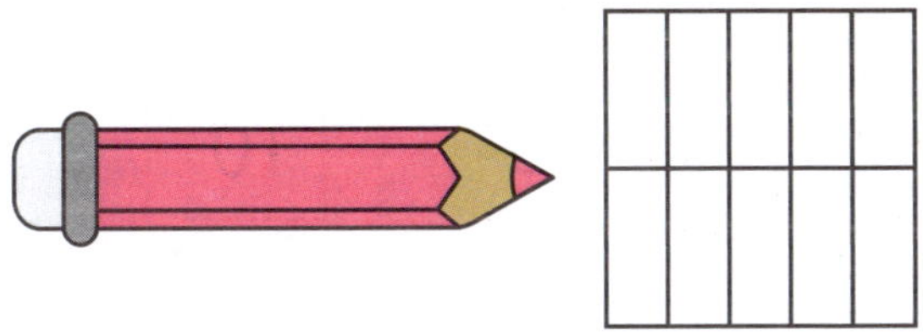

750 Help kids to the school.

751 Colour the correct number box.

1 4 9

6 2 4

7 3 5

10 8 6

752 Count, choose and write.

	+		
	+		
	+		
	+		
	+		

3 1 5 2 4

753 Decode the 5-letter words.

3 E	5 M	1 C	2 R	4 A
1	2	3	4	5

5 L	3 I	4 L	1 G	2 R
1	2	3	4	5

754 Colour the number of cells as given.

755 Circle the corresponding letter.

Q S H Z

M E C I

R P O G

A R U M

756 On the planet Zet held a space conference. Go through the maze for each alien.

757 Write the action words.

758 Join and colour.

759 Write the remaining.

 = ☐

 = ☐

 = ☐

 = ☐

760 Fill in the missing numbers.

761 Find the path from 1 to 10.

5	8	2	6	7	3		
4	6	7	8	4	2		
8	2	5	4	2	5	1	1
7	10	6	9	6	5	3	2
		10	9	8	7	4	5
		9	7	8	6	5	7

762 What do they say?

CHUMP | OINK OINK | WOOF WOOF | NEIGH | MOO | MEOW

763 Who follow next?

764 Yes or no?

Whales live in an aquarium?

YES NO

Cats eat fish?

YES NO

Does a chicken swim in water?

YES NO

765 Match if they join.

a b c d

a b c d

766 Count and match.

6

2

9

4

10

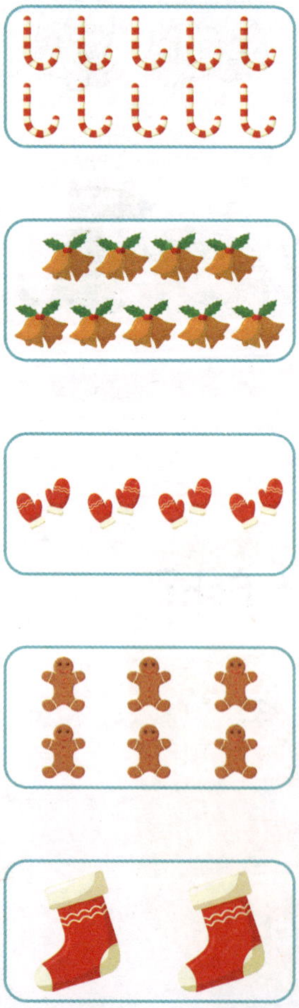

767 Calculate and write.

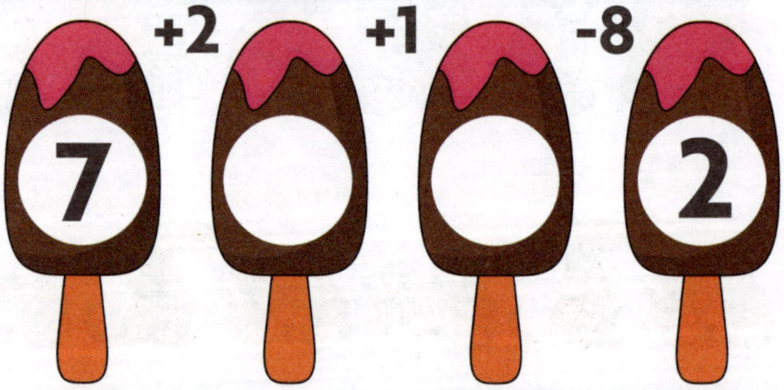

768 Which goes together?

769 Colour the picture using colour codes.

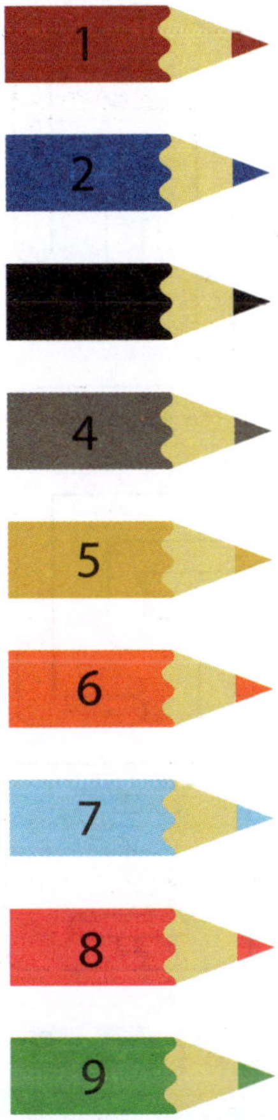

770 Match the following.

bl-  brown
broun

fr-  block
bläk

tr-  crab
krab

cr-  drum
drəm

dr-  train
trān

oa-  fruit
fro͞ot

771 Finish the pattern.

772 Find pairs.

773 From small z to capital Z

774 Match little girls and umbrellas.

775 Find and colour all the parallelograms.

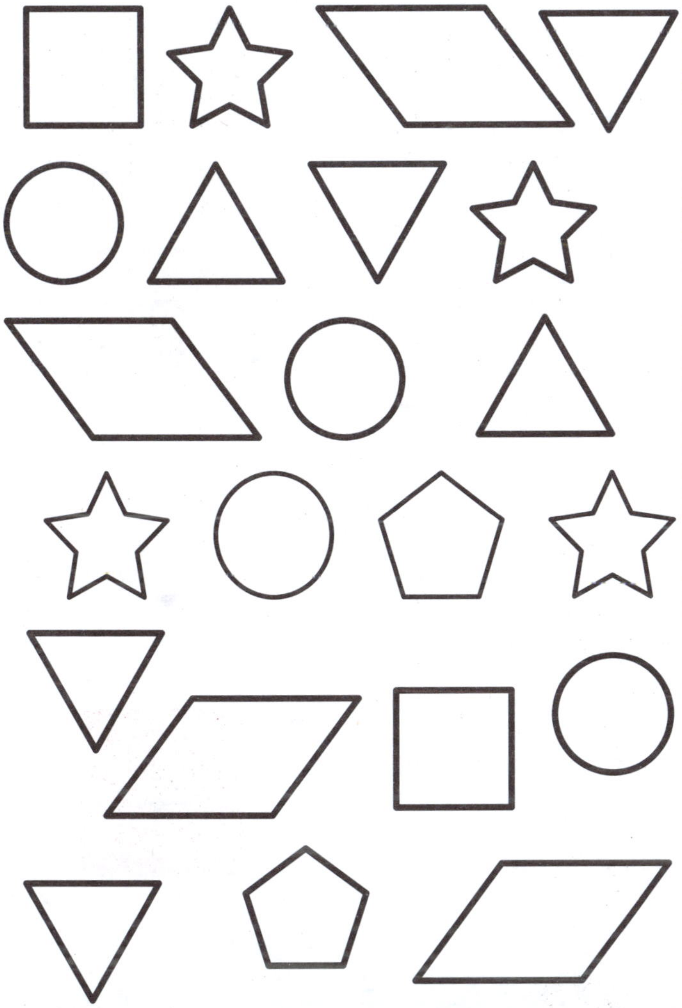

777 Halloween crossword

776 Add and match with the correct sum.

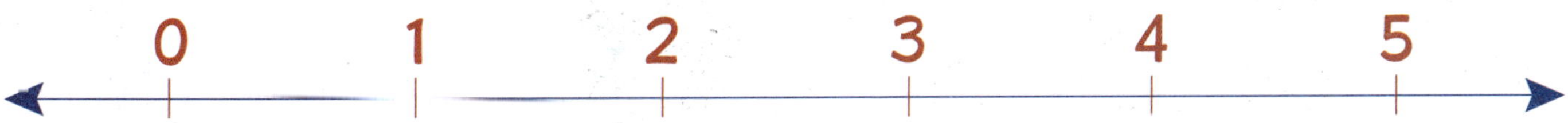

778 Colour and reveal the hidden.

1	2	1	2	1	2	1	2	1	2
3	3	3	3	3	3	3	3	3	3
3	4	3	3	4	3	4	4	4	3
3	4	3	3	4	3	3	4	3	3
3	4	4	4	4	3	3	4	3	3
3	4	3	3	4	3	3	4	3	3
3	4	3	3	4	3	4	4	4	3
3	3	3	3	3	3	3	3	3	3
1	2	1	2	1	2	1	2	1	2

1

2

3

4

779 Colour the xylophone.

780 Match by shape.

781 Animal sounds

782 Match letters and pictures.

 A

 B

 C

 D

 E

783 + or - ?

6 ◯ 2 = 8

5 ◯ 3 = 2

7 ◯ 1 = 8

3 ◯ 3 = 0

784 Can you find any differences?

785 What comes last?

786 Trace and colour.

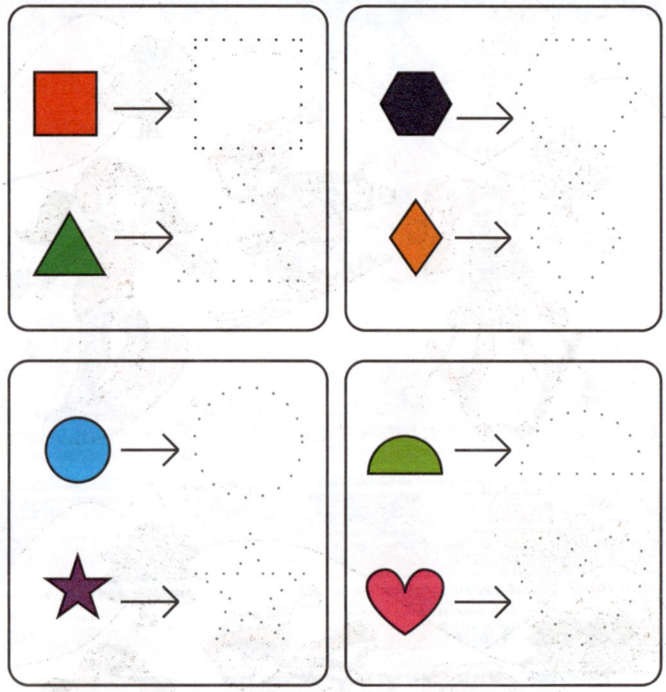

788 How many?

787 Draw clock hands.

789 Fill in the blanks.

_lue

_host

ma_ic

en_ine

790 Follow to colour.

791 Fill in the circles.

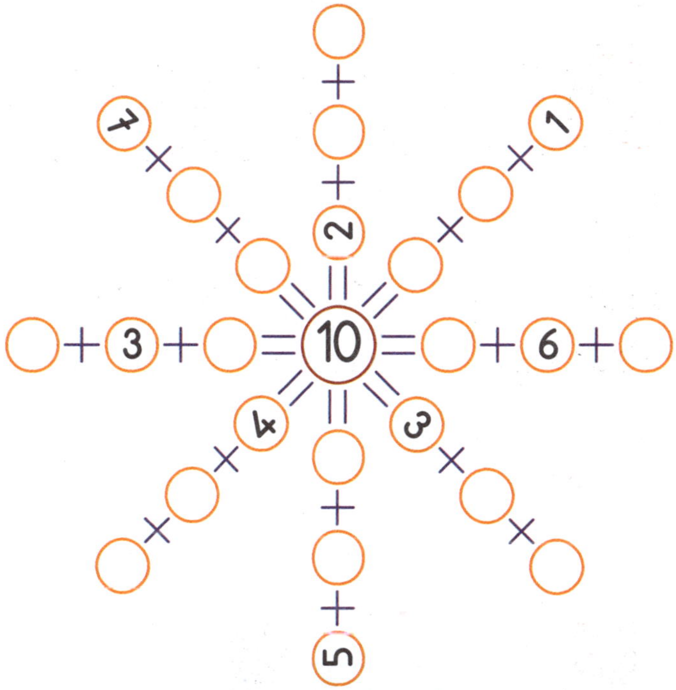

792 Easter crossword

793 Trace the numbers.

1 1 1 1 1 1 1 1 1 1 1 1

2 2 2 2 2 2 2 2 2 2 2 2

3 3 3 3 3 3 3 3 3 3 3 3

4 4 4 4 4 4 4 4 4 4 4 4

5 5 5 5 5 5 5 5 5 5 5 5

794 Colour the butterfly.

795 Count and match.

796 How many?

797 Sudoku

798 Count and write.

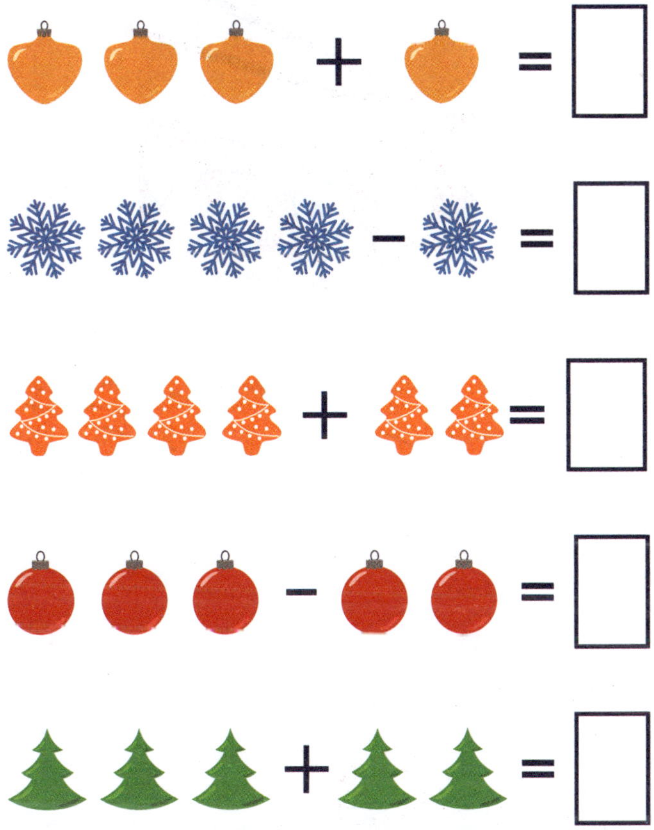

799 Help the bear find the path to the beehive.

800 Colour the drum.

802 Cross (×) big mugs and circle small cups.

801 Complete the pattern.

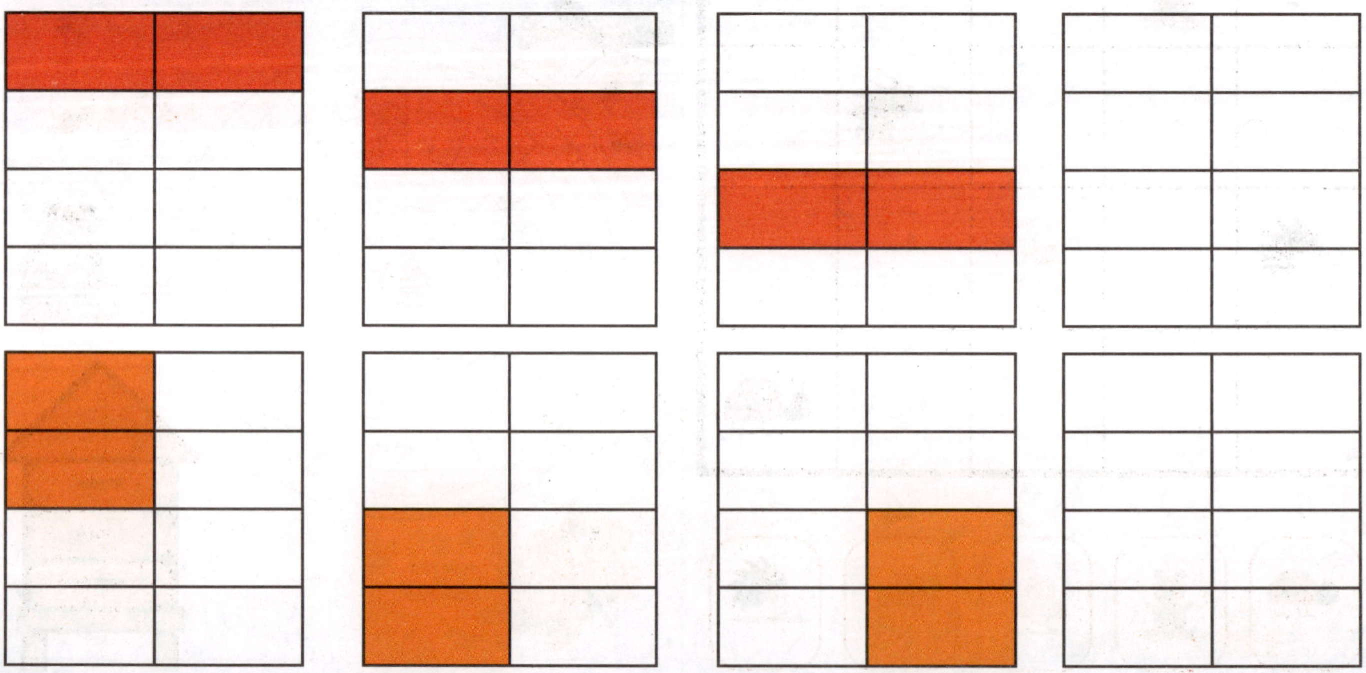

803 Letter writing practice

y

yo-yo

y y y y y

y y y y y

y y y y y

806 Add and subtract.

3	−	3	=	◯
+		+		+
◯		0		9
=		=		=
◯	+	◯	=	9

13 − ◯ = 6

804 Look at the time and draw the hands on the clocks.

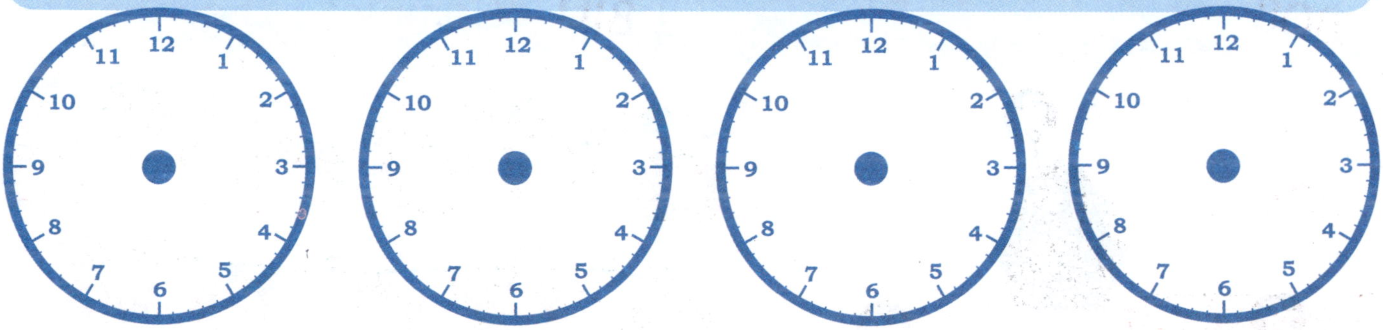

1:30 5:00 3:15 12:30

805 Count and colour.

807 Match the highlighted.

6

10

8

1

809 Word search

F	H	F	L	Y	D	X	U	W	U
U	A	T	Y	L	F	M	S	I	M
Q	P	I	W	K	H	D	H	J	C
B	Q	T	L	C	O	P	F	F	G
T	C	I	X	H	R	I	O	D	G
C	N	P	A	I	S	I	O	J	C
Q	M	R	Y	C	E	S	R	C	O
F	P	X	G	K	D	Y	C	K	W
V	O	S	H	E	E	P	Y	N	Z
V	O	D	O	N	K	E	Y	R	R

808 Find the correct shadow.

810 Complete the vine.

811 Which is the missing letter?

S

N

A

_anta Claus

814 Whose house is it?

812 Follow to colour.

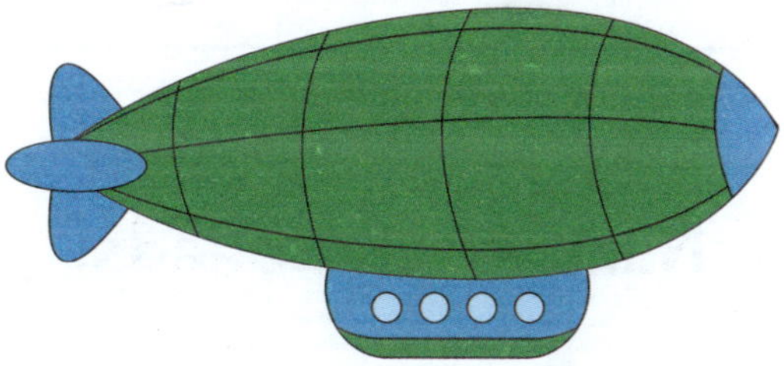

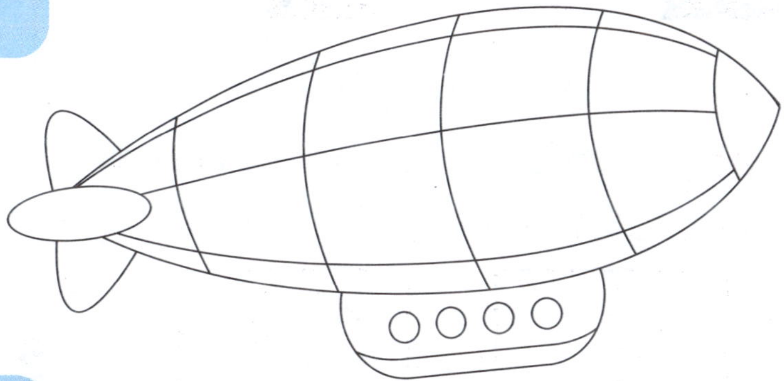

813 Crossword

815 Match by shape.

816 Count the fingers and circle the correct answer.

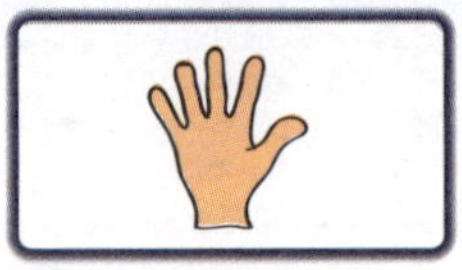

5 6 7 8 9

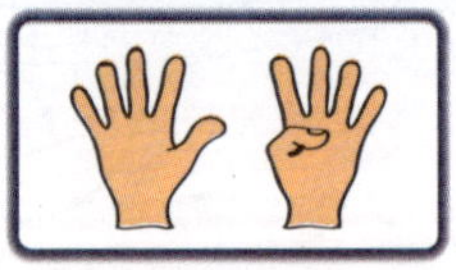

6 7 8 9 10

2 3 4 5 6

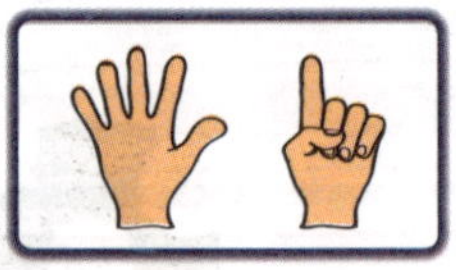

5 6 7 8 9

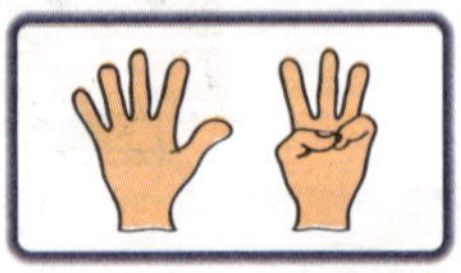

5 6 7 8 9

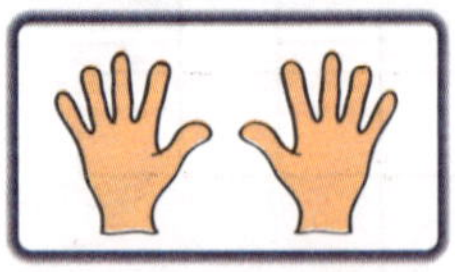

6 7 8 9 10

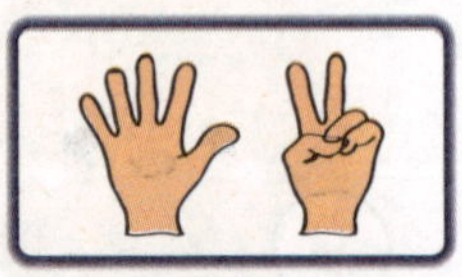

6 7 8 9 10

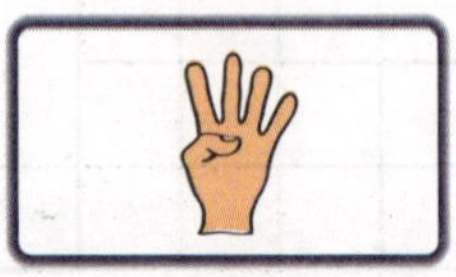

3 4 5 6 7

817 Trace and colour.

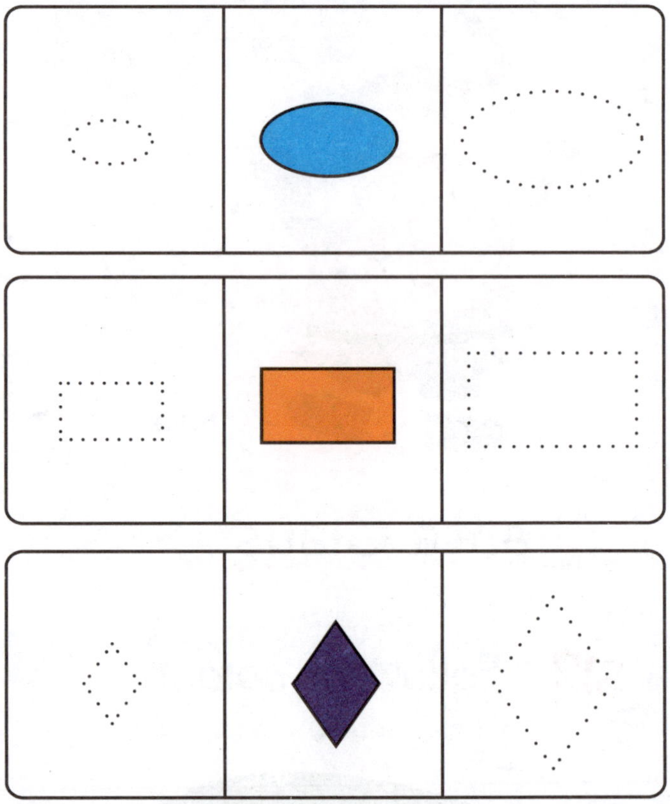

818 Number the beads.

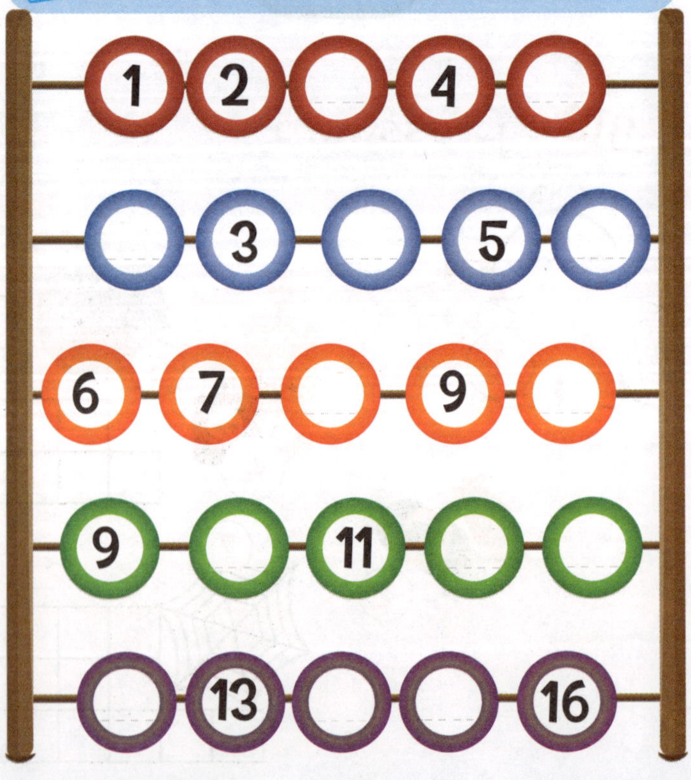

819 Compare the two numbers in each row. Trace more or less to complete each sentence correctly.

10	is	More / Less	Than	7
8	is	More / Less	Than	5
2	is	More / Less	Than	9
4	is	More / Less	Than	6

820 Write the action words.

821 Worms decided to eat fruit. Feed them through all the mazes.

822 Colour by number.

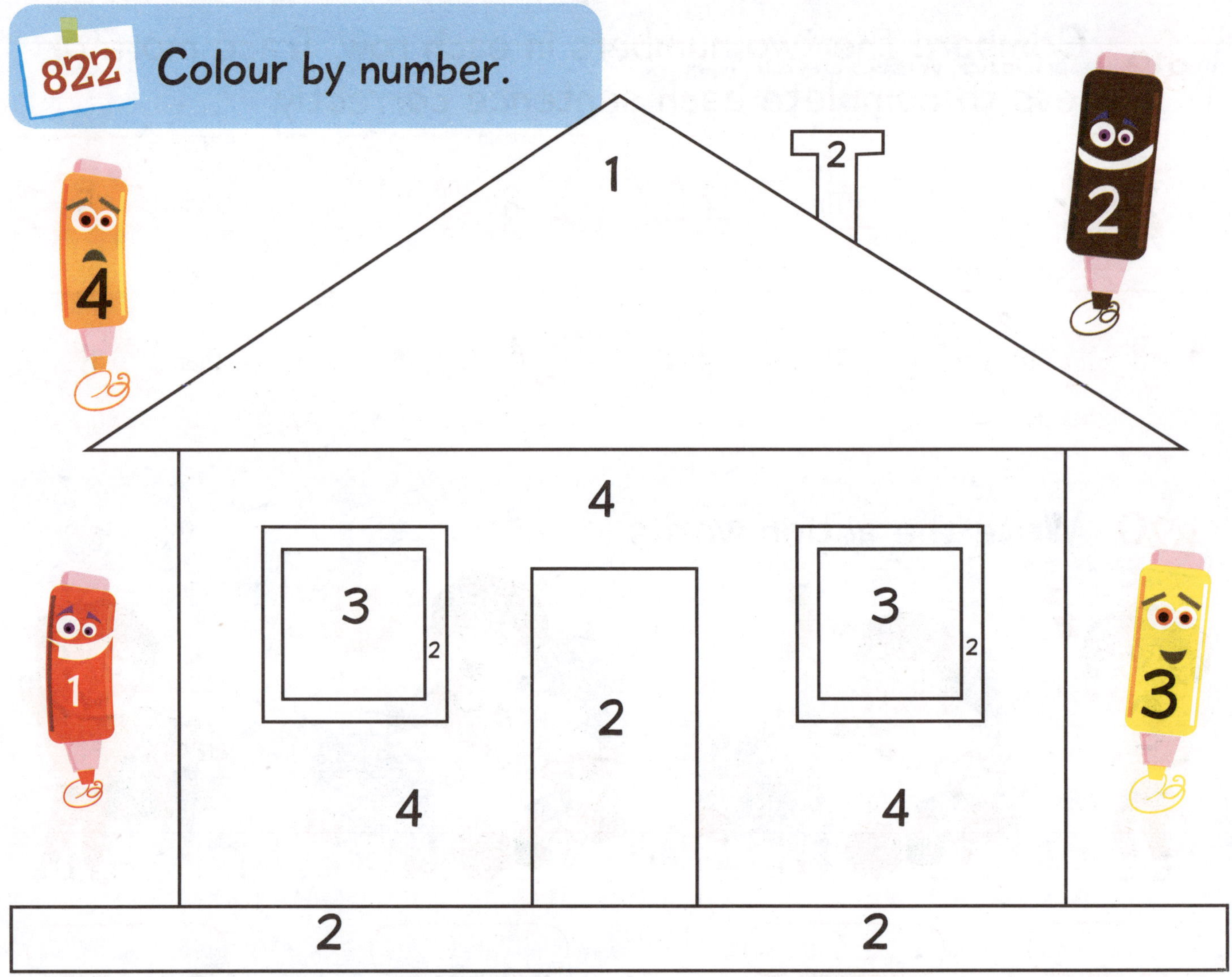

823 Christmas crossword

824 Guess whose name?

B			
D			

825 Decode the 5-letter words.

3 O	5 Y	1 S	2 T	4 R
1	2	3	4	5

4 I	1 F	2 R	5 T	3 U
1	2	3	4	5

826 Maths puzzle

	+		=	11
−		+		−
		1		
=		=		=
	+	3	=	7

	−	1	=	2
−		+		+
				7
=		=		=
1	+		=	

827 How many?

828 + or × ?

(+) (×) 1 ◯ 1 = 1

(+) (×) 7 ◯ 2 = 9

(+) (×) 5 ◯ 2 = 10

(+) (×) 3 ◯ 1 = 4

829 Complete number sentences.

☐	+	☐	=	4
+		+		+
☐	+	9	=	☐
=		=		=
6	+	☐	=	18

831 Right way to exit?

A

B

C

830 Find their numbers.

4 5 3 6 7

832 Trace to their initials.

834 Which goes together?

833 Mirror image matching

835 Match numbers and pictures.

836 Calculate and fill.

837 Which is related?

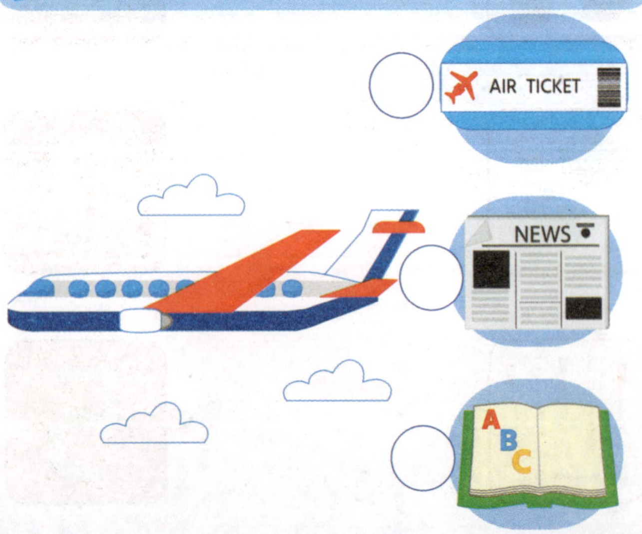

838 Count and write.

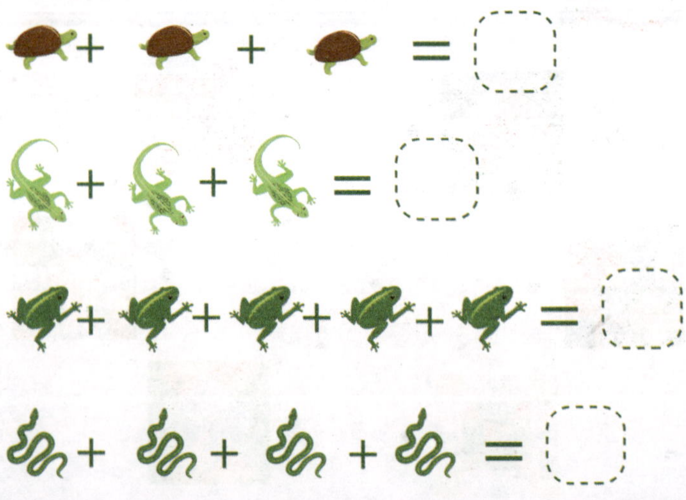

839 Windy, hot, cold or rainy?

840 How many?

841 Colour as indicated.

square rectangle triangle Circle

842 Join and colour.

843 Match the right answer.

844 Colour the next.

845 Colour the different-sized shapes.

846 Find the answers.

37 − 8 = ☐

24 − 12 = ☐

68 − 29 = ☐

95 − 30 = ☐

847 What does the abacus show?

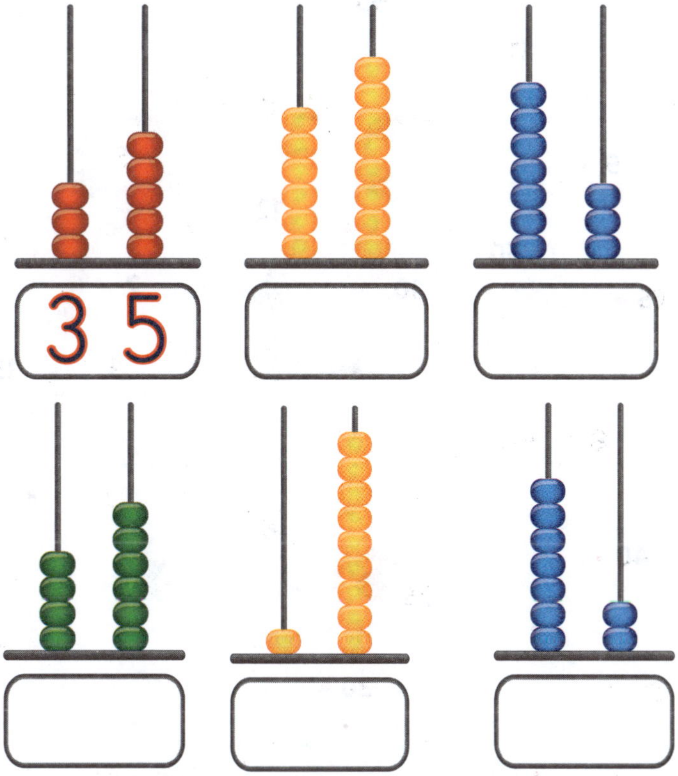

848 Honeycomb puzzle

849 Clock riddle

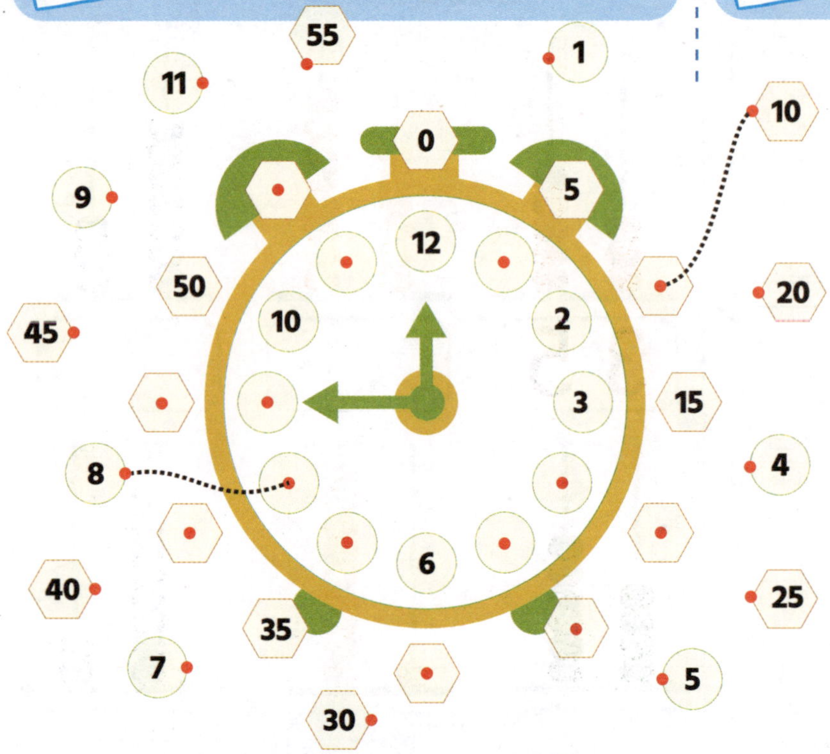

851 Circle the corresponding letter.

H T R D

A B H R

D P N T

B C L N

850 Count and match.

852 Help the bunny count the baby plants.

853 Count backwards and write the numbers.

854 How many?

855 Use the clues to finish the pattern.

856 Solve and match.

7

4

5

9

8

857 Find the value.

= 30

= 16

= 5

= ☐

858 Finish the rest.

859 Match by pattern.

861 Word search

Z	W	E	P	S	H	O	V	E	L
Q	B	E	V	I	N	H	Q	O	F
M	U	I	R	F	E	N	C	E	S
M	C	H	I	V	E	W	P	Z	W
H	K	R	K	G	Y	A	Q	Y	G
E	E	S	E	E	D	S	B	F	S
Q	T	J	A	O	U	T	H	X	Z
F	L	O	W	E	R	S	O	R	M
D	B	V	B	O	O	T	S	B	E
W	B	H	Q	N	Y	F	M	P	N

860 Letter writing practice

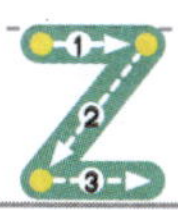

zebra

862 Match pairs.

863 Match the yarns.

866 Add in the hut.

5	+		=	6
+		+		+
	+	4	=	7
=		=		=
8	+		=	

864 Give values.

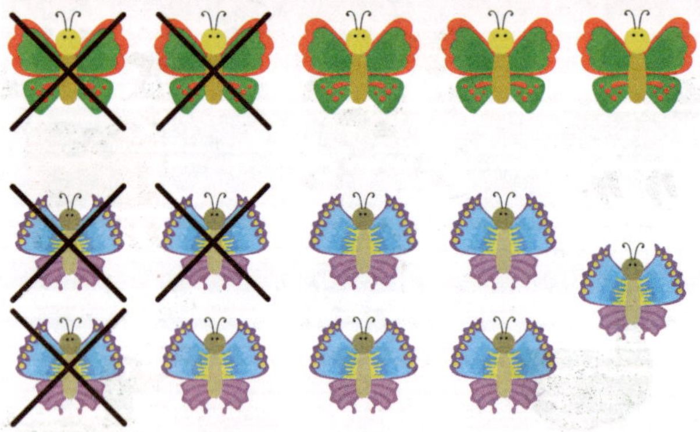

□ – □ = □

□ – □ = □

865 In which picture is not a triangle, not a circle, not a square?

867 Circle the corresponding letter.

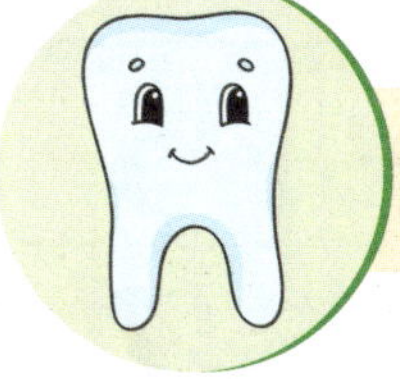

M I T A

E W F P

P K S C

Y T G R

869 Count and fill in the box.

868 Choose and complete the sudoku.

870 Word search

G	K	F	L	O	W	E	R	L
N	U	G	S	O	P	T	X	B
I	H	R	E	T	S	A	E	U
R	E	G	G	A	G	P	C	N
P	M	E	L	B	H	R	O	N
S	P	H	G	H	U	N	T	Y
N	H	B	A	S	K	E	T	P
B	Q	K	D	O	I	B	W	O
W	O	C	H	I	C	K	E	N

CHICKEN SPRING HUNT
BUNNY EGG
EASTER FLOWER BASKET

871 Join the dots and colour.

872 Count and colour.

873 Count and circle the correct number.

5
7
4
6

4
5
3
2

874 Find the correct shadow.

A. 

B. 

C. 

875 Animal wheel

878 How many cubes?

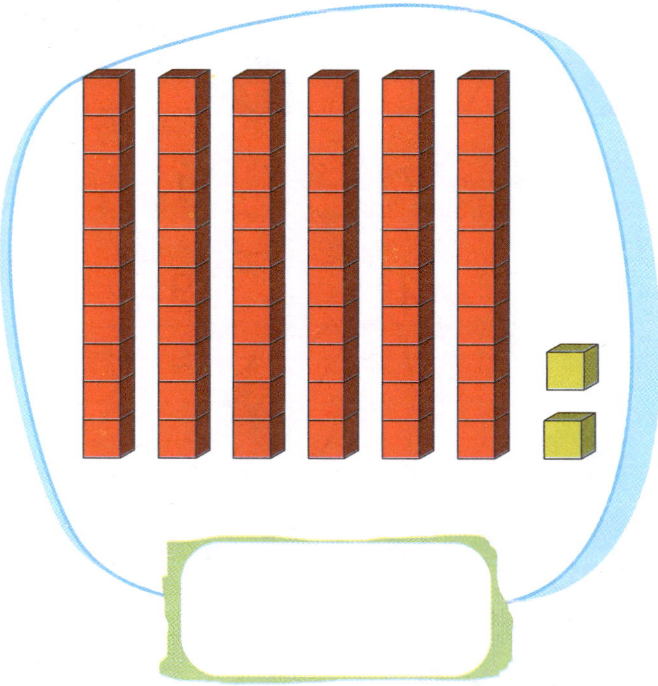

876 Count and write.

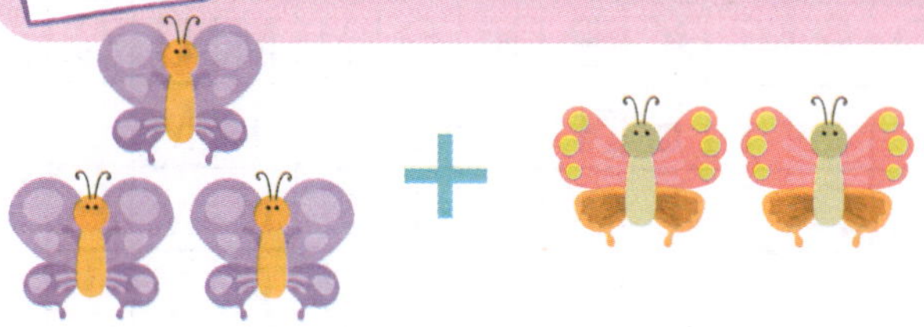

☐ + ☐ = ☐

☐ + ☐ = ☐

877 Colour the blocks according to the numbers written on the apples.

879 Match baubles and numbers.

880 Count toucans on each branch.

881 Which goes together?

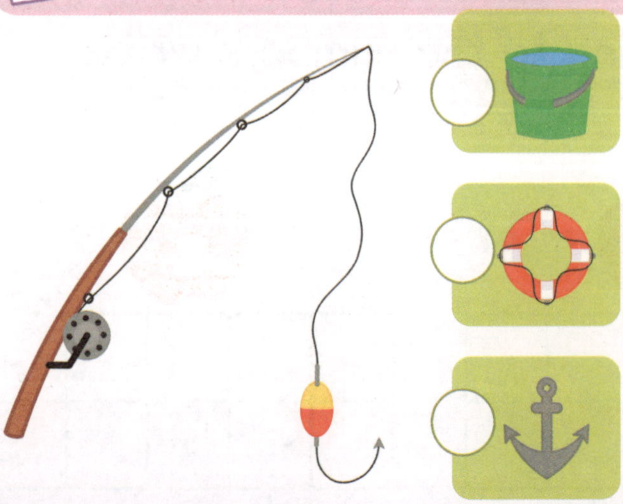

882 Word search

L	Z	N	H	A	U	G	L	V	I	D
C	A	T	S	G	S	H	A	C	M	X
O	R	G	K	B	K	O	N	M	U	C
F	I	I	E	I	M	S	T	I	M	S
F	O	B	L	X	S	T	E	N	M	P
I	C	D	E	L	C	H	R	P	Y	I
N	T	E	T	M	Y	O	N	O	F	D
N	O	M	O	O	T	U	N	T	H	E
A	B	O	N	O	H	S	H	I	A	R
B	E	N	S	N	E	E	S	O	T	N
N	R	T	R	E	E	W	F	N	X	Z

883 How many flowers?

884 Maths puzzle

10	−		=	
−		−		−
8				3
=		=		=
	−	1	=	

6	+		=	12
+		−		−
=		=		=
8	+	1	=	

885 Draw and complete.

886 Match by size.

887 Add the following.

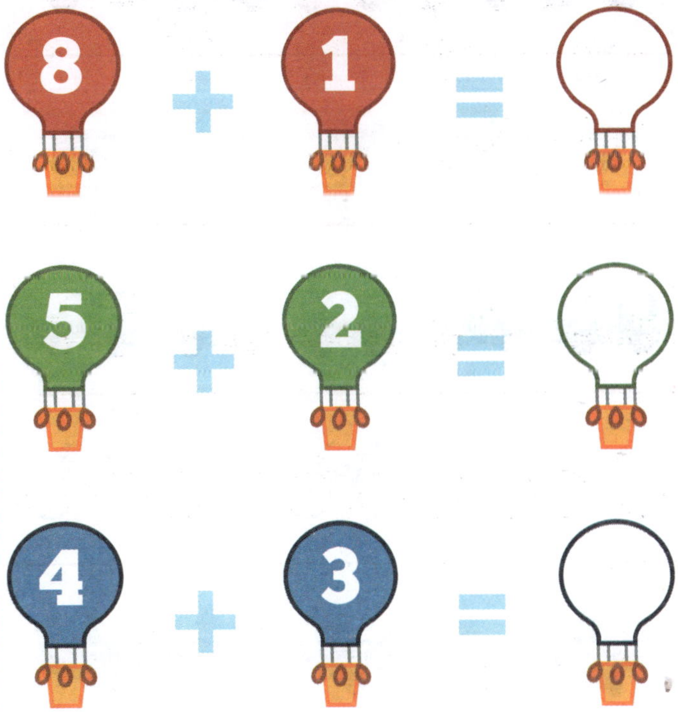

888 A or an?

○ a
○ an
eagle

○ a
○ an
duck

○ a
○ an
soap

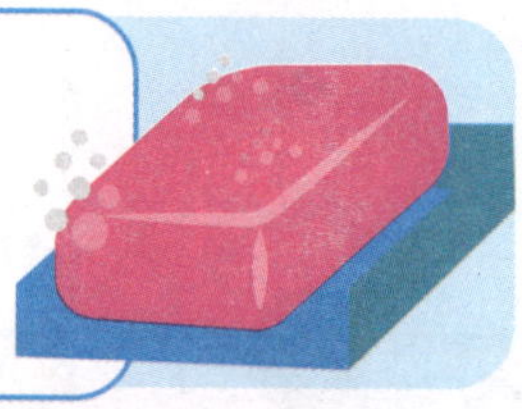

889 Odd one out

890 Add fractions.

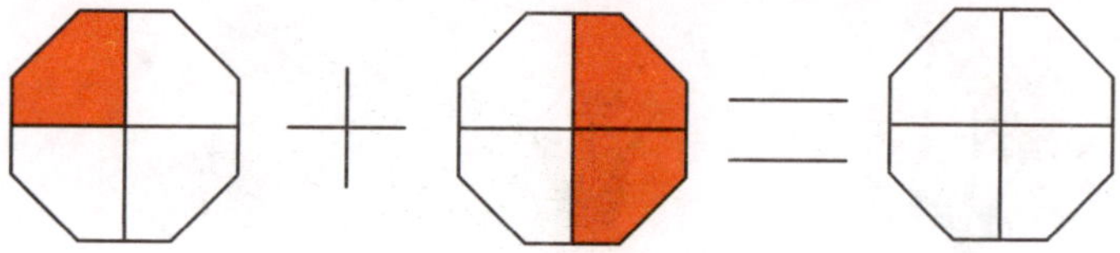

$$\frac{1}{4} + \frac{2}{4} = \frac{\square}{\square}$$

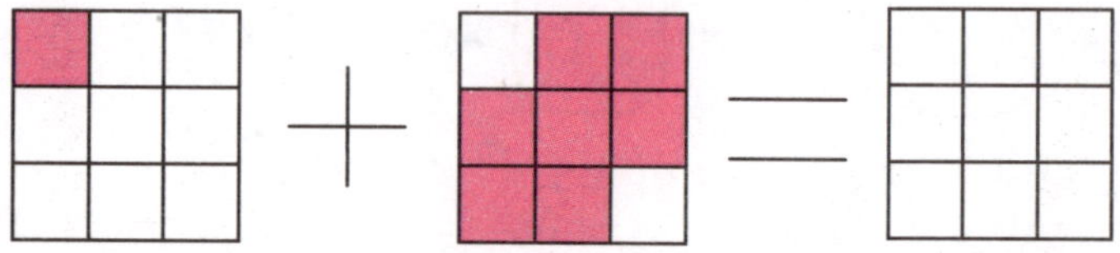

$$\frac{1}{9} + \frac{7}{9} = \frac{\square}{\square}$$

891 Word search

S	E	A	H	O	R	S	E
E	M	C	R	C	L	T	P
A	E	R	A	E	I	A	D
I	R	A	D	A	P	R	D
D	M	B	I	N	H	F	O
F	I	S	N	U	O	I	L
O	C	T	O	P	U	S	P
F	R	E	N	D	I	H	H
A	A	P	E	A	R	L	I
M	E	R	M	A	I	D	N

MERMAID
OCTOPUS
OCEAN
STARFISH
SEAHORSE
PEARL
CRAB
SEA
DOLPHIN

892 Add in the apple.

2	+	( )	=	5
+		+		+
( )	+	( )	=	( )
=		=		=
7	+	3	=	( )

893 Which goes together?

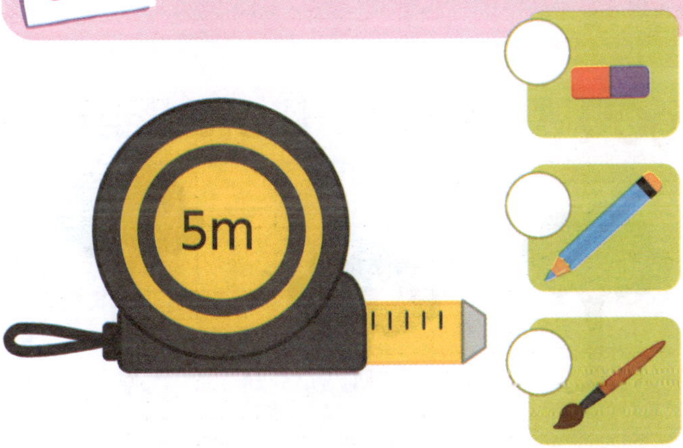

894 Compare.

895 Draw to complete.

896 Subtraction

7 5	4 6
− 3 1	− 2 1
( ) ( )	( ) ( )

8 6	6 4
− 4 0	− 1 2
( ) ( )	( ) ( )

897 Find its name.

11	14	9	6	5

a	b	c	d	e	f	g	h	i	j	k	l	m
1	2	3	4	5	6	7	8	9	10	11	12	13

n	o	p	q	r	s	t	u	v	w	x	y	z
14	15	16	17	18	19	20	21	22	23	24	25	26

898 Copy the picture.

899 Match the pendants.

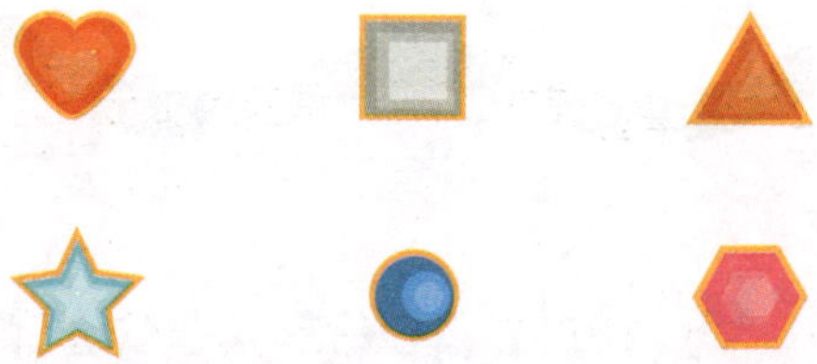

900 Underline the tallest.

901 Count and add.

902 Match with fruit baskets.

903 Find the value.

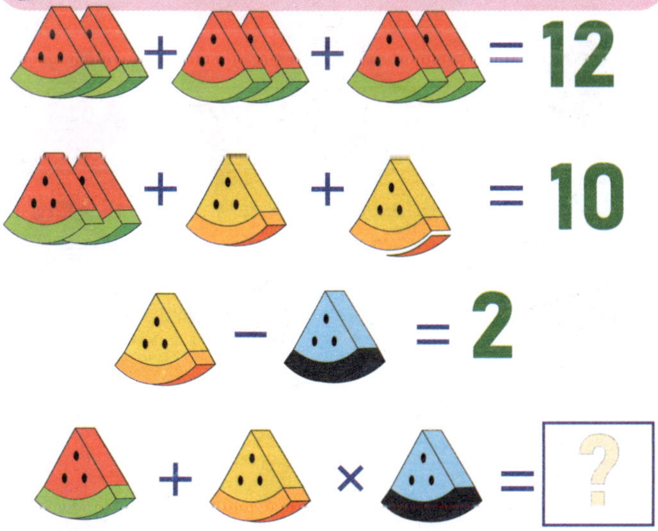

904 Crossword

905 What is it used for?

906 How many?

907 Write numbers before and after.

14

16

7

11

19

10

908 Count and circle the correct number.

6
7
4
5

9
8
7
6

909 Write their count.

910 Solve the rebus.

911 How old are they?

912 Complete the pattern.

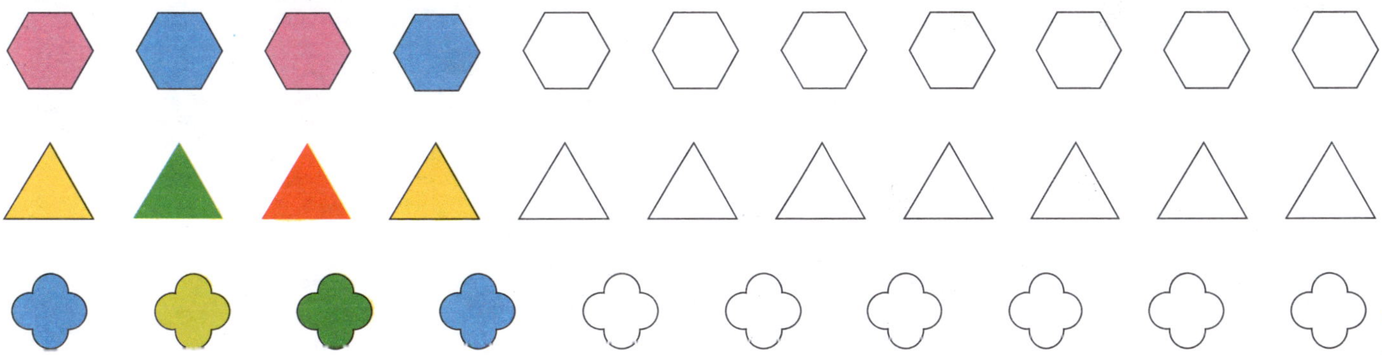

913 Add and subtract the notes.

914 What is it used for?

915 Match the pieces.

916 Colour the shapes as indicated.

917 Fill in the missing numbers.

1	2	3		5		7		9	10
11		13	14		16	17	18		20
21	22	23		25	26		28	29	
	32	33	34		36	37		39	40
41	42		44	45		47	48		50
	52	53	54		56	57		59	60
61		63		65	66		68	69	
71	72		74	75		77	78		80
	82	83		85	86		88	89	
91	92		94		96	97	98		100

918 Match the numbers.

6

4

7

3

5

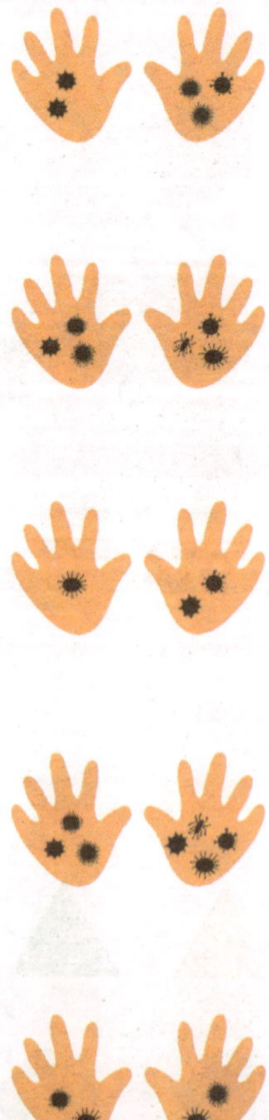

919 Subtract and match.

20 − 1	• •	1
3 − 2	• •	19
7 − 4	• •	2
5 − 3	• •	3

920 Subtract the currency.

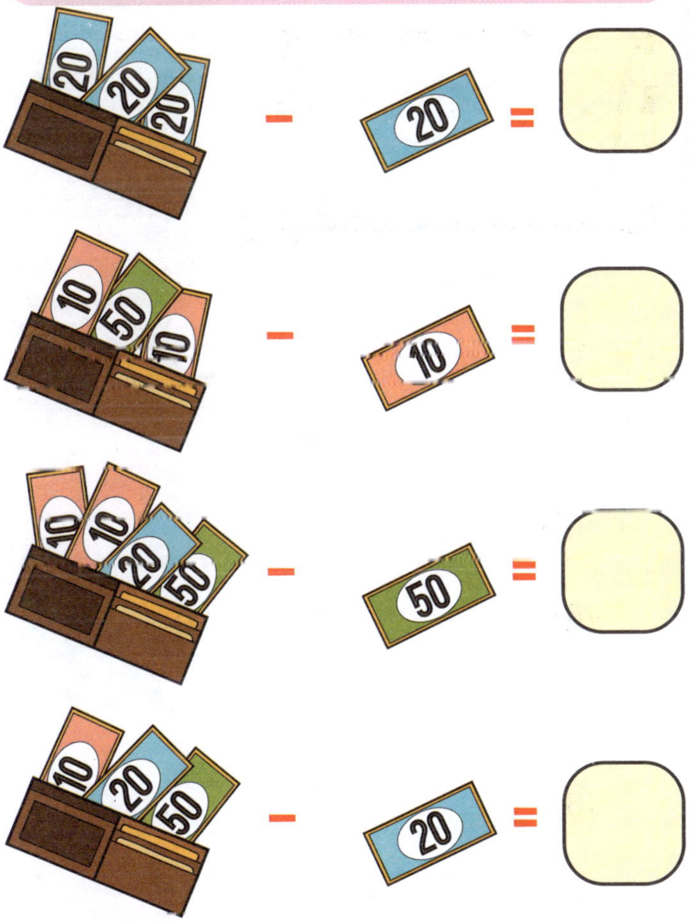

921 Help the postman find the houses to drop the letters.

922 Riddle with numbers.

923 Connect the dots and colour.

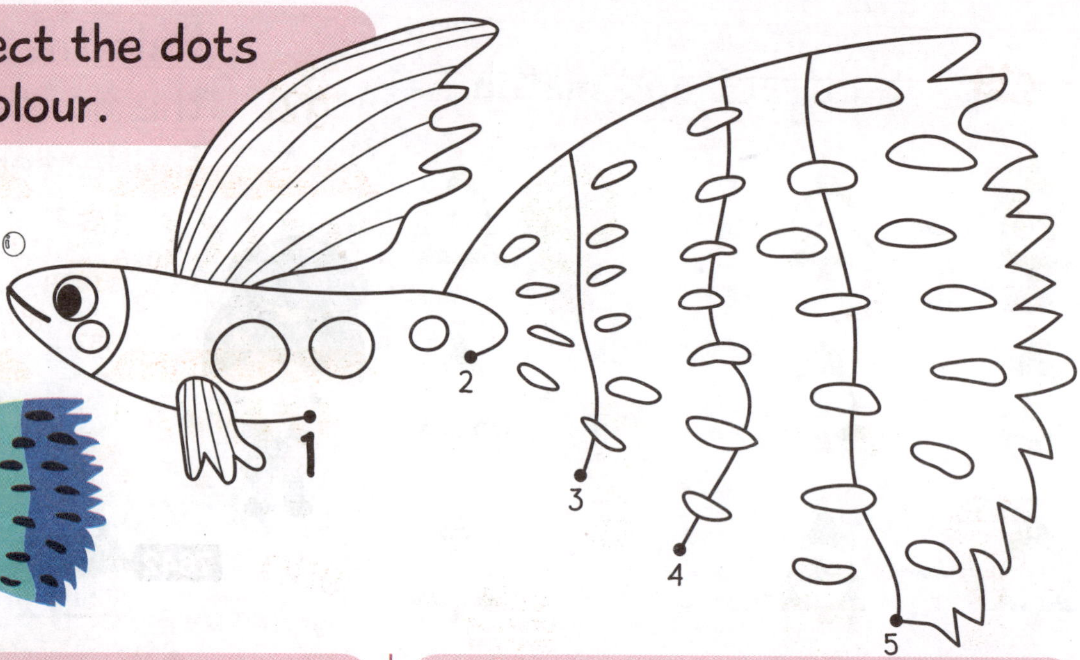

924 Find the missing numbers.

926 Which goes together?

925 Find the correct shadow.

Ⓐ 

Ⓑ 

Ⓒ 

Ⓐ 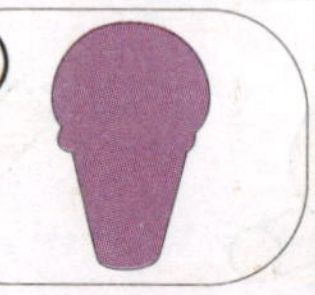

Ⓑ 

Ⓒ 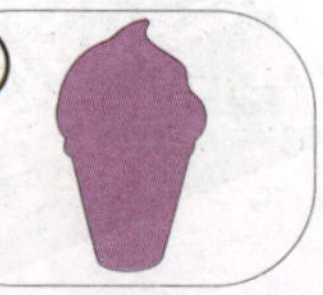

927 Find one balloon without a copy.

928 Find the way home.

929 Count and fill in the circles.

930 Find number 6.

2	4	9	7	8	7	10	1	2
5	5	7	8	3	1	3	4	9
4	3	1	5	10	6	6	2	1
9	6	2	10	8	9	6	2	5
8	10	4	7	8	2	5	7	1
4	6	1	3	9	1	6	1	3

931 Trace and colour

932 Complete the missing parts of the sudoku.

Level 1

+	−		×
=		+	−
×	=	−	
	+	×	=

Level 2

=		−	
−	+	×	
+			×
	=	+	

933 Find the correct shadow.

○ ○ ○ ○

○ ○ ○ ○

934 Find the correct values.

☐	+	☐	+	☐	=	10
+		+		+		
☐	+	3	+	☐	=	10
+		+		+		
☐	+	☐	+	☐	=	10
=		=		=		
10		10		10		

935 What is it used for?

936 A or an?

○ a
○ an
igloo

○ a
○ an
knife

○ a
○ an
bear

937 Colour the shapes by number.

1 2 3 4

938 Solve the rebus.

939 Calculate and match with the difference.

17-7 13 20-9

11-7 5

4

11

15-2 10 13-8

940 Help baby elephants.

941 Join and colour.

942 How many?

943 Riddle with numbers.

944 Which goes together?

945 Ho ho ho! Help Santa!

946 Vegetables crossword

947 Solve the task.

9 →(−5) ◯ →(+4) ◯ →(−7) 1

3 →(+2) ◯ →(−4) ◯ →(+6) 7

948 Measurement: How long?

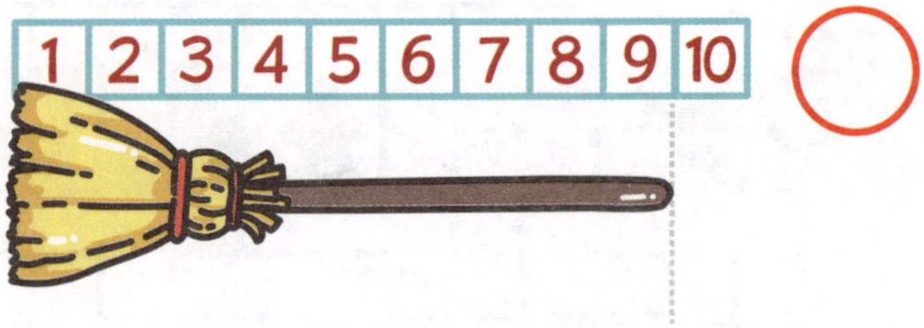

949 Match with the correct shadow.

951 Colour by number.

950 Circle the correct fractions.

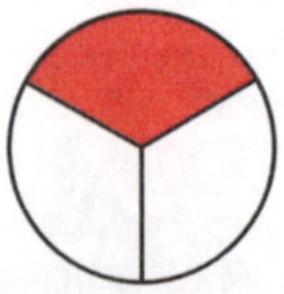 $\frac{1}{3}$ $\frac{3}{1}$ $\frac{2}{3}$ $\frac{4}{1}$

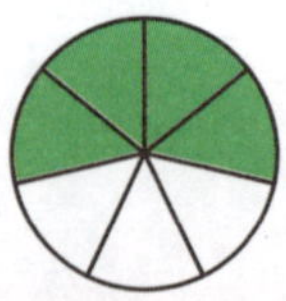 $\frac{4}{8}$ $\frac{7}{4}$ $\frac{4}{6}$ $\frac{4}{7}$

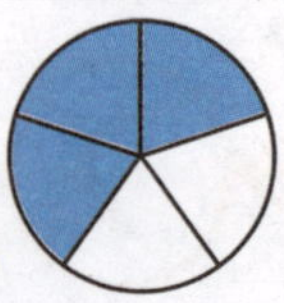 $\frac{4}{6}$ $\frac{5}{4}$ $\frac{3}{5}$ $\frac{5}{3}$

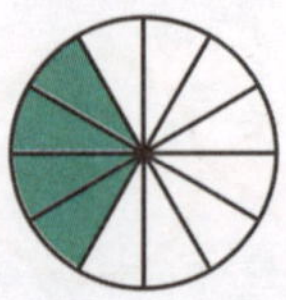 $\frac{4}{10}$ $\frac{5}{12}$ $\frac{4}{14}$ $\frac{4}{12}$

952 Riddle with numbers.

953 What comes next?

1 2 3 1 2 3 1 ___

4 5 4 5 4 5 4 ___

6 7 6 7 6 7 6 ___

8 8 8 8 8 8 8 ___

9 4 9 9 4 9 9 ___

4 1 3 4 1 3 4 ___

954 Match names.

- dental floss
- toothbrush
- mouthwash
- tooth
- toothpaste
- candy

955 Find 7 differences.

956 Connect number-wise and colour.

958 Find the missing numbers.

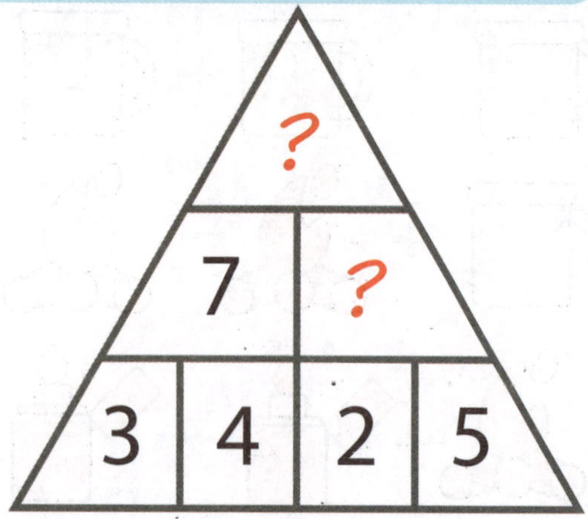

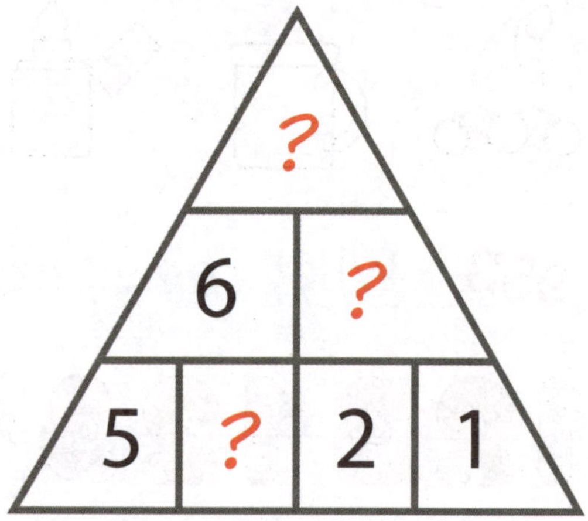

957 What replaces the question mark?

959 What is being knit?

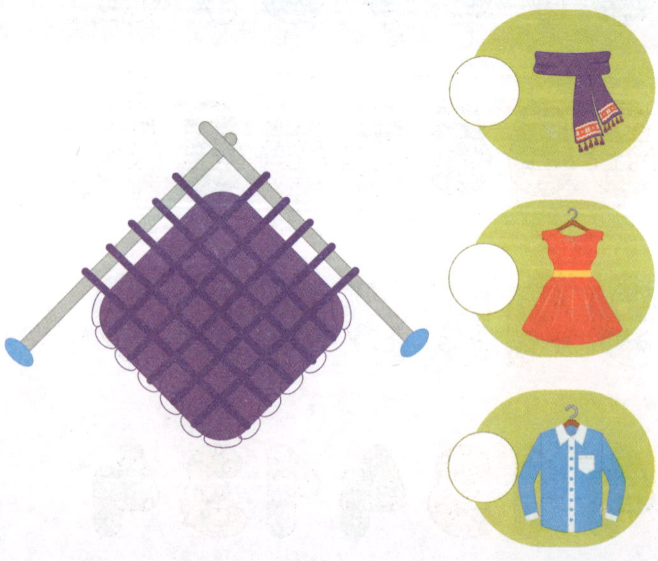

960 Connect the dots and colour.

961 Circle the correct fraction.

$\frac{3}{4}$ $\frac{1}{3}$ $\frac{1}{4}$ $\frac{1}{5}$

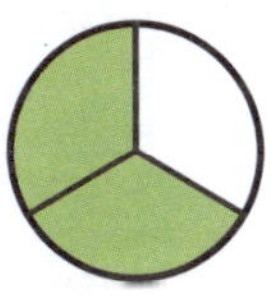

$\frac{2}{3}$ $\frac{2}{8}$ $\frac{3}{4}$ $\frac{1}{3}$

$\frac{7}{8}$ $\frac{5}{6}$ $\frac{7}{7}$ $\frac{3}{5}$

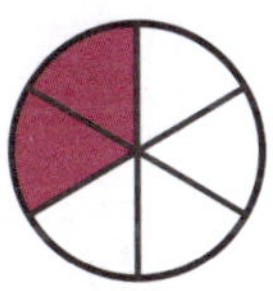

$\frac{4}{6}$ $\frac{3}{5}$ $\frac{2}{6}$ $\frac{5}{7}$

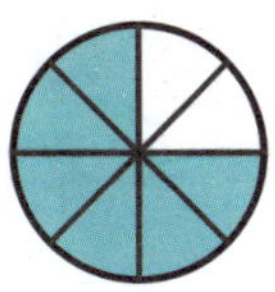

$\frac{6}{8}$ $\frac{6}{7}$ $\frac{5}{6}$ $\frac{4}{8}$

962 Count and add.

963 Decode the 5-letter words.

2 Y	4 U	5 P	1 S	3 R
1	2	3	4	5

5 E	3 A	4 P	1 G	2 R
1	2	3	4	5

964 Subtract and match.

19 – 11	•	•	3
10 – 8	•	•	4
7 – 3	•	•	8
12 – 9	•	•	2

965 Maths puzzle

5	–	4	=	☐
+		+		+
3		☐		☐
=		=		=
☐	–	6	=	☐

☐	+	☐	=	1
+		+		+
3		☐		☐
=		=		=
☐	+	7	=	10

966 Find the missing element.

967 What replaces the question mark?

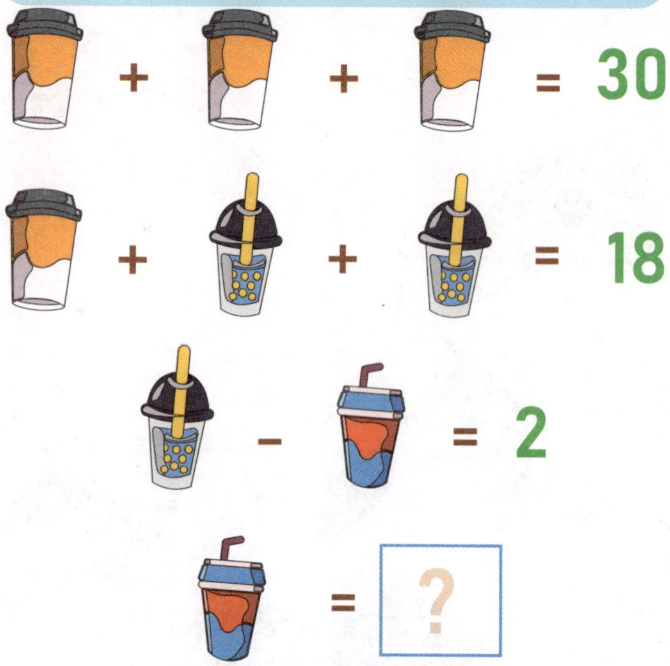

968 Write the corresponding letters.

969 Finish the other half.

970 What is being sewn?

971 What is it?

e c n p i l

□ □ □ □ □ □

972 Join the numbers and colour the Christmas tree.

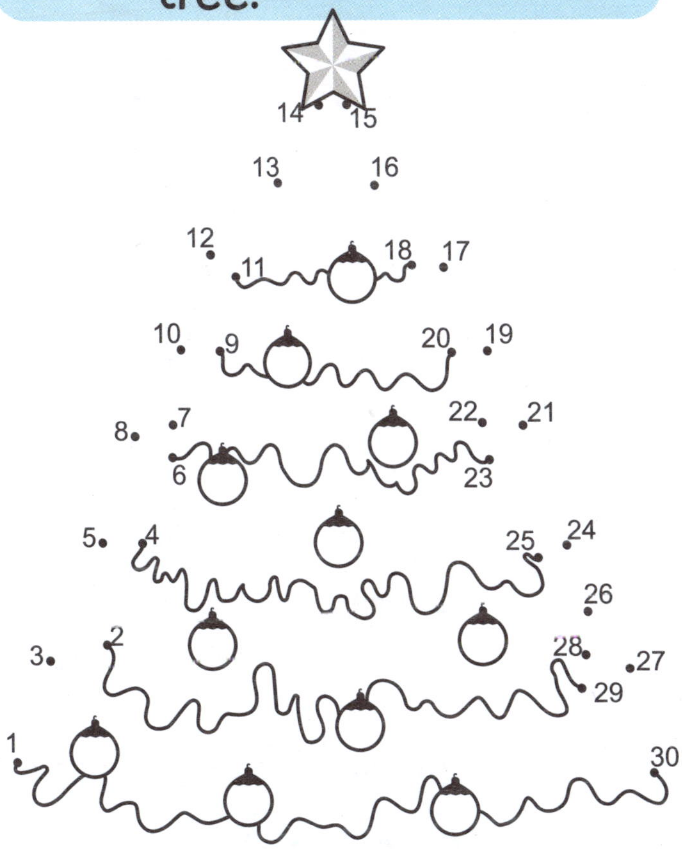

973 Compare the numbers.

1	>	0	5	□	3
2	□	2	0	□	9
2	□	3	1	□	1
7	□	6	1	□	3
6	□	0	7	□	8
2	□	1	2	□	1
3	□	5	7	□	5

974 A or an?

- ◯ a
- ◯ an

jacket

- ◯ a
- ◯ an

frog

- ◯ a
- ◯ an

comb

975 Add, match and colour the apples.

976 Match with the correct shadow.

977 Household crossword

978 Multiply the following.

$1 \times 1 =$ ◯	$3 \times 1 =$ ◯
$5 \times 1 =$ ◯	$4 \times 2 =$ ◯
$3 \times 3 =$ ◯	$2 \times 3 =$ ◯
$2 \times 1 =$ ◯	$2 \times 2 =$ ◯

981 Find the missing part.

979 Which sofa is not yellow, not red, not blue?

980 Subtract and match.

14 7 16 8 13

12 1 15 4 10

4 3 6 2 1

982 Join and colour.

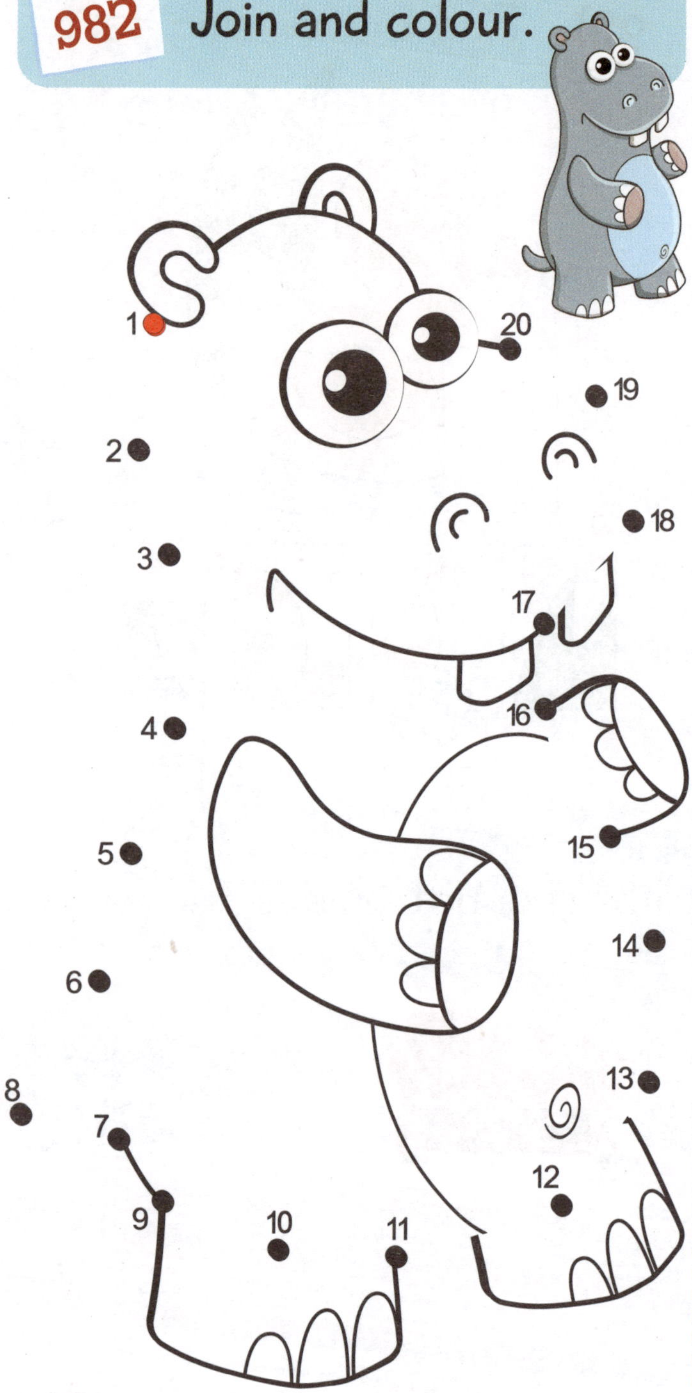

984 Count and cross.

985 Find two same-flavoured cupcakes.

983 Handwriting practice

986 Addition

+	1	2	3
1	2		
2			
3			
4			

988 Calculate and match the products.

12   5X6   3X6

60

4X9   36   2X6

18   10X6   30

987 Colour according to the code.

2+2 =

4+2 =

7+1 =

9-7 =

2+3 =

6-3 =

2+5 =

5+4 =

989 Trace and colour.

990 Help the turtle swim across by the given rule.

				2	5	6	8	3	10
				➡	1	4	9	7	9
13	11	8	10	8	4	7	10	12	14
17	12	16	14	11	9	11	13	9	11
24	25	20	18	13	14	15	16	22	26
27	21	19	31	28	25	22	19	28	30
22	23	30	34	39	21	23	26	29	32
28	25	27	37	20	23	27	30	33	36
39	37	34	40	43	46	49	➡		
42	40	38	33	35	37	40	42		

992 Repeat the lines.

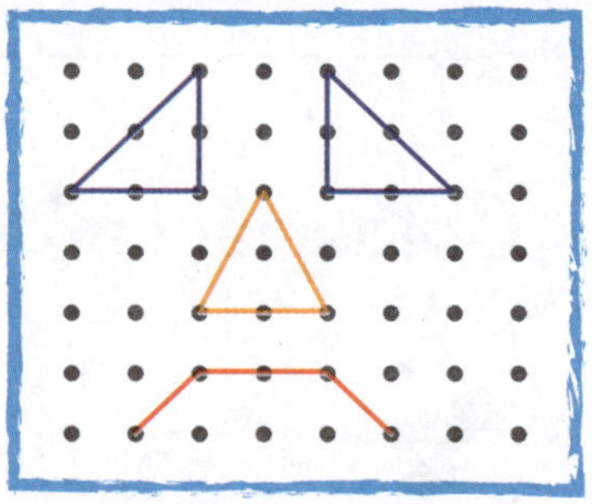

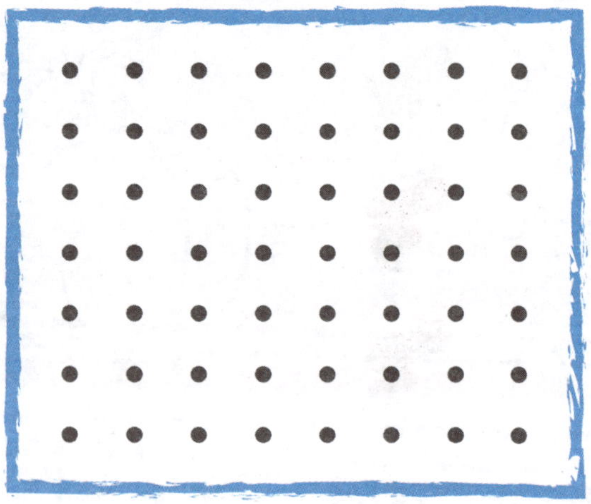

991 Complete the pattern.

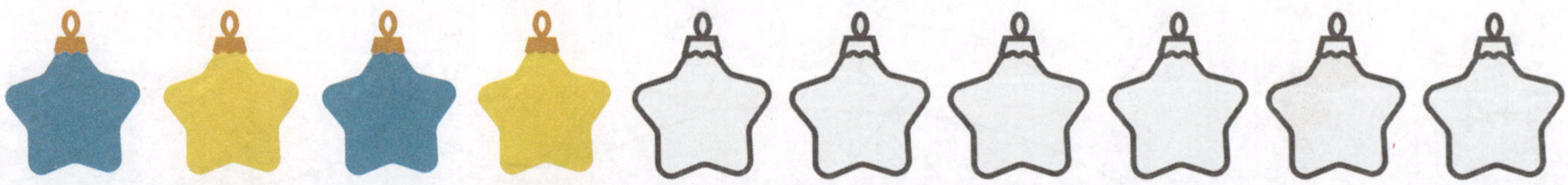

993 Solve the rebus and colour.

996 Shape match

994 Shadow match

997 Find 6 differences.

995 Count and write.

998 After and before

999 A or an?

a
an
mirror

a
an
bee

a
an
towel

1001 Write the fractions.

1000 Tell the time.